PLANNING

THE PRIMARY NATIONAL CURRICULUM

Sara Miller McCune founded SAGE Publishing in 1965 to support the dissemination of usable knowledge and educate a global community. SAGE publishes more than 1000 journals and over 800 new books each year, spanning a wide range of subject areas. Our growing selection of library products includes archives, data, case studies and video. SAGE remains majority owned by our founder and after her lifetime will become owned by a charitable trust that secures the company's continued independence.

Los Angeles | London | New Delhi | Singapore | Washington DC | Melbourne

KEIRA SEWELL

PLANNING

THE PRIMARY NATIONAL CURRICULUM

A COMPLETE GUIDE FOR TRAINEES AND TEACHERS

SECOND EDITION

Learning Matters
An imprint of SAGE Publications Ltd
1 Oliver's Yard
55 City Road
London EC1Y 1SP

SAGE Publications Inc.
2455 Teller Road
Thousand Oaks, California 91320

SAGE Publications India Pvt Ltd
B 1/I 1 Mohan Cooperative Industrial Area
Mathura Road
New Delhi 110 044

SAGE Publications Asia-Pacific Pte Ltd
3 Church Street
#10-04 Samsung Hub
Singapore 049483

Editor: Amy Thornton
Production editor: Chris Marke
Marketing manager: Dilhara Attygalle
Cover design: Wendy Scott
Typeset by: C&M Digitals (P) Ltd, Chennai, India
Printed in the UK

Library of Congress Control Number: 2017957599

British Library Cataloguing in Publication Data

A catalogue record for this book is available from the British Library

ISBN 978-1-5264-2067-1
ISBN 978-1-5264-2068-8 (pbk)

At SAGE we take sustainability seriously. Most of our products are printed in the UK using FSC papers and boards. When we print overseas we ensure sustainable papers are used as measured by the PREPS grading system. We undertake an annual audit to monitor our sustainability.

Contents

Note: The contents listed in grey are sections of the national curriculum framework for England, key stages one and two.

About the authors

Keira Sewell is an independent educational consultant at Visionary Education (**www.visionary-education.co.uk**). She has over 25 years' experience of supporting the professional development of both trainee and experienced teachers and specialises in science education.

Deborah Wilkinson is a senior lecturer in education at the University of Chichester. She is a qualified primary school teacher and has over 15 years of experience working in educational settings.

Linda Cooper is a senior lecturer in primary education specialising in humanities at the University of Chichester. She has 18 years of educational experience working in both schools and initial teacher training institutions.

Karen Hosack Janes is an education consultant and an experienced author. She has a specialist knowledge in creative curriculum development and teaching and learning through the visual arts. She has taught as a senior member of staff in schools and at university level, and was formerly Head of Schools at the National Gallery, London.

Alison Daubney is a part-time teacher educator at the University of Sussex. She also works on a freelance basis supporting hubs, schools and organisations with curriculum development, pedagogy, assessment, evaluation and training.

Duncan Mackrill is a senior lecturer, music education curriculum tutor and Director of Teaching and Learning in the School of Education and Social Work at the University of Sussex.

Kristy Howells is the Faculty of Education Director of Physical Education at Canterbury Christ Church University. Her research area is physical activity and the impact of physical education lessons on the contribution to children's physical activity levels. She lectures to primary education student teachers and specialises in physical education.

Helen Caldwell is the Curriculum Lead for Primary Computing at the University of Northampton, where she teaches both trainee and experienced teachers. Other areas of interest are assistive technologies for SEND and the use of mobile devices.

Sue Dutson worked in agricultural research before training to teach. After 20 years in primary and middle schools she became a local authority advisor and OFSTED inspector before moving into initial teacher education. Her specialisms are science and design technology education.

Laura Quinton Maryon is a primary school teacher, literacy subject leader and SENCo who specialises in the development of early reading and reading for pleasure. She has also worked in primary teacher education.

Sam Parkes is a school improvement specialist for mathematics at the University of Chichester. She designs and delivers a range of professional development programmes to support mathematics teaching in local primary and secondary schools and academies, and teaches on trainee teacher programmes and MA courses. She is a primary mathematics specialist and has over 12 years' experience of teaching and leading mathematics across the primary age range and of teaching mathematics and supporting departmental improvement at a secondary level.

Sway Grantham (@SwayGrantham) is a specialist leader in education for the Milton Keynes area focusing on computing and ICT. She teaches full-time in a primary school and shares a range of learning ideas and pedagogy for computing, ICT and many other curriculum areas on her blog (**www.swaygrantham.co.uk**).

Kelly Stock is a senior lecturer at Anglia Ruskin University. She has taught primary and secondary languages and is also an additional inspector working on behalf of OFSTED. She is currently studying at doctoral level at the University of Cambridge in the area of 'outstanding teaching'.

How to use this book

This book will help you think about what principles and philosophies underpin effective planning. It provides guidance on how to plan each subject and includes the national curriculum framework for key stages 1 and 2. On the contents page the framework is listed in grey text to help you identify which is guidance and which parts are taken directly from the framework.

Section 1 provides an overview of planning. Begin by reading **Chapter 1** as this outlines the context of the national curriculum to help you understand what changes the revised curriculum of 2014 brought to planning in schools. It explains the way in which the national curriculum is structured and how this contributes to the development of a school's curriculum. This chapter also explores how the Teachers' Standards relate to planning and encourages you to reflect on what philosophical stance you adopt when considering what primary education should offer children.

Chapter 2 extends this by exploring the foundations of good planning for all subject areas. It unpicks what effective planning should include and what theories underpin this and explores the key elements of effective classroom management. It is important that you read this chapter in association with each of the subject-specific chapters.

Chapter 3 explores mastery in the Primary National Curriculum. It asks the question 'What is mastery?' in relation to progression, understanding and depth of learning. The chapter then goes on to give guidance on planning for and assessing mastery and includes a separate section on recording mastery.

Section 2 extends the ideas explored in Section 1 by examining each subject area individually in the order they appear within the national curriculum. Each chapter contains three sections.

- **Principles of planning** explores the aspects of planning specific to that subject area.
- **Examples of planning** illustrates these ideas through a sequence of three annotated lesson plans so that you can see what these look like in practice.
- **The framework** is the part of the national curriculum which applies to the subject area. It is taken directly from the national curriculum framework for England and includes both the statutory and non-statutory guidance.

This means that you can read the ideas and approaches to planning in each subject, look at how these are put into practice in your planning and then use the national curriculum to plan your own lessons. Each chapter signposts you to further reading and useful resources to help you continue to develop your understanding of pedagogy in each of the national curriculum subjects.

Section 3 extends these ideas by looking at longer-term planning. It explores the role of each stage within the planning process and considers how schools can put together a creative curriculum. A number of ideas are provided as a starting point for you to develop your own creative curriculum.

We know that the skills required to plan effectively take time to develop and we hope that this book will support you throughout your teaching career. It should make you think about current approaches, philosophies and theories in education and how these impact on your own practice. Being reflective is critical to becoming a more effective teacher and knowing not only *what* you are teaching but *why* is an essential part of this process.

Section 1

Overview of planning

This section will explore the structure and organisation of the national curriculum, providing a context for planning and the related Teachers' Standards. Generic principles of planning will be discussed in Chapter 2.

1 The planning context

Keira Sewell

Context 1 Implementing the national curriculum

The requirements for the national curriculum for England are laid out in the framework document. Not all schools need to teach the national curriculum and, even when they are required to or choose to teach it, the national curriculum should be considered as only one part of a broad and balanced curriculum.

The first national curriculum was introduced in 1989 and comprised of nine subjects. Since then there have been a number of revisions, the most recent being the framework document for the national curriculum in England implemented from September 2014.

It is likely that you will be training and working in some schools where minor changes have been made to reflect the revised curriculum and in others where the curriculum has been completely rewritten. It is important, therefore, that you understand the changes made in the revised framework so that you can ensure your planning reflects these and complies with the statutory requirements.

Key changes

The changes made in the revised national curriculum (DfE, 2014) can be summarised as follows.

- The national curriculum is only statutory for maintained schools in England and these schools must publish their curriculum by subject and year group online each year. Academies can choose whether to follow the national curriculum.
- The national curriculum is to be considered one part of the curriculum offered by a school and no further guidance will be given by the government on how to plan or teach the curriculum offered.
- English, mathematics and science remain as core subjects but with an expectation that numeracy and literacy will be taught through all subject areas. There is an emphasis on phonics in the early teaching of reading.
- Art and design, design and technology, geography, history, music and physical education remain as foundation subjects. Information and communications technology has been replaced by computing with an expectation that ICT should

permeate all subjects. Languages are now included in the national curriculum for key stages 2 and 3.

- There remains an expectation that personal, social and health education (PSHE) and religious education (RE) will be part of any school provision although the content of this remains, largely, within the control of each school. Sex and relationship education is not statutory in the primary phase. Citizenship and sex and relationship education are statutory from key stage 3.
- In assessment, levels have been removed and schools are free to choose their own system of reporting. Children will be expected to understand and apply the concepts, skills and processes outlined in the programmes of study appropriate for their year group or key stage. Schools will still be required to report progress to parents at the end of each key stage, and end of key stage tests will remain.

Structure of the national curriculum

The overall structure and requirements of the national curriculum are laid out in Section 2 of this chapter and you should read this to better understand the requirements. However, in summary, the national curriculum framework for primary schools is comprised of three core subjects:

- English
- mathematics
- science

and eight foundation subjects:

- art and design
- computing
- design and technology
- geography
- history
- languages
- music
- physical education.

Each of the subjects has a programme of study, identified as 'statutory requirements' or 'subject content', and some subjects also include non-statutory guidance or examples. You do not need to use these examples but they provide an illustration of what you might do or how you might teach the content.

The core subject programmes of study are laid out for each year group or, in some cases, for two years (i.e. lower and upper key stage 2). The foundation subjects programmes of study are laid out for each key stage.

For assessment purposes, attainment is based on achievement of the programmes of study by the end of the period of study (either year or key stage). The 2014 national curriculum is different to previous documents in that the statements in the programmes of study should be considered learning **outcomes** rather than learning **objectives**. We will explore this further in Chapter 2.

The revised national curriculum gives schools much greater freedom in terms of planning and assessment and encourages them to respond to local agendas and needs and to incorporate regional and national agendas and events. For a number of years schools have taken much greater ownership of the curricula offered and you will find a good deal of variance between the approaches to planning and assessment adopted by schools. For this reason, while it is critical that you understand the statutory requirements of the national curriculum to ensure what you offer is compliant, you need to understand the rationale underpinning the approaches each school takes. As part of this, you will need to develop a personal philosophy of education.

Developing a personal philosophy

Consider the following.

- What do you think education is? Is it a process or a product? Is schooling the same as education? (Read Sewell and Newman (2014) to reflect on some of these ideas.)
- Does the purpose of education change from the primary to the secondary phase and, if so, why and in what ways?
- What do you think children should be able to know, understand, do and be by the end of the primary phase?
- How should a primary curriculum reflect these ideas? (Read Hedges (2014) to reflect on this.)
- What principles can you apply to your planning to reflect your personal philosophy of education?

Draw up a list of principles that you would wish to underpin all of your planning in schools and keep them in the front of your planning folder. Refer back to them regularly to ensure they are still current and relevant. Your views will evolve as you become more experienced and knowledgeable and as a result of changes to our understanding of education as a society. A good starting point in considering your personal philosophy is the Teachers' Standards (DfE, 2013).

Teachers' Standards

The Standards which measure the development of any teacher are used for a variety of reasons including accountability, pay levels, quality assurance and achievement of Qualified Teacher Status (QTS) and the induction period. They are presented in two parts:

- Part 1: Teaching
- Part 2: Personal and professional conduct

Consider the eight headings for part 1 of the Standards which state that a teacher must:

1. set high expectations which inspire, motivate and challenge pupils;
2. promote good progress and outcomes by pupils;
3. demonstrate good subject and curriculum knowledge;
4. plan and teach well-structured lessons;
5. adapt teaching to respond to the strengths and needs of all pupils;
6. make accurate and productive use of assessment;
7. manage behaviour effectively to ensure a good and safe learning environment;
8. fulfil wider professional responsibilities.

Why do you think these are the minimum requirements of a teacher at any level and how should these principles underpin your planning? Add these ideas to your personal philosophy notes.

Now consider part 2 of the Standards which state:

A teacher is expected to demonstrate consistently high standards of personal and professional conduct. The following statements define the behaviour and attitudes which set the required standard for conduct throughout a teacher's career.

- Teachers uphold public trust in the profession and maintain high standards of ethics and behaviour, within and outside school, by:
  - treating pupils with dignity, building relationships rooted in mutual respect, and at all times observing proper boundaries appropriate to a teacher's professional position;
  - having regard for the need to safeguard pupils' well-being, in accordance with statutory provisions;
  - showing tolerance of and respect for the rights of others;
  - not undermining fundamental British values, including democracy, the rule of law, individual liberty and mutual respect, and tolerance of those with different faiths and beliefs;
  - ensuring that personal beliefs are not expressed in ways which exploit pupils' vulnerability or might lead them to break the law.

- Teachers must have proper and professional regard for the ethos, policies and practices of the school in which they teach, and maintain high standards in their own attendance and punctuality.
- Teachers must have an understanding of, and always act within, the statutory frameworks which set out their professional duties and responsibilities.

How do these Standards contribute to your own personal philosophy and how will these be reflected in your planning? Add these ideas to your notes.

You should now have a clearer idea about what you are trying to achieve in your planning and how this might be put into effect. Review your reflections regularly to ensure they remain current and relevant.

Further reading

DfE (2013) *Teachers' Standards*. Available at: **www.gov.uk/government/collections/teachers-standards**

DfE (2014) *The National Curriculum in England: Framework Document*. London: DfE.

Hedges, C. (2104) The curriculum. In Curtis, W., Ward, S., Sharp, J. and Hankin, L. (eds) *Education Studies: An Issue Based Approach* (3rd edition). London: Sage/Learning Matters.

Sewell, K. and Newman, S. (2014) What is education? In Curtis, W., Ward, S., Sharp, J. and Hankin, L. (eds) *Education Studies: An Issue Based Approach* (3rd edition). London: Sage/Learning Matters.

FROM THE FRAMEWORK

Context 2 The framework for the national curriculum

1. Introduction

1.1 This document sets out the framework for the national curriculum and includes:

- contextual information about both the overall school curriculum and the statutory national curriculum, including the statutory basis of the latter
- aims for the statutory national curriculum
- statements on inclusion, and on the development of pupils' competence in numeracy and mathematics, language and literacy across the school curriculum
- programmes of study for all the national curriculum subjects other than for key stage 4 science, which will follow.

2. The school curriculum in England

2.1 Every state-funded school must offer a curriculum which is balanced and broadly based and which:

- promotes the spiritual, moral, cultural, mental and physical development of pupils at the school and of society, and
- prepares pupils at the school for the opportunities, responsibilities and experiences of later life.

2.2 The school curriculum comprises all learning and other experiences that each school plans for its pupils. The national curriculum forms one part of the school curriculum.

2.3 All state schools are also required to make provision for a daily act of collective worship and must teach religious education to pupils at every key stage and sex and relationship education to pupils in secondary education.

2.4 Maintained schools in England are legally required to follow the statutory national curriculum which sets out in programmes of study, on the basis of key stages, subject content for those subjects that should be taught to all pupils. All schools must publish their school curriculum by subject and academic year online.

2.5 All schools should make provision for personal, social, health and economic education (PSHE), drawing on good practice. Schools are also free to include other subjects or topics of their choice in planning and designing their own programme of education.

3. The national curriculum in England

Aims

3.1 The national curriculum provides pupils with an introduction to the essential knowledge that they need to be educated citizens. It introduces pupils to the best that has been thought and said; and helps engender an appreciation of human creativity and achievement.

3.2   The national curriculum is just one element in the education of every child. There is time and space in the school day and in each week, term and year to range beyond the national curriculum specifications. The national curriculum provides an outline of core knowledge around which teachers can develop exciting and stimulating lessons to promote the development of pupils' knowledge, understanding and skills as part of the wider school curriculum.

Structure

3.3   Pupils of compulsory school age in community and foundation schools, including community special schools and foundation special schools, and in voluntary aided and voluntary controlled schools, must follow the national curriculum. It is organised on the basis of four key stages and twelve subjects, classified in legal terms as 'core' and 'other foundation' subjects.

3.4   The Secretary of State for Education is required to publish programmes of study for each national curriculum subject, setting out the 'matters, skills and processes' to be taught at each key stage. Schools are free to choose how they organise their school day, as long as the content of the national curriculum programmes of study is taught to all pupils.

3.5   The structure of the national curriculum, in terms of which subjects are compulsory at each key stage, is set out in the table below.

	Key stage 1	Key stage 2	Key stage 3	Key stage 4
Age	5–7	7–11	11–14	14–16
Year groups	1–2	3–6	7–9	10–11
Core subjects				
English	✓	✓	✓	✓
Mathematics	✓	✓	✓	✓
Science	✓	✓	✓	✓
Foundation subjects				
Art and design	✓	✓	✓	
Citizenship			✓	✓
Computing	✓	✓	✓	✓
Design and technology	✓	✓	✓	
Languages*		✓	✓	
Geography	✓	✓	✓	
History	✓	✓	✓	
Music	✓	✓	✓	
Physical education	✓	✓	✓	✓

Figure 1.1   Structure of the national curriculum

*Note: At key stage 2 the subject title is 'foreign language'; at key stage 3 it is 'modern foreign language'.

3.6   All schools are also required to teach religious education at all key stages. Secondary schools must provide sex and relationship education.

	Key stage 1	Key stage 2	Key stage 3	Key stage 4
Age	5–7	7–11	11–14	14–16
Year groups	1–2	3–6	7–9	10–11
Religious education	✓	✓	✓	✓
Sex and relationship education			✓	✓

Figure 1.2   Statutory teaching of religious education and sex and relationship education

2 Principles of planning

Keira Sewell

Principles 1 Generic principles of planning

This unit outlines some of the generic principles of planning, whatever the subject. It should be read in conjunction with the appropriate subject chapter in Section 2 of this book. Reference will also be made to the generic principles outlined in the framework for the national curriculum, found in Section 2 of this chapter.

Overview

Planning is the cornerstone to effective learning but it is also one of the most challenging aspects of teaching. Getting it right can be difficult but careful thought can help you avoid some of the common mistakes and improve the ways in which you support and promote learning in the classroom.

The Teachers' Standards (DfE, 2013) define the minimum level of practice from the point of being awarded Qualified Teacher Status (QTS) and must be achieved by the end of any period of teacher training in order to qualify as a teacher and begin the induction period. Although the interconnected nature of the Standards makes it difficult to separate them out, there are clear Standards relating to planning and it is the achievement of these which will be the focus of this chapter.

The Teachers' Standards which relate to planning are as follows.

- Plan and teach well-structured lessons.
- Impart knowledge and develop understanding through effective use of lesson time.
- Promote a love of learning and children's intellectual curiosity.
- Set homework and plan other out-of-class activities to consolidate and extend the knowledge and understanding pupils have acquired.
- Reflect systematically on the effectiveness of lessons and approaches to teaching.
- Contribute to the design and provision of an engaging curriculum within the relevant subject area(s).

Planning effective lessons

It is important to remember that teaching does not necessarily equal learning and planning effectively requires careful thought to ensure what we do in our lessons/activities supports and promotes learning and enables children to make progress. This requires an understanding of how we develop as professionals; a good model to start with is the relationship between theory, research and practice.

A quick glance at the internet will provide many examples of activities which can be done in the classroom or even outside it. Many of these are exciting and fun but not all promote learning. While exciting and fun is a good starting point, learning is challenging and needs to be underpinned by a clear rationale.

Putting into practice effective planning requires us to think about the theories which underpin effective learning. It is likely that you will have studied learning theories such as behaviourism, constructivism and social contructivism but new theories of learning located in the neurosciences are emerging and influencing our thinking about how learning can best be supported in the classroom. These emerging theories are informed by current research in a range of different areas and subjects, enabling us to draw information from a wide spectrum and formulate new ways of thinking and working. It is important that you keep up-to-date with current theories and research as teaching is not formulaic; what works well in one situation, on one day with one group of children may not be so effective in another context. Therefore, your planning must be informed by current thinking and by your knowledge of the children you are teaching.

In order to explore the ways in which the Teachers' Standards relating to planning can be achieved this chapter will focus on three aspects through which the relationship between theory, research and practice can be explored. These are:

- lesson content and structure;
- classroom organisation;
- teaching strategies.

For the purposes of this section we are looking only at short-term planning but Section 3 of this book explores planning structures which are longer term.

1. Lesson content and structure

There are many ways of planning lessons and it is likely that your training institution or school will have adopted a structure which suits their needs. As you look through this book you will see that the planning structure has been adapted to suit the needs of each subject area and that the format may look slightly different; however, you will also see that each example of planning has areas in common. As a trainee, you will usually need to follow very detailed planning structures which will help support you during what can be a very challenging and often stressful time. As you become more experienced your planning may become less detailed and more long term. Whatever planning format you use it is important to consider what should be included and why.

Organisational details

It is important to include sections where you can record the date and time of the lesson, the group you are teaching, the number of children, the subject or topic focus and the national curriculum reference or context of study. You may also include reference to prior learning or the context of your planning. All this provides easy reference to all the information about the lesson and allows you to annotate your plans should things change (as they often do in the primary classroom). Your planning files should be a working document and it is good practice to annotate your plans to show how you are responding to different circumstances and to children's progress.

Focus on learning

This is **the** most important part of any planning and must be done first. If you do not know what you are intending children to learn then you will not know what activities to choose.

Begin by identifying what you want children to learn. This should build on previous learning or identified areas of misconception. You will find that different schools call this different names ('learning objectives', 'intended learning', 'learning outcomes', etc.) but they all equate to one thing – what will children learn from your planned lesson or activity? For the purposes of this book we will use the phrase *intended learning*.

The focus of learning will, initially, be drawn from the statutory programmes of study in the national curriculum. These are learning outcomes rather than learning objectives and should be thought of as the learning children will need to have achieved at the end of the year or key stage. This means, in most cases, you will need to break these down into smaller steps to identify the progression within these ideas and the learning for each lesson. Consider the following:

- *Children will be taught to:*
  develop positive attitudes towards and stamina for writing by: . . .writing for different purposes (English programme of study, Year 2, writing composition, DfE, 2013)

What learning does this identify? Could this be done in one lesson? What are 'positive attitudes' and what kinds of 'different purposes' are there for writing? Reading the non-statutory guidance is a very useful starting point as this provides further information about what and how these areas can be taught.

You will also notice that the national curriculum uses the phrase 'children will be taught to . . .' which sometimes means that we have to work harder to consider what children will learn from this teaching. Remember teaching does not always equal learning. Good subject knowledge is essential. This will enable you to break down large ideas and concepts into smaller steps and better understand progression in learning.

Let us imagine we want children to learn how to write a formal letter and that we decide to use the context of writing to the manager of a local supermarket asking her about the packaging of products. Our intended learning might read:

- *Children will learn to compose a formal letter*

It is usual for lessons to have no more than three objectives for learning although there may be occasions when you have more, particularly if the lesson is addressing more than one subject area. Your objectives may also include aspects which are not part of the national curriculum but reflect local needs, the needs of individual children or specific skills or attitudes you wish to develop. For example, you may wish children to learn to work as part of a team.

Once we have established what we want children to learn we need to consider how we will know when this has been achieved. In order to do this we need to identify what constitutes success. Again there are many phrases used to describe this but for the purposes of this book we will use the phrase *success criteria*. Success in composing a formal letter may be identified if children:

- *place their own address correctly*
- *date the letter correctly*
- *use a formal style of writing to convey meaning*
- *sign the letter correctly.*

A good way to review the effectiveness of success criteria is to use the acronym we often use for setting goals – SMART:

Specific – to the children and to the intended learning.
Measurable – in terms of progress against learning.
Attainable – for all children.
Realistic – within the time parameters and the learning challenge.
Timely – clear outcomes within a given timeframe.

Good success criteria enable you to quickly make a decision about whether a child has achieved the learning intended and, if not, what aspect they are finding challenging. Avoid woolly statements like 'continue to', 'experience', 'develop' as it is difficult to identify when these have been achieved.

The third stage of identifying learning is to determine how you will assess what has been learned – we will call this the *assessment strategy*. In the example of intended learning from English it is obvious that the most sensible approach would be to collect in and mark children's letters. However, it is important to remember that there are many strategies you could choose from and that not all evidence will be permanent. The evidence arising from some strategies, such as observation and questioning, will be more ephemeral. Remember that your lesson plan is a large part of your evidence for assessment as it details what constitutes success in learning and how this was assessed. We do not always need a product from children in order to record their achievements.

As you can see, there is a clear route through identifying learning.

Intended learning → success criteria → assessment strategy

It is important you get all these things in place before deciding how you will teach as each step impacts on classroom organisation and choice of teaching and learning strategies.

As you become more experienced you will be able to provide differentiated learning to accommodate individual needs of the children in your class. Sometimes these will be differentiated by outcome and may be identified by success criteria which begin 'all children will . . .', 'some children will . . .' and 'a few children will . . .'. In other cases differentiation will be by task and your intended learning will be different for different individuals or groups of children.

Lesson structure

Once you have established intended learning it is likely that you have already thought of some ideas about how you might like to achieve this. You will have some teaching approaches in mind and have some idea about how the lesson will flow. We will cover teaching and learning strategies in more detail later in this chapter but it is important also to consider the overall structure of the lesson.

Think about how your lesson will begin. Different learning will require different introductions but the important thing is to consider how you can engage children in the activity right from the start. Sometimes we call this the 'hook'. As you look through the example lessons provided in the subject sections of this book you will see different 'hooks', all of which have been designed specifically to introduce an area of learning and engage children. Think carefully about the impact of the introduction to your lesson. For example, it is common for schools to begin lessons with children sitting on the carpet; while this has advantages, such as being able to gather children around a resource (e.g. an interactive whiteboard), it also presents some organisational issues. Many classrooms are not large enough for children to sit in a clear space and this can lead to behaviour management issues when children sit too close together or behind/between tables. It also takes time to move children to the carpet and move them back again, which may not justify the potential for learning. Finally, sitting on a carpet in a cold classroom may not be the most comfortable way to begin the lesson. Think carefully about how you could use a range of strategies to introduce a lesson in order to ensure children are engaged and on task right from the start.

Consider then how your lesson will progress. Will it follow the format of introduction, main activity and plenary or is there potential for doing shorter activities with mini-plenaries to clarify, monitor or assess learning? Not all lessons should follow the same format and the structure should be determined by the intended learning.

At each point you should think about three things.

- What will the teacher be teaching and why?
- What will the children be doing in order to learn?
- How long will it take to do both of these?

These questions enable you to think through the ideas about which strategies best promote learning, which learning theories underpin these and how best to engage children in their learning.

Timings are a really important thing to put on your lesson plans. They enable you to manage your time effectively and allow you to set clear expectations with time limits which can be communicated to your children. For example, 'you have fifteen minutes to write one paragraph of your letter'. It is likely that, at first, your lessons will be either too long or too short as timings are quite difficult to judge with a new class. For this reason it is often useful to have extension activities planned just in case the children finish much earlier than planned.

Vocabulary

Your lesson plans should identify the new vocabulary you are intending children to learn. This is important as it is likely that the concepts or processes you are teaching will be associated with specific vocabulary and you will need to think about how to teach this. Be wary here of identifying all the words you or the children will be using and focus solely on the vocabulary linked to the intended learning. This does not restrict you to these words but does ensure these are a focus of the lesson and that you have thought through what they mean before you begin teaching.

Resources

Identifying the resources you will need for the lesson helps you to be prepared. Good lessons begin long before you start teaching and careful preparation ensures you are not rushing around at the last minute trying to collect what you need. The following areas are for you to consider.

- Which resources will best support the intended learning? This may mean ordering resources from an outside source (e.g. visiting speaker, health education unit) or booking resources within the school (e.g. the laptops, the hall/gym).
- Which resources do you need to make or prepare?
- Where do you wish to hold the lesson? Would it work best outside the classroom and, if so, where? If you are working outside, particularly off-site, you will need to follow your school's risk assessment procedures and adhere to the recommended pupil:staff ratio.
- How will you organise the resources? Will they be accessible to children from the start or will they be given out or collected when required? How will this affect the extent to which children can be independent in their learning and how will it affect behaviour management in the classroom?
- Have you checked that all the resources you intend to use are safe for use within the classroom? Are there any children who may react negatively to some resources (e.g. some children hate puppets and others hate working outdoors)?
- Are there any resources which may exclude children, create barriers to learning or which promote or suggest stereotypes?

Homework

Your school will have a homework policy which you will need to adhere to. This will include details on how much and what types of homework each school administers. If your school does have a homework requirement then think carefully about how any homework given contributes to the learning of either this lesson or the sequence of lessons. Children are more likely to see the benefit of homework if they can see value in it and engage accordingly. Homework does not have to be a written record but could be an activity which involves the whole family, some research, watching a particular television programme or accessing a particular website. Be creative!

Evaluation

An important part of your lesson plan will be the evaluation. Planning is cyclical and your evaluation from the previous lesson should inform future planning. Most training institutions will have their own format but these will have two areas which will be common to all: children's learning and the effectiveness of the teaching approach.

At first you will be required to complete very detailed evaluations of at least some of the teaching you do. This is important as it ensures you reflect carefully on your own teaching and the impact it has had on learning. It also contributes to the assessments you make of individual, group and class learning.

A common error in evaluations is that teachers identify all the aspects of their teaching which have had a negative impact on learning rather than also including aspects which have supported or promoted learning. It is often easier to identify what we do not do well than it is to identify our strengths, often because these come more naturally to us and are more intuitive. Make sure your evaluations are balanced and realistic. For example, if you are still in the early stages of delivering lessons it is unlikely that differentiated learning is going to be a strength at this time. Be honest in your evaluations. Are children misbehaving because they are badly behaved or because they are disengaged with you and your lesson? Look at how they respond to other adults in the classroom; do they respond differently and what do these adults do to engender this? Once you evaluate effectively you can use your reflections to inform your future planning and set yourself realistic targets for your own professional development.

2. Classroom organisation

Organising your classroom well can greatly impact on the effectiveness of your lesson. For the purposes of this book we will focus on grouping, seating arrangements, teacher role and additional support, all of which need to be considered in effective planning.

Grouping

Perhaps one of the greatest impacts on how we group children was the work of Piaget and Vygotsky through their theories of constructivism and social constructivism. Both these theories of learning stressed the importance of others in learning and this has led to a more collaborative approach in the classroom. However, research has given rise to a number of debates around grouping, namely whether group work works equally for children with different levels of attainment, gender or learning needs and whether all work should be collaborative.

The best way to address this is to be aware of the research relating to grouping in the classroom and to consider the best way to support learning. Individual learning opportunities have great value in the classroom and should be part of your repertoire of classroom organisation. However, grouping also supports collaborative learning very effectively but consider what type of grouping may work best (e.g. by attainment, friendship, interests, gender, etc.).

If you do group children, think about the size of the group. Often, group tables in the classroom mean group sizes can be as large as eight children, but is it possible for all these children to work collaboratively on the same project or do they tend to break into smaller groups?

Consider what role children will take in a group. Are children's strengths being used effectively or are areas of weakness being developed? Do the same children always do the practical element of an activity and do others always act as scribes? Are all children engaged in the activity or do some metaphorically or physically remove themselves? One approach is to allocate roles which change according to the activity or the areas you want to develop within the group or for individual children.

Seating arrangements

You may find that classroom seating arrangements remain the same regardless of the activity but effective planning considers how best to arrange seating so that it accommodates the teaching and learning approaches adopted. Obviously one of the factors which will determine this is whether you want children to work as groups or individually. Do not feel that you have to change your classroom every time you deliver a different lesson but experiment with different arrangements to see how they work for you. You could try the following.

- Horseshoe – useful for debates, discussions and practical music making.
- Small group tables – useful for practical activities which require small groups (up to 4) to work together.
- Large group tables – useful for collaborative activities where contributions from a number of children is effective.
- Rows – useful for individual working or more delivery mode activities.
- L-shape or F-shape – useful for enabling exchange across different groups of children but also allowing for pair or individual work.
- Open plan floor work with tables and chairs pushed to the sides of the room – useful for large practical activities which require space, circle time in PSHE and practical music making.

However you decide to organise your classroom the emphasis should be on learning – how will your chosen arrangement support children making progress?

Teacher role

Effective teachers need to manage the group of learners, the activities within the lesson and the learning simultaneously; not an easy role! Good teachers make this look effortless but they have worked hard to adopt roles which enable effective management of teaching and learning and transition seamlessly from one to another. Planning out how you might adopt different roles enables you to anticipate what might happen in a lesson. Roles you may adopt include:

- managing;
- modelling;
- coaching;
- facilitating;
- observing;
- assessing;
- prompting;
- questioning.

A useful approach is to have two columns in your planning – 'What the teacher will do' and 'What the children will do'. This enables you to think through the roles you will adopt and how they may promote learning. One good question to ask when planning a lesson is 'Who will work hardest?' Should it be you or the children?

Additional support

Whether your additional adult support is a parent, a learning mentor, a teaching assistant or a learning support assistant, who may be assigned to a specific child or children, you need to plan how they will support specific individuals or groups of children and you will need to ensure they are clear about their role and purpose within the classroom. There is great debate around this issue, most commonly around whether additional support should be assigned to low attaining or high attaining groups. There are advantages and disadvantages to both but any approach will only be effective if your adult support understands the learning intended and how best to support children in achieving this. This means that you must share your planning with them and prepare any assessment structures (including key ideas and questions) you wish them to use.

Remember also that support is not confined only to lower or higher attainers; there is a danger that we ignore those middle attainers who could achieve more if given appropriate support.

3. Teaching strategies

There are many teaching strategies we could use and to mention them all is way beyond the scope of this book; however, there are key elements which are central to current thinking in education and one way to break this down is to think of three elements.

- Content – **what** will be taught.
- Approach to teaching and learning – **how** it is taught and learned.
- Rationale – the underpinning philosophies, values and theories of **why** it will be taught.

Whilst the 'what', 'how' and 'why' may vary for each subject, something which will be explored further in the following subject-specific chapters in Section 2 of this book, there are some generic ideas and this section will focus on the following.

- Promoting a love of learning.
- Inclusion.
- Dialogic learning.
- Literacy and numeracy.
- Information and communications technology.

Promoting a love of learning

We often hear that children have a 'natural curiosity' but is this necessarily true and is it true they are curious about all things? The answer is probably 'no'; not all children are interested in what we want them to be interested in and not all children love learning. Think about your own learning; is it easy and comfortable or is it challenging and sometimes uncomfortable? Do you need time to assimilate new learning or is it instantaneous? A large part of choosing effective teaching strategies is about determining what will engage children and how they will enjoy learning to learn.

When choosing a teaching strategy the central premise should be that it will promote learning. This means that every decision you make about 'what', 'how' and 'why' should be underpinned by clearly thought through principles on how this will enable children to learn more effectively. Think about what engages you in learning new things. Is it the way it relates to you personally, your interests, your expertise? Is it the way in which it is presented to you, the ideas used, the choice of media? Is it the level of challenge? This does not suggest that we should only use teaching strategies which are within the children's zone of interest but knowing our children well does enable us to tailor activities to their specific needs and to respond to personal or community interests or issues. This may mean bringing in expertise from the local community or using the local football pitch as a context for learning, it may mean using social networks or blogs to share findings or it may mean using stories as a way of exploring historical contexts.

Recently, greater emphasis has been placed on enabling children to learn how to learn with significant success. These ideas build on current research around how we learn and aim to equip children with the thinking skills, behaviours and attitudes of learning. Work by Guy Claxton, Natasha Serrett and Mary Budd Rowe are good starting points when thinking how you will create opportunities within your planning for children to develop these skills (see further reading). For example, learner independence can be encouraged by creating space within a lesson for independent enquiry and resilience can be developed by providing children with strategies to manage distractions. Encouraging, ordering and recording thinking can be encouraged by a variety of approaches and you may find reading work around De Bono's six thinking hats (De Bono, 2009), mind mapping (Buzan, 2003), the habits of mind (Costa, 2008) and taxonomy of learning (Bloom, 1956) useful starting points.

Essentially, the possibilities are endless in terms of teaching approaches but consider how the strategy itself promotes learning. A useful starting point is to think about the following.

- Differentiation.
- Active learning.
- Creativity.
- Out of classroom learning.
- Peer education.
- Co-operative and collaborative learning.
- ICT in education.
- Learning to learn.

It should be noted, however, that there are common pitfalls associated with choosing teaching strategies. First, the strategy itself becomes the focus rather than the learning it should facilitate. For example, the use of interactive whiteboards became a common teaching approach when the government funded their installation in all primary classrooms; however, the extent to which they were used effectively varies enormously from school to school. As a display resource they can be a fun way of presenting something (as long as we avoid the 'death by PowerPoint' route) but making the transition to effective learning can be more challenging. How can we use the 'interactive' element more effectively? Second, there is also a danger that the level of resource preparation required in certain approaches greatly outweighs the overall learning gain leaving teachers planning and preparing for hours on end with no significant outcome. Third, some approaches are more easily (and comfortably) used by some teachers and not others. For example, when drama-based approaches such as 'hot seating' are used well they can be very effective but, used badly, they can quickly lose the interest and engagement of the children.

Inclusion

The national curriculum is very clear about inclusion in that it identifies that teachers should:

- have high expectations of all children;
- adhere to the appropriate equal opportunities legislation and roles and duties of the profession;
- ensure there are no barriers to learning and provide access to learning under the SEN Code of Practice where appropriate.

In your planning you will need to ensure that you adhere to government, local and school policies regarding inclusion and that you are sensitive to the needs of children in your class. This will mean considering how you will provide appropriate challenge in your lessons for *all* learners, how you will organise and manage resources (including supporting adults), how you will ensure all children can communicate learning effectively, how you will engage and support children, how you will group children and what contexts for learning you might use. Reference to the Teachers' Standards (DfE, 2013) outlines further how you will be expected to meet the needs of all your learners.

Dialogic learning

Dialogue has long been seen as an important factor in education; however, many educators have recently begun to look more critically at the extent to which effective dialogue is actually a part of our classrooms. Research has shown that classroom talk tends to be dominated by teachers and that interactions are more likely to be teacher–pupil–teacher rather than encouraging pupil–pupil dialogue. The importance of dialogue in learning and the different types of talk have been explored by a number of authors but the work of Alexander (2008 and 2010), Mercer (1996) and Mortimer and Scott (2003) are useful starting points when considering how you might promote dialogic learning in your classroom.

Improving dialogue in the classroom is not just a matter of using specific teaching approaches; it requires thought about classroom organisation and ethos, groupings, peer and adult support, development of the interpersonal skills required for collaboration and discussion and learning context. A study by Baines et al. (2009) provides a useful insight into the complexity of this; however, there are some teaching approaches you can incorporate into your planning to achieve a more dialogic classroom which include:

- small group work;
- paired talk;
- open questions – make sure you write them on your plan;
- wonder walls;
- no hands up policy (use lolly sticks to target specific children or use strategies such as 'phone a friend');
- whiteboards to record ideas for discussion;
- prompts for discussion (e.g. concept maps or cartoons);
- different audiences or initiators (e.g. hot seating, role play, puppets).

Critically, you must ensure the timings in your planning allow for 'wait time' when asking questions or encouraging discussion. You should also consider how you will manage more open discussions which can go somewhat off track!

Look down your lesson plan – how much time do you anticipate you will be talking, how much time do you anticipate children will be talking, how much time do you anticipate there will be no talk at all? When do children get thinking time in your lesson?

Literacy and numeracy

A key element of the national curriculum is that every opportunity should be used to develop children's numerical and literary skills, even if these are not the primary subject focus of the lesson (see Principles 2, Points 4 and 5). This means that you should use opportunities to exploit this and teach two or more subjects through one lesson or activity. Not only is this good practice in terms of demonstrating the relationship between areas of learning, it also leaves time to explore other areas of interest or local importance. Further exploration of this is provided in Section 3.

Achieving this is often relatively easy if a little thought is given during the initial stages of planning. As can be seen from the earlier section on dialogic learning, spoken language can be developed in a variety of ways. For example, in music the emphasis is on oracy, with children encouraged to 'show me' rather than 'tell me' through the dominant language of sound. In the same way reading and writing can make use of the variety of contexts and genres provided through other subject areas. Identifying the vocabulary you are teaching has already been discussed earlier in this chapter. Identifying mathematical links can be more easily achieved in some subjects, for example science, than others and therefore you should not try and force links where they do not exist. The important element is to consider where you would like to locate new teaching in literacy and numeracy; is it best taught within a literacy or numeracy lesson and then practised and demonstrated in a lesson which focuses on a different subject area or is there scope for teaching more than one subject in a single lesson? Consider extended projects which enable you to build on ideas developed through a number of different activities which have a core focus.

Information and communications technology

The revisions to the national curriculum saw a change in name from information and communications technology (ICT) to computing. This saw a shift in focus within the curriculum to teaching specific computing skills with a greater emphasis on using and applying digital technology across the curriculum. Planning in each subject will need to reflect on the use of ICT, in its broadest sense, to ensure children have the opportunity to develop their understanding and application of ICT within the real world.

There are many examples in the non-statutory guidance of how ICT can be used effectively to support and promote learning across the curriculum. The rate of technological development is often difficult to keep abreast with but your planning will need to reflect new technologies and new ways of learning. ICT should engage learners and enhance learning opportunities if it is to be incorporated in your planning to best effect.

Further reading

Alexander, R. J. (2008) *Towards Dialogic Teaching: Rethinking Classroom Talk* (4th edition). Dialogos.

Alexander, R. J. (2010) *Dialogic Teaching Essentials.* [online] Available at: **www.nie.edu.sg/files/oer/FINAL%20Dialogic%20Teaching%20Essentials.pdf**

Baines, E., Rubie-Davies, C. and Blatchford, P. (2009) Improving pupil group work interaction and dialogue in primary classrooms: Results from a year-long intervention study. *Cambridge Journal of Education,* 39(1): 95–117.

Bloom, B. S. (ed.) (1956) *Taxonomy of Educational Objectives, the Classification of Educational Goals – Handbook I: Cognitive Domain.* New York: McKay.

Budd Rowe, M. (1986) Wait time: Slowing down may be a way of speeding up! *Journal of Teacher Education,* 37, 43–50.

Buzan, T. (2003) *Mind Maps for Kids: An Introduction.* London: Harper Thorsons.

Claxton, G. (1999) *Wise Up: The Challenges of Lifelong Learning.* London: Bloomsbury (Stafford Educational Press, 2001).

Claxton, G. *Building Learning Power.* [online] Available at: **www.buildinglearningpower.co.uk**

Costa, A. L. (2008) Describing the habits of mind. In Costa, A. L. and Kallick, B. (eds) *Learning and Leading with Habits of Mind: 16 Essential Characteristics for Success.* Alexandria: Association for Supervision & Curriculum Development.

DfE (2013) *Teachers' Standards.* [online] Available at **www.gov.uk/government/collections/teachers-standards**

Mercer, N. (1996) Sociocultural perspectives and the study of classroom discourse. In Coll, C. and Edwards, D. (eds) *Discourse and Learning in the Classroom.* Madrid: Infancia and Aprendizaje, 13–23.

Mortimer, E. F. and Scott, P. H. (2003) *Meaning Making in Secondary Science Classrooms.* Maidenhead: Open University Press.

Serret, N. (2006) Developing children's thinking in primary science. In Harlen, W. (ed.) *ASE Guide to Primary Science Education.* Hatfield: ASE.

Principles 2 The framework for the national curriculum

4. Inclusion

Setting suitable challenges

4.1 Teachers should set high expectations for every pupil. They should plan stretching work for pupils whose attainment is significantly above the expected standard. They have an even greater obligation to plan lessons for pupils who have low levels of prior attainment or come from disadvantaged backgrounds. Teachers should use appropriate assessment to set targets which are deliberately ambitious.

Responding to pupils' needs and overcoming potential barriers for individuals and groups of pupils

4.2 Teachers should take account of their duties under equal opportunities legislation that covers race, disability, sex, religion or belief, sexual orientation, pregnancy and maternity, and gender reassignment.

4.3 A wide range of pupils have special educational needs, many of whom also have disabilities. Lessons should be planned to ensure that there are no barriers to *every* pupil achieving. In many cases, such planning will mean that these pupils will be able to study the full national curriculum. The SEN Code of Practice includes advice on approaches to identification of need which can support this. A minority of pupils will need access to specialist equipment and different approaches. The SEN Code of Practice outlines what needs to be done for them.

4.4 With the right teaching, that recognises their individual needs, many disabled pupils may have little need for additional resources beyond the aids which they use as part of their daily life. Teachers must plan lessons so that these pupils can study every national curriculum subject. Potential areas of difficulty should be identified and addressed at the outset of work.

4.5 Teachers must also take account of the needs of pupils whose first language is not English. Monitoring of progress should take account of the pupil's age, length of time in this country, previous educational experience and ability in other languages.

4.6 The ability of pupils for whom English is an additional language to take part in the national curriculum may be in advance of their communication skills in English. Teachers should plan teaching opportunities to help pupils develop their English and should aim to provide the support pupils need to take part in all subjects.

5. Numeracy and mathematics

5.1 Teachers should use every relevant subject to develop pupils' mathematical fluency. Confidence in numeracy and other mathematical skills is a precondition of success across the national curriculum.

5.2   Teachers should develop pupils' numeracy and mathematical reasoning in all subjects so that they understand and appreciate the importance of mathematics. Pupils should be taught to apply arithmetic fluently to problems, understand and use measures, make estimates and sense check their work. Pupils should apply their geometric and algebraic understanding, and relate their understanding of probability to the notions of risk and uncertainty. They should also understand the cycle of collecting, presenting and analysing data. They should be taught to apply their mathematics to both routine and non-routine problems, including breaking down more complex problems into a series of simpler steps.

6. Language and literacy

6.1   Teachers should develop pupils' spoken language, reading, writing and vocabulary as integral aspects of the teaching of every subject. English is both a subject in its own right and the medium for teaching; for pupils, understanding the language provides access to the whole curriculum. Fluency in the English language is an essential foundation for success in all subjects.

Spoken language

6.2   Pupils should be taught to speak clearly and convey ideas confidently using Standard English. They should learn to justify ideas with reasons; ask questions to check understanding; develop vocabulary and build knowledge; negotiate; evaluate and build on the ideas of others; and select the appropriate register for effective communication. They should be taught to give well-structured descriptions and explanations and develop their understanding through speculating, hypothesising and exploring ideas. This will enable them to clarify their thinking as well as organise their ideas for writing.

Reading and writing

6.3   Teachers should develop pupils' reading and writing in all subjects to support their acquisition of knowledge. Pupils should be taught to read fluently, understand extended prose (both fiction and non-fiction) and be encouraged to read for pleasure. Schools should do everything to promote wider reading. They should provide library facilities and set ambitious expectations for reading at home. Pupils should develop the stamina and skills to write at length, with accurate spelling and punctuation. They should be taught the correct use of grammar. They should build on what they have been taught to expand the range of their writing and the variety of the grammar they use. The writing they do should include narratives, explanations, descriptions, comparisons, summaries and evaluations: such writing supports them in rehearsing, understanding and consolidating what they have heard or read.

Vocabulary development

6.4 Pupils' acquisition and command of vocabulary are key to their learning and progress across the whole curriculum. Teachers should therefore develop vocabulary actively, building systematically on pupils' current knowledge. They should increase pupils' store of words in general; simultaneously, they should also make links between known and new vocabulary and discuss the shades of meaning in similar words. In this way, pupils expand the vocabulary choices that are available to them when they write. In addition, it is vital for pupils' comprehension that they understand the meanings of words they meet in their reading across all subjects, and older pupils should be taught the meaning of instruction verbs that they may meet in examination questions. It is particularly important to induct pupils into the language which defines each subject in its own right, such as accurate mathematical and scientific language.

3 Mastery in the national curriculum

Keira Sewell

What is mastery?

The revision of the national curriculum in 2014 (DfE, 2014) brought with it an alternative way of reviewing learning. For the first time since the implementation of the national curriculum the levels were removed. Many educationalists had argued that these levels were not a dependable way of defining achievement, giving rise to a multitude of interpretations and resulting in inconsistent use. There was also concern that the statements of attainment lent themselves to a somewhat arbitrary 'tick box' approach to assessment, which was at odds with the concept of deep learning.

The revised curriculum gave much greater focus to progression of understanding and depth of learning rather than focusing on a more formulaic idea of progression, which simply moved children to the next set of content. The idea of 'mastery level' came from the publication of the performance levels soon after the implementation of the revised curriculum. Since then this has been replaced with the descriptor 'working at greater depth' in the current Teacher assessment frameworks for key stages 1 and 2 for use in the 2017 to 2018 academic year (STA, 2017). These frameworks are only available for English, mathematics and science. The descriptors 'working towards the expected standard', 'working at the expected standard' and 'working at greater depth within the expected standard' are used for English and mathematics, while science only has descriptors for 'working at the expected standard'.

Whilst it is expected that all children will achieve the learning identified in the national curriculum for their age group, some children will demonstrate different depths of learning. Those working at greater depth exhibit learning characteristics associated with mastery, such as a deep learning of key constructs and ideas, which can be recalled over time and used and applied in a range of contexts, the ability to make sound links between ideas and constructs, both in the same subject and with other relevant subjects, and the ability to use skills and processes drawn from a variety of sources. Section 3 provides examples of cross-curricular planning that enables children to demonstrate their developing mastery.

Planning for mastery

Effective planning enables children to make progress and the revised curriculum was designed to enhance this in two key ways.

First, the content was revised to better reflect expected learning for a specific age group. In most subjects this resulted in a reduction of content, so that more time could be spent on embedding key ideas and principles before progressing to the next level of learning. In order to understand this, it can help if we remember learning is neither neat nor linear. Think of learning as building a wall, rather than building a tower. For a wall to be strong and long lasting the structure must be sound and the foundations firm. Whilst we can build up different sections of the wall at different times, we do not want to leave major gaps as this would limit the height to which we can build. It is this approach that enables children to develop an understanding of the 'big ideas' and key principles of learning, such as understanding genres in literature or understanding forces in science. That is not to say there can be no bricks missing at all; all of us have small gaps in our knowledge or understanding which may not impede our progression in understanding. However, if there are significant gaps this will impact on our future progression.

Second, there was much greater focus on progression in the language used within statements of attainment. Look carefully at the words used in the national curriculum and consider what they mean in terms of learning, as they are good indicators of what should be taught.

Bloom's taxonomy of learning domains is a useful starting point when understanding progression and the route to mastery. Devised as a means of promoting higher level learning, his identification of six categories within the cognitive domain has underpinned approaches to teaching for many years. Figure 3.1 provides a summary of the key principles and the key words associated with each category.

To move from the two lower levels to the higher levels associated with mastery, children must have a sound knowledge base of the subject. This requires the teacher to also have a good understanding of the subject, so that they can identify misconceptions and plan learning opportunities that enable children to continue to make progress. Each subject chapter in Section 2 provides references to subject knowledge texts that will support you.

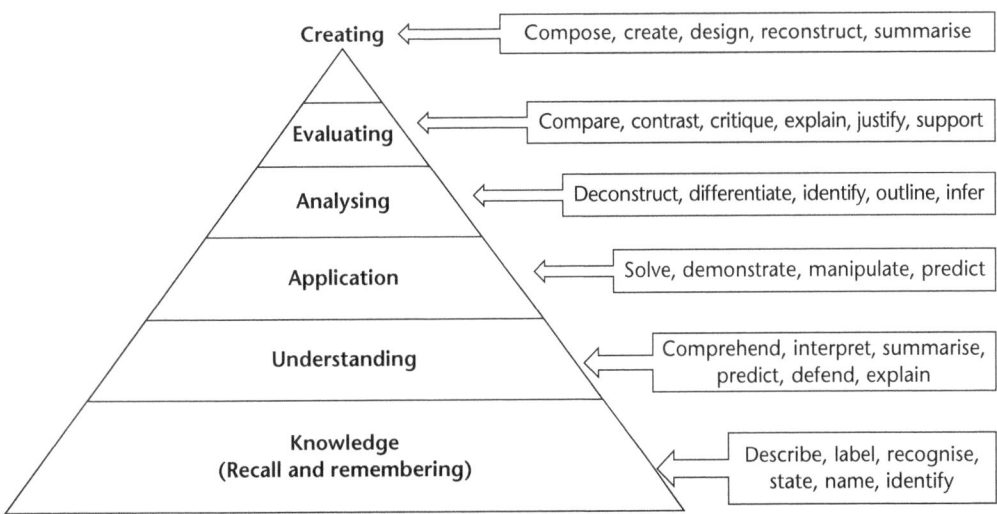

Figure 3.1   Bloom's categories in the cognitive domain

Reflective task

Consider the following statements of attainment from the science curriculum for Year 4 and Year 6.

- Recognise that a switch opens and closes a circuit and associate this with whether or not a lamp lights in a simple series circuit. (Year 4 Programme of study, DFE, 2014)
- Compare and give reasons for variations in how components function, including the brightness of bulbs, the loudness of buzzers and the on/off position of switches. (Year 6 Programme of study, DFE, 2014)

In the first the children are required to observe an effect whilst, in the second, children will need to compare the effects of varying components in circuits and begin to develop principles of circuits and the flow of electrical current which can be applied in a range of contexts. They will need to draw on ideas of circuits, conductivity, voltage and resistance, all of which are much more complex ideas and require much deeper understanding of the effects of electricity.

Using the categories in Bloom's cognitive domain and the words associated with each level, what activity could you plan to enable children to demonstrate progression to Bloom's level of application in their understanding of the concept of electricity?

Chapter 2, in this section, outlined the principles of effective planning and emphasised the need to focus on learning. Clear learning objectives are critical to promoting mastery in your classroom, but equally critical is the need to employ a variety of teaching approaches that enable children to develop, not only their conceptual or procedural understanding, but also the skills and attitudes deep learning requires. These include:

- independence;
- a willingness to fail (trial and error is an essential part of learning);
- the ability to apply learning both within a subject and across subjects;
- the ability to apply learning without reminders or pre-teaching;
- the ability to teach others;
- resilience.

Achieving this will require you to move from being the instructor to the facilitator of learning and to differentiate your planning to scaffold children developing their learning skills. The subject-focused chapters in Section 2 will help you consider how you might use a range of teaching strategies to promote these characteristics in your learners.

Assessing mastery

The published teacher assessment frameworks for key stages 1 and 2 (STA, 2017) are a useful reference point to identify the level at which children are working. However, assessment of learning is a much more complex process than simply identifying what children can do. It can be difficult to assess deep understanding. Think about the following when planning your schemes of work.

First, you will need to provide a range of opportunities for children to demonstrate the extent of their learning, rather than relying on single lessons that are assessed in isolation. Think about Bruner's idea of the spiral curriculum where learning programmes enable children to develop an understanding of increasingly more complex ideas. Assessment of this may take place at specific points, which will enable you to monitor progress, identify misconceptions and diagnose barriers to learning. As a result, you will be able to plan differentiated activities that support children in their continued progress. Summative methods of assessment should be planned to enable children to understand, demonstrate and celebrate their achievements. For an example of this look at the Teacher Assessment in Primary Science (TAPS) project (TAPS, online).

Second, you will need to critically evaluate your planning to ensure you are using strategies that enable children to demonstrate mastery. The iterative cycle of formative assessment often begins with a more teacher-led approach where the teacher describes, explains or demonstrates concepts or skills, alongside modelling effective learning strategies with the aim of providing children with the skills to assess their own progress and become more independent learners. Assessments provide an important insight into how effective your teaching strategies are for your whole class, for specific groups of children and for individuals. You should ensure that you regularly critically evaluate both individual lessons and your medium-term planning to ensure you are not limiting learning by your own actions. Section 2 provides ideas about effective strategies for individual subjects, but you may also wish to consider how you promote good learning behaviours. For example, many schools' mission or vision statements assert that children are encouraged to become independent learners, but what actions does everyone in the school take to achieve this and how is this monitored?

Reflective task

Draw three columns on a piece of paper. In the first write down all the things you think children should demonstrate when they are considered to be independent. In the second column write down the behaviour(s) children will demonstrate when they are working independently and in the third write down all the behaviour(s) teachers will demonstrate when they are encouraging independence.

For example: 1. Resilience, 2. willingness to try something new/different, ability to persevere, even if they fail, 3. effective use of praise to promote confidence, provides new contexts for learning.

Think about other behaviours of effective learners and do the same exercise to help you reflect on how you might promote these in your classroom.

Third, feedback should be focused on learning and aim to provide the children with the skills to become self-aware and self-critical. Think about when feedback is appropriate and what type of feedback is relevant to each individual child and in each context for learning.

Finally, moderation is essential. You will need to discuss your judgements about children's learning with other colleagues, both within your own school and from other schools. This will enable you to establish a much clearer idea of what learning at different levels looks like and help to support children to make progress both within the primary phase and beyond.

Recording mastery

The removal of levels has not necessarily removed numerical assessment records and there are good reasons for this. Numerical systems make it easy to produce data that can be used to quickly and easily monitor progress across cohorts, for specific groups of pupils and for individuals. Deep learning is much more complex and, consequently, more difficult to record numerically. However, you will find many schools still ascribe a numerical value to achievement, the most common being a system of 1 to 3 marks, with 3 being mastery and 1 being entry level learning. There is no issue with this if the record of assessment fulfils its requirement; that is, does it enable the teacher or the school to monitor individual and group progress and enable learners to continue to make progress? Critically, if it does not inform learning then it is of no use.

When considering any recording system used by a school it is important to remember the difference between **assessment** and **recording**. It is the process of assessment which should drive the system of recording, not the other way around. It is easy to fall into the trap of having a wonderful, colour-coded record of assessment, which can take hours to complete, but have little value. You will need to develop a purposeful and manageable system of recording your assessments, which can be used both across your own school and across different phases of education. It is unlikely that you will be able to record mastery in a simple tick box or as a number without exemplifying your judgements. Again, moderation with colleagues is critical to this process.

In summary, mastery is recognised as the demonstration of learning beyond the expected level. It is characterised by certain learner behaviours and the ability to use and apply knowledge. Read the 'principles of planning' sections for each subject in Section 2 to better understand how to teach effectively and look closely at the examples of planning provided to see how these are put into practice.

Further Reading

Standards and Testing Agency (2017) *Teacher assessment frameworks at the end of key stage 1.* Available at: **www.gov.uk/government/publications/teacher-assessment-frameworks-at-the-end-of-key-stage-1**

Standards and Testing Agency (2017) *Teacher assessment frameworks at the end of key stage 2.* Available at: **www.gov.uk/government/publications/teacher-assessment-frameworks-at-the-end-of-key-stage-2**

Teacher Assessment in Primary Science (TAPS) project. Available at: **https://pstt.org.uk/resources/curriculum-materials/assessment**

Section 2

Subject planning

This section will look at each of the national curriculum subjects to identify specific ideas relating to each subject. The programmes of study for each subject are included to help you plan and sample lesson plans illustrate the ideas discussed.

Section 2

4 English

Planning English in the national curriculum

Laura Quinton Maryon

English 1 Principles of planning

This section looks at the key factors which are specific to planning effective English lessons. It builds on the generic factors for planning found in Chapter 1 and should be read in conjunction with these ideas.

The English teaching sequence

As with all planning, it is vital to first consider what you want the outcomes to be from the teaching sequence. What is it that you want the children to know and understand by the end of the sequence, and what might they produce or do to demonstrate this knowledge and understanding? Although you are planning for English, the end product doesn't necessarily need to be a piece of written work. Think creatively. Always start with your learning objectives and then plan your activities to support these. Ensure your planning allows for development over all four modes of language: speaking and listening, reading and writing.

Begin your teaching sequence with a high-quality text that allows children to develop their reading skills and provides a model for a final outcome. This text may be an oral story, picture book, comic, film, poem, novel . . . the possibilities are endless. Becoming a teacher-reader is vital in selecting the right texts to use with your class – texts that will spark children's interest, be suitable for their comprehension levels, and contain interesting language features and a variety of narrative structures. Read as widely as you can. Good places to look for children's book recommendations are *Books for Keeps* and the United Kingdom Literary Association's (UKLA) *English 4–11*. Don't forget to follow children's books prizes as well, particularly the UKLA, Carnegie and Greenaway medals. The Centre for Literacy in Primary Education (CLPE) publishes a core book list each year which suggests high-quality titles for each primary age range. Gamble's (2013) *Exploring Children's Literature: Reading with Pleasure and Purpose* is essential reading for understanding a variety of texts and genres on both a theoretical and pedagogical level.

Bearne (2002, page 32) suggests a useful diagram to follow when planning your English sequence, beginning with familiarisation with the genre or text type. Spend time sharing and discussing your original text/text type and ensure children understand the features of the text type. It is useful to share a variety of texts of the same type at this stage of the sequence. Consider language and grammar. Why has the author chosen certain words and phrases? What is the impact on the reader?

In the second part of the sequence, children can begin sharing ideas for their own text orally. Speaking allows children to organise their thoughts and try out new ideas before writing them down. Pie Corbett is a well-respected advocate of Talk for Writing and you will find his resources online and in books if you would like more information on this approach. You might begin by asking children to re-tell the original story or text, allowing them to rehearse and internalise its narrative and language structures. They could then move on to changing one or two aspects of the text (for example, the setting) or inventing an entirely new text of the type you are studying.

You need to plan for shared, guided and independent writing in your teaching sequence, with focused objectives for each approach. Your objectives may be at text, sentence or word level, or a combination. Shared writing takes place as a whole class with the teacher scribing on the board. The class makes suggestions and alterations, but the session is led by the teacher. Guided writing allows for a personalised writing curriculum, and involves the teacher working with small groups of children (no more than six) on a focused learning objective. Children are grouped according to need. The final step of the sequence is independent writing. Through exploration of a given text type, oral rehearsal and teacher demonstration and guidance, children will now be well equipped to create their own text.

Grammar and spelling

There is a renewed focus on grammar and spelling in the current national curriculum and with the advent of the Grammar, Punctuation and Spelling standardised assessment tests. It is important you have a good understanding of grammar, punctuation and spelling yourself and there are several texts that can help you to develop your subject knowledge in this area, such as Seely (2007) *Grammar for Teachers*. Although some aspects of grammar and punctuation need to be taught separately, it is also important to take a holistic route to developing this knowledge through immersion in high-quality texts. Ensure grammar is identified in your planning. As a class, always consider the language choices an author has made in their writing and what impact this has on the reader. This is much more effective than rote learning of the separate parts. Children can then be encouraged to use these same linguistic devices in their own writing. UKLA has published an excellent guide to the teaching of grammar in context, *Teaching Grammar Effectively in Primary Schools* (Reedy and Bearne, 2013), which details how to plan and teach grammar across the primary age range in a meaningful way.

Learning spelling patterns and rules through spelling investigations is more effective than rote-learning spelling lists. In a spelling investigation children explore a spelling rule or pattern, often looking at a family of words. They have the opportunity to discuss and explore spelling patterns with their group, collaborating together to enhance engagement and understanding. For more information on this approach to the planning and teaching of spelling see Martin (2010) *Talk for Spelling*.

The development of reading

An understanding of the development of reading is vital for any English teacher. While current initiatives focus on systematic synthetic phonics as the only strategy to teach when decoding words, it is vital that language comprehension and a love of reading is developed alongside this. To learn more about the debate around the focus on systematic synthetic phonics read Dombey's (2010) booklet *Teaching Reading: What the Evidence Says.*

The Independent Review of the Teaching of Early Reading (DfES, 2006), more commonly referred to as *The Rose Review*, sets out clear guidelines regarding the planning and teaching of systematic synthetic phonics. Rose recommends a 'first and fast' approach to the teaching of systematic synthetic phonics, meaning that phonics should be the first approach when teaching children how to decode and that this should be achieved by the end of year 2. He recommends a daily, discrete phonics lesson of 20 minutes, consisting of four sections: revisit and review, teach, practise, apply (see lesson plan for more details). Phonics lessons should be fun, high quality, systematic, multi-sensory, fast-paced and active, and provide opportunity for daily blending and segmenting practice. Each phoneme (sound) and grapheme (how the sound is written) should be taught systematically. The *Letters and Sounds* document (Primary National Strategy, 2007) is a good place to start when planning your phonics lessons.

The Rose Review stresses that phonics must be taught as part of a *language-rich environment*. There is much more to reading than simply decoding the words on the page. Ensure you identify in your planning how you will teach language comprehension and develop enjoyment of reading. Book talk and drama activities are a great way of developing children's understanding of what they are reading. Baldwin and Fleming (2003) offer many suggestions for using drama as a way into texts.

Guided reading allows children to practise and apply their reading skills in small groups of no more than six, led by the teacher. Like guided writing, guided reading sessions should have a focused learning objective, which could be based on word recognition or language comprehension. When planning your session, decide on the aim – for example, developing reading strategies, or developing understanding of a certain aspect of the text. Plan the kinds of questions you might ask and include questions that require literal, inferential and deductive reading. Guided reading is most often planned separately to the whole-class English lesson.

Assessment

Identify formative and summative assessment opportunities throughout your English planning cycle. As with any planning, always be clear on what the children need to do to succeed. Creating checklists and success criteria together is an effective way of ensuring children remain focused in their English work.

Resources

High-quality children's literature should form the bulk of your resources for English. Ensure you have texts that all abilities in your class can access and that are also physically accessible to the class. Consider also any other resources that will encourage, support or enhance reading, writing, speaking and listening. For example, story sacks are an excellent way of deepening children's understanding

of a text and supporting discussion. Also consider how ICT resources can be used to inspire or support learning. You might use cameras to capture and review drama activities, software to create storyboards, or apps to encourage reading for pleasure (the interactive Morris Lessmore book for the iPad is a must here). The possibilities are endless.

Further reading

Baldwin, P. and Fleming, K. (2003) *Teaching Literacy Through Drama: Creative Approaches*. London: Routledge.

Bearne, E. (2002) *Making Progress in Writing*. London: Routledge.

Books for Keeps. [online] Available at: **www.http://booksforkeeps.co.uk**

Browne, A. (2009) *Developing Language and Literacy 3–8* (3rd edition). London: Sage.

Centre for Literacy in Primary Education. [online] Available at: **www.clpe.org.uk**

Chambers, A. (2011) *Tell Me (Children, Reading & Talk) with The Reading Environment*. Stroud: Thimble Press.

Corbett, P. (2010) *Jumpstart! Literacy*. Abingdon: Routledge.

Cremin, T. (2009) *Teaching English Creatively*. Abingdon: Routledge.

DfES (2006) *Independent Review of the Teaching of Early Reading*. [online] Available at: **http://webarchive.nationalarchives.gov.uk/20100526143644/http:/standards.dcsf.gov.uk/phonics/report.pdf**

Dombey, H. (2010) *Teaching Reading: What the Evidence Says*. Leicester: UKLA.

Gamble, N. (2013) *Exploring Children's Literature: Reading with Pleasure and Purpose*. London: Sage.

Joliffe, W. and Waugh, D. (2012) *Teaching Systematic Synthetic Phonics in the Primary School*. London: Sage.

Martin, T. (2010) *Talk for Spelling*. Leicester: UKLA.

Primary National Strategy (2007) *Letters and Sounds: Principles and Practice of High Quality Phonics*. [online] Available at: **www.gov.uk/government/uploads/system/uploads/attachment_data/file/190599/Letters_and_Sounds_-_DFES-00281-2007.pdf**

Reedy, D. and Bearne, E. (2013) *Teaching Grammar Effectively in Primary Schools*. Leicester: UKLA.

Seely, J. (2007) *Grammar for Teachers*. Tiverton: Oxpecker Press.

Tandy, M. and Howell, J. (2008) *Creating Writers in the Primary Classroom: Practical Approaches to Inspire Teachers and Their Pupils*. London: Routledge.

English 2 Examples of planning

The following lesson plans are provided as examples of planning in English. They do not contain the detail you will probably wish to have on your plans but do illustrate some of the points discussed previously. The first lesson plan focuses on reading and response, the second on writing and the third is an example of a phonics lesson plan. The first two plans are created around the text The Lost Thing *by Shaun Tan.*

Lesson One: Reading and response

Subject/topic: English (reading)	Date: 23/10/2016 Time: 11.00 a.m.	Teaching group/set: Y5 No. of pupils: 28	
Intended learning: Children will learn: • to make predictions about a text based on given knowledge • to develop and utilise skills of inference and deduction • to give reasons for their opinions with direct reference to a text • to identify patterns within a text/s.			**NC reference/ context:** Reading – comprehension
Success criteria: • I can explain what might happen in *The Lost Thing* based on the front page. • I can explain what I like and dislike about *The Lost Thing* and give reasons for these opinions, referring directly to the text. • I can identify patterns in *The Lost Thing* and make links between *The Lost Thing* and other texts. Differentiation: Children will work in differentiated groups. Differentiation will be by outcome.			**Assessment strategy:** • Observation of group work • Observation of individual children during book talk

There may be specific children you would want to focus on and you could identify them here.

All children will be able to access this lesson as it is based on a picture book and the teacher will read the story aloud. Children will have different levels of response to the text.

Key vocabulary: n/a	Resources: *The Lost Thing* by Shaun Tan Coloured copies of picture from the front page featuring The Lost Thing, one for each group of six in the class (ensure the title of the book is not showing)	Risk assessment: n/a

Time	Teacher focus	Pupil focus
15 mins	Create excitement and intrigue around the text. Start by exploring the character of The Lost Thing. Don't reveal the name of the character to begin with. Teacher to assess children's discussions and provide support to groups where needed.	Working in differentiated groups of approximately six, each group to have a picture of The Lost Thing. Annotate the picture with what they might predict about the character. What kind of character do they think The Lost Thing will be? What might his/her role be in the story? Do not refer to the character by name at this stage. Each group to share some of their ideas about The Lost Thing.

| 10 mins | Reveal the entire front page of the text, including the name, The Lost Thing.

Facilitate discussion to elicit key ideas emerging. | Children to discuss as a class their new thoughts about The Lost Thing. Has knowing the title/name of the character changed their ideas about him/her? |
|---|---|---|
| 15 mins | Share text of *The Lost Thing* with the class. Allow for some discussion throughout without breaking the flow of the narrative. | Children to listen to the story of *The Lost Thing* as a class. They may wish to discuss certain parts of the story/illustrations during the reading. |
| 20 mins | Facilitate book talk discussion around *The Lost Thing*, using Chambers' style.

Possible questions for discussion:

What do you like about the text? What do you dislike? Were there any puzzles in the text or questions that you might ask? Were there any patterns in the text or links that you can make to other texts?

Assess children's response to the text, including inference and deduction and comprehension. | Children reflect on and respond to the text through class discussion. |

For more information on this style of book talk please see Chambers (2011).

Lesson Two: Writing in response to reading

| Subject/topic:

English (writing) | Date: 27/10/2016

Time: 10.30 a.m. | Teaching group/set: Y5

No. of pupils: 28 |
|---|---|---|
| **Intended learning:**

Children will learn:

• to use questions to further understand a character
• how to write in role, using the first person and past tense.

In the guided-writing group children will learn to use connectives to extend their sentences. | | **NC reference/context:**

Writing – composition |
| **Success criteria:**

• I can ask questions to further understand The Lost Thing.
• I can write in role as The Lost Thing, using the first person and the past tense. | | **Assessment strategy:**

• Observation of children's understanding of the text during hot-seating activity
• Observation of children's contributions during shared writing
• Peer assessment of writing
• Teacher marking of writing |
| **Key vocabulary:**

First person

Past tense | **Resources:**

The Lost Thing by Shaun Tan

Images from page 6 (one per child) | **Risk assessment:**

n/a |

Your guided-writing group could focus on any objective relevant to their needs.

Further success criteria will be suggested by the children after the shared-writing session. It is up to you how much you direct this and some of it will depend on discussion during shared writing.

Time	Teacher focus	Pupil focus
5 mins	Facilitate short class discussion of feeling lost and alone. Has there ever been a time when you were lost? How did it feel?	Children to participate in discussion around being lost. Draw on past experiences and link these to the text.
10 mins	Choose one child to be The Lost Thing. Carry out hot-seating drama activity to develop an understanding of the character of The Lost Thing. Encourage children to focus on the start of the book and what might have happened before then. How did The Lost Thing end up at the beach?	Work in differentiated pairs to make notes on small whiteboards together: What do we know about The Lost Thing? What would we like to know about The Lost Thing? Children to ask questions of The Lost Thing to try and understand more about his character.
15 mins	Display page 3 of the text (depicting The Lost Thing at the beach). Facilitate shared-writing session. Demonstrate writing in role as The Lost Thing at this point in the story. Focus on writing in the first person and use of past tense. What might he be thinking/feeling at this point in the text? Create checklist/success criteria as a class for the children to assess their work against. What are we looking for when we are writing in role?	Participate in shared-writing session, asking questions and offering suggestions.
20 mins	Provide children with images of page 6 of the text (the moment when the boy plays with The Lost Thing). Work with a guided group whose needs have been previously identified.	Independent writing in role as The Lost Thing when he first meets the boy. Refer to the checklist/success criteria throughout writing.
10 mins	Facilitate peer assessment of children's writing. Encourage children to adhere directly to the success criteria when marking their partner's work.	Children to assess a partner's work against the success criteria. They give their partner two stars (two things they have done well in their writing) and a wish (one thing they might improve next time).

Creating success criteria together gives children ownership over the task and expectations. Ensure these remain displayed throughout their independent work so that they can refer back to them when needed.

This peer assessment could be done orally or could be written. Ensure that children are given time to respond to comments in the next lesson.

Example phonics lesson plan

Phase 5 (Year 1)	Objectives: To learn the /ph/ grapheme.
Revisit and review	Revision of graphemes from Phases 3 and 4 using the following interactive game on the interactive whiteboard: **www.ictgames.com/phonemePopLS_v2.html**
Teach	Teach the new grapheme /ph/. Practise the sound and write on the board. Show Between the Lions, 'The "ph" song': **www.youtube.com/watch?v=-PhJe5kJkX8**

Phase 5 (Year 1)	Objectives: To learn the /ph/ grapheme.
	Play again and ask children to join in the song.
	Can children think of any other words that have /ph/ in? Add these to the list.
Practise	Practise reading words containing /ph/. Have pre-prepared words for the children to read.
Apply	Read sentences containing at least one high frequency word and the grapheme /ph/. Have pre-prepared sentences for the children to read – e.g. 'The alphabet starts with the letter "a".' They could read these sentences to a partner initially.

There are opportunities for differentiation during the practise and apply sections of the lesson. Here you could give children easier or harder words to read depending on their ability.

English 3 The framework for English

Purpose of study

English has a pre-eminent place in education and in society. A high-quality education in English will teach pupils to speak and write fluently so that they can communicate their ideas and emotions to others and through their reading and listening, others can communicate with them. Through reading in particular, pupils have a chance to develop culturally, emotionally, intellectually, socially and spiritually. Literature, especially, plays a key role in such development. Reading also enables pupils both to acquire knowledge and to build on what they already know. All the skills of language are essential to participating fully as a member of society; pupils, therefore, who do not learn to speak, read and write fluently and confidently are effectively disenfranchised.

Aims

The overarching aim for English in the national curriculum is to promote high standards of language and literacy by equipping pupils with a strong command of the spoken and written word, and to develop their love of literature through widespread reading for enjoyment. The national curriculum for English aims to ensure that all pupils:

- read easily, fluently and with good understanding
- develop the habit of reading widely and often, for both pleasure and information
- acquire a wide vocabulary, an understanding of grammar and knowledge of linguistic conventions for reading, writing and spoken language
- appreciate our rich and varied literary heritage
- write clearly, accurately and coherently, adapting their language and style in and for a range of contexts, purposes and audiences
- use discussion in order to learn; they should be able to elaborate and explain clearly their understanding and ideas
- are competent in the arts of speaking and listening, making formal presentations, demonstrating to others and participating in debate.

Spoken language

The national curriculum for English reflects the importance of spoken language in pupils' development across the whole curriculum – cognitively, socially and linguistically. Spoken language underpins the development of reading and writing. The quality and variety of language that pupils hear and speak are vital for developing their vocabulary and grammar and their understanding for reading and writing. Teachers should therefore ensure the continual development of pupils' confidence and competence in spoken language and listening skills. Pupils should develop a capacity to explain their understanding of books and other reading, and to prepare their ideas before they write. They must be assisted in making their thinking clear to themselves as well as to others and teachers should ensure that pupils build secure foundations by using discussion to probe and remedy their misconceptions. Pupils should also be taught to understand and use the conventions for discussion and debate.

All pupils should be enabled to participate in and gain knowledge, skills and understanding associated with the artistic practice of drama. Pupils should be able to adopt, create and sustain a range of roles, responding appropriately to others in role. They should have opportunities to improvise, devise and script drama for one another and a range of audiences, as well as to rehearse, refine, share and respond thoughtfully to drama and theatre performances.

Statutory requirements which underpin all aspects of spoken language across the six years of primary education form part of the national curriculum. These are reflected and contextualised within the reading and writing domains which follow.

Reading

The programmes of study for reading at key stages 1 and 2 consist of two dimensions:

- word reading
- comprehension (both listening and reading).

It is essential that teaching focuses on developing pupils' competence in both dimensions; different kinds of teaching are needed for each.

Skilled word reading involves both the speedy working out of the pronunciation of unfamiliar printed words (decoding) and the speedy recognition of familiar printed words. Underpinning both is the understanding that the letters on the page represent the sounds in spoken words. This is why phonics should be emphasised in the early teaching of reading to beginners (i.e. unskilled readers) when they start school.

Good comprehension draws from linguistic knowledge (in particular of vocabulary and grammar) and on knowledge of the world. Comprehension skills develop through pupils' experience of high-quality discussion with the teacher, as well as from reading and discussing a range of stories, poems and non-fiction. All pupils must be encouraged to read widely across both fiction and non-fiction to develop their knowledge of themselves and the world in which they live, to establish an appreciation and love of reading, and to gain knowledge across the curriculum. Reading widely and often increases pupils' vocabulary because they encounter words they would rarely hear or use in everyday speech. Reading also feeds pupils' imagination and opens up a treasure-house of wonder and joy for curious young minds.

It is essential that, by the end of their primary education, all pupils are able to read fluently, and with confidence, in any subject in their forthcoming secondary education.

Writing

The programmes of study for writing at key stages 1 and 2 are constructed similarly to those for reading:

- transcription (spelling and handwriting)
- composition (articulating ideas and structuring them in speech and writing).

It is essential that teaching develops pupils' competence in these two dimensions. In addition, pupils should be taught how to plan, revise and evaluate their writing. These aspects of writing have been incorporated into the programmes of study for composition.

Writing down ideas fluently depends on effective transcription: that is, on spelling quickly and accurately through knowing the relationship between sounds and letters (phonics) and understanding the morphology (word structure) and orthography (spelling structure) of words. Effective composition involves forming, articulating and communicating ideas, and then organising them coherently for a reader. This requires clarity, awareness of the audience, purpose and context, and an increasingly wide knowledge of vocabulary and grammar. Writing also depends on fluent, legible and, eventually, speedy handwriting.

Spelling, vocabulary, grammar, punctuation and glossary

The two statutory appendices – on spelling and on vocabulary, grammar and punctuation – give an overview of the specific features that should be included in teaching the programmes of study.

Opportunities for teachers to enhance pupils' vocabulary arise naturally from their reading and writing. As vocabulary increases, teachers should show pupils how to understand the relationships between words, how to understand nuances in meaning, and how to develop their understanding of, and ability to use, figurative language. They should also teach pupils how to work out and clarify the meanings of unknown words and words with more than one meaning. References to developing pupils' vocabulary are also included within the appendices.

Pupils should be taught to control their speaking and writing consciously and to use Standard English. They should be taught to use the elements of spelling, grammar, punctuation and 'language about language' listed. This is not intended to constrain or restrict teachers' creativity, but simply to provide the structure on which they can construct exciting lessons. A non-statutory Glossary is provided for teachers.

Throughout the programmes of study, teachers should teach pupils the vocabulary they need to discuss their reading, writing and spoken language. It is important that pupils learn the correct grammatical terms in English and that these terms are integrated within teaching.

School curriculum

The programmes of study for English are set out year-by-year for key stage 1 and two-yearly for key stage 2. The single year blocks at key stage 1 reflect the rapid pace of development in word reading during these two years. Schools are, however, only required to teach the relevant programme of study by the end of the key stage. Within each key stage, schools therefore have the flexibility to introduce content earlier or later than set out in the programme of study. In addition, schools can introduce key stage content during an earlier key stage if appropriate. All schools are also required to set out their school curriculum for English on a year-by-year basis and make this information available online.

Attainment targets

By the end of each key stage, pupils are expected to know, apply and understand the matters, skills and processes specified in the relevant programme of study.

Schools are not required by law to teach the example content in [square brackets] or the content indicated as being 'non-statutory'.

Spoken language – years 1 to 6

Spoken language

Statutory requirements

Pupils should be taught to:

- listen and respond appropriately to adults and their peers
- ask relevant questions to extend their understanding and knowledge
- use relevant strategies to build their vocabulary
- articulate and justify answers, arguments and opinions
- give well-structured descriptions, explanations and narratives for different purposes, including for expressing feelings
- maintain attention and participate actively in collaborative conversations, staying on topic and initiating and responding to comments
- use spoken language to develop understanding through speculating, hypothesising, imagining and exploring ideas
- speak audibly and fluently with an increasing command of Standard English
- participate in discussions, presentations, performances, role play, improvisations and debates
- gain, maintain and monitor the interest of the listener(s)
- consider and evaluate different viewpoints, attending to and building on the contributions of others
- select and use appropriate registers for effective communication.

Notes and guidance (non-statutory)

These statements apply to all years. The content should be taught at a level appropriate to the age of the pupils. Pupils should build on the oral language skills that have been taught in preceding years.

Pupils should be taught to develop their competence in spoken language and listening to enhance the effectiveness with which they are able to communicate across a range of contexts and to a range of audiences. They should therefore have opportunities to work in groups of different sizes – in pairs, small groups, large groups and as a whole class. Pupils should understand how to take turns and when and how to participate constructively in conversations and debates.

Attention should also be paid to increasing pupils' vocabulary, ranging from describing their immediate world and feelings to developing a broader, deeper and richer vocabulary to discuss abstract concepts and a wider range of topics, and to enhancing their knowledge about language as a whole.

Pupils should receive constructive feedback on their spoken language and listening, not only to improve their knowledge and skills but also to establish secure foundations for effective spoken language in their studies at primary school, helping them to achieve in secondary education and beyond.

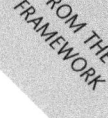

Key stage 1 – year 1

During year 1, teachers should build on work from the Early Years Foundation Stage, making sure that pupils can sound and blend unfamiliar printed words quickly and accurately using the phonic knowledge and skills that they have already learnt. Teachers should also ensure that pupils continue to learn new grapheme-phoneme correspondences (GPCs) and revise and consolidate those learnt earlier. The understanding that the letter(s) on the page represent the sounds in spoken words should underpin pupils' reading and spelling of all words. This includes common words containing unusual GPCs. The term 'common exception words' is used throughout the programmes of study for such words.

Alongside this knowledge of GPCs, pupils need to develop the skill of blending the sounds into words for reading and establish the habit of applying this skill whenever they encounter new words. This will be supported by practice in reading books consistent with their developing phonic knowledge and skill and their knowledge of common exception words. At the same time they will need to hear, share and discuss a wide range of high-quality books to develop a love of reading and broaden their vocabulary.

Pupils should be helped to read words without overt sounding and blending after a few encounters. Those who are slow to develop this skill should have extra practice.

Pupils' writing during year 1 will generally develop at a slower pace than their reading. This is because they need to encode the sounds they hear in words (spelling skills), develop the physical skill needed for handwriting, and learn how to organise their ideas in writing.

Pupils entering year 1 who have not yet met the early learning goals for literacy should continue to follow their school's curriculum for the Early Years Foundation Stage to develop their word reading, spelling and language skills. However, these pupils should follow the year 1 programme of study in terms of the books they listen to and discuss, so that they develop their vocabulary and understanding of grammar, as well as their knowledge more generally across the curriculum. If they are still struggling to decode and spell, they need to be taught to do this urgently through a rigorous and systematic phonics programme so that they catch up rapidly.

Teachers should ensure that their teaching develops pupils' oral vocabulary as well as their ability to understand and use a variety of grammatical structures, giving particular support to pupils whose oral language skills are insufficiently developed.

Year 1 programme of study

Reading – word reading

Statutory requirements

Pupils should be taught to:

- apply phonic knowledge and skills as the route to decode words
- respond speedily with the correct sound to graphemes (letters or groups of letters) for all 40+ phonemes, including, where applicable, alternative sounds for graphemes
- read accurately by blending sounds in unfamiliar words containing GPCs that have been taught
- read common exception words, noting unusual correspondences between spelling and sound and where these occur in the word
- read words containing taught GPCs and –s, –es, –ing, –ed, –er and –est endings
- read other words of more than one syllable that contain taught GPCs

(Continued)

(Continued)

- read words with contractions [for example, I'm, I'll, we'll], and understand that the apostrophe represents the omitted letter(s)
- read aloud accurately books that are consistent with their developing phonic knowledge and that do not require them to use other strategies to work out words
- re-read these books to build up their fluency and confidence in word reading.

Notes and guidance (non-statutory)

Pupils should revise and consolidate the GPCs and the common exception words taught in Reception. As soon as they can read words comprising the year 1 GPCs accurately and speedily, they should move on to the year 2 programme of study for word reading.

The number, order and choice of exception words taught will vary according to the phonics programme being used. Ensuring that pupils are aware of the GPCs they contain, however unusual these are, supports spelling later.

Young readers encounter words that they have not seen before much more frequently than experienced readers do, and they may not know the meaning of some of these. Practice at reading such words by sounding and blending can provide opportunities not only for pupils to develop confidence in their decoding skills, but also for teachers to explain the meaning and thus develop pupils' vocabulary.

Pupils should be taught how to read words with suffixes by being helped to build on the root words that they can read already. Pupils' reading and re-reading of books that are closely matched to their developing phonic knowledge and knowledge of common exception words supports their fluency, as well as increasing their confidence in their reading skills. Fluent word reading greatly assists comprehension, especially when pupils come to read longer books.

Reading – comprehension

Statutory requirements

Pupils should be taught to:

- develop pleasure in reading, motivation to read, vocabulary and understanding by:
  - listening to and discussing a wide range of poems, stories and non-fiction at a level beyond that at which they can read independently
  - being encouraged to link what they read or hear read to their own experiences
  - becoming very familiar with key stories, fairy stories and traditional tales, retelling them and considering their particular characteristics
  - recognising and joining in with predictable phrases
  - learning to appreciate rhymes and poems, and to recite some by heart
  - discussing word meanings, linking new meanings to those already known
- understand both the books they can already read accurately and fluently and those they listen to by:
  - drawing on what they already know or on background information and vocabulary provided by the teacher
  - checking that the text makes sense to them as they read and correcting inaccurate reading
  - discussing the significance of the title and events

- o making inferences on the basis of what is being said and done
- o predicting what might happen on the basis of what has been read so far

- participate in discussion about what is read to them, taking turns and listening to what others say
- explain clearly their understanding of what is read to them.

Notes and guidance (non-statutory)

Pupils should have extensive experience of listening to, sharing and discussing a wide range of high-quality books with the teacher, other adults and each other to engender a love of reading at the same time as they are reading independently.

Pupils' vocabulary should be developed when they listen to books read aloud and when they discuss what they have heard. Such vocabulary can also feed into their writing. Knowing the meaning of more words increases pupils' chances of understanding when they read by themselves. The meaning of some new words should be introduced to pupils before they start to read on their own, so that these unknown words do not hold up their comprehension.

However, once pupils have already decoded words successfully, the meaning of those that are new to them can be discussed with them, so contributing to developing their early skills of inference. By listening frequently to stories, poems and non-fiction that they cannot yet read for themselves, pupils begin to understand how written language can be structured in order, for example, to build surprise in narratives or to present facts in non-fiction. Listening to and discussing information books and other non-fiction establishes the foundations for their learning in other subjects. Pupils should be shown some of the processes for finding out information.

Through listening, pupils also start to learn how language sounds and increase their vocabulary and awareness of grammatical structures. In due course, they will be able to draw on such grammar in their own writing.

Rules for effective discussions should be agreed with and demonstrated for pupils. They should help to develop and evaluate them, with the expectation that everyone takes part. Pupils should be helped to consider the opinions of others.

Role-play can help pupils to identify with and explore characters and to try out the language they have listened to.

Writing – transcription

Statutory requirements

Spelling (see English Appendix 1)

Pupils should be taught to:

- spell:
  - o words containing each of the 40+ phonemes already taught
  - o common exception words
  - o the days of the week
- name the letters of the alphabet:
  - o naming the letters of the alphabet in order
  - o using letter names to distinguish between alternative spellings of the same sound

(Continued)

(Continued)

- add prefixes and suffixes:

  o using the spelling rule for adding –s or –es as the plural marker for nouns and the third person singular marker for verbs
  o using the prefix un–
  o using –ing, –ed, –er and –est where no change is needed in the spelling of root words [for example, helping, helped, helper, eating, quicker, quickest]

- apply simple spelling rules and guidance, as listed in English Appendix 1
- write from memory simple sentences dictated by the teacher that include words using the GPCs and common exception words taught so far.

Notes and guidance (non-statutory)

Reading should be taught alongside spelling, so that pupils understand that they can read back words they have spelt.

Pupils should be shown how to segment spoken words into individual phonemes and then how to represent the phonemes by the appropriate grapheme(s). It is important to recognise that phoneme-grapheme correspondences (which underpin spelling) are more variable than grapheme-phoneme correspondences (which underpin reading). For this reason, pupils need to do much more word-specific rehearsal for spelling than for reading.

At this stage pupils will be spelling some words in a phonically plausible way, even if sometimes incorrectly. Misspellings of words that pupils have been taught to spell should be corrected; other misspelt words should be used to teach pupils about alternative ways of representing those sounds.

Writing simple dictated sentences that include words taught so far gives pupils opportunities to apply and practise their spelling.

Statutory requirements

Handwriting

Pupils should be taught to:

- sit correctly at a table, holding a pencil comfortably and correctly
- begin to form lower-case letters in the correct direction, starting and finishing in the right place
- form capital letters
- form digits 0-9
- understand which letters belong to which handwriting 'families' (i.e. letters that are formed in similar ways) and to practise these.

Notes and guidance (non-statutory)

Handwriting requires frequent and discrete, direct teaching. Pupils should be able to form letters correctly and confidently. The size of the writing implement (pencil, pen) should not be too large for a young pupil's hand. Whatever is being used should allow the pupil to hold it easily and correctly so that bad habits are avoided.

Left-handed pupils should receive specific teaching to meet their needs.

Writing – composition

Statutory requirements

Pupils should be taught to:

- write sentences by:
  - saying out loud what they are going to write about
  - composing a sentence orally before writing it
  - sequencing sentences to form short narratives
  - re-reading what they have written to check that it makes sense
- discuss what they have written with the teacher or other pupils
- read aloud their writing clearly enough to be heard by their peers and the teacher.

Notes and guidance (non-statutory)

At the beginning of year 1, not all pupils will have the spelling and handwriting skills they need to write down everything that they can compose out loud.

Pupils should understand, through demonstration, the skills and processes essential to writing: that is, thinking aloud as they collect ideas, drafting, and re-reading to check their meaning is clear.

Writing – vocabulary, grammar and punctuation

Statutory requirements

Pupils should be taught to:

- develop their understanding of the concepts set out in English Appendix 2 by:
  - leaving spaces between words
  - joining words and joining clauses using and
  - beginning to punctuate sentences using a capital letter and a full stop, question mark or exclamation mark
  - using a capital letter for names of people, places, the days of the week, and the personal pronoun 'I'
  - learning the grammar for year 1 in English Appendix 2
- use the grammatical terminology in English Appendix 2 in discussing their writing.

Notes and guidance (non-statutory)

Pupils should be taught to recognise sentence boundaries in spoken sentences and to use the vocabulary listed in English Appendix 2 ('Terminology for pupils') when their writing is discussed.

Pupils should begin to use some of the distinctive features of Standard English in their writing. 'Standard English' is defined in the Glossary.

Key stage 1 – year 2

By the beginning of year 2, pupils should be able to read all common graphemes. They should be able to read unfamiliar words containing these graphemes, accurately and without undue hesitation, by sounding them out in books that are matched closely to each pupil's level of word reading knowledge. They should also be able to read many common words containing GPCs taught so far [for example, shout, hand, stop, or dream], without needing to blend the sounds out loud first. Pupils' reading of common exception words [for example, you, could, many, or people], should be secure. Pupils will increase their fluency by being able to read these words easily and automatically. Finally, pupils should be able to retell some familiar stories that have been read to and discussed with them or that they have acted out during year 1.

During year 2, teachers should continue to focus on establishing pupils' accurate and speedy word reading skills. They should also make sure that pupils listen to and discuss a wide range of stories, poems, plays and information books; this should include whole books. The sooner that pupils can read well and do so frequently, the sooner they will be able to increase their vocabulary, comprehension and their knowledge across the wider curriculum.

In writing, pupils at the beginning of year 2 should be able to compose individual sentences orally and then write them down. They should be able to spell correctly many of the words covered in year 1 (see English Appendix 1). They should also be able to make phonically plausible attempts to spell words they have not yet learnt. Finally, they should be able to form individual letters correctly, so establishing good handwriting habits from the beginning.

It is important to recognise that pupils begin to meet extra challenges in terms of spelling during year 2. Increasingly, they should learn that there is not always an obvious connection between the way a word is said and the way it is spelt. Variations include different ways of spelling the same sound, the use of so-called silent letters and groups of letters in some words and, sometimes, spelling that has become separated from the way that words are now pronounced, such as the 'le' ending in table. Pupils' motor skills also need to be sufficiently advanced for them to write down ideas that they may be able to compose orally. In addition, writing is intrinsically harder than reading: pupils are likely to be able to read and understand more complex writing (in terms of its vocabulary and structure) than they are capable of producing themselves.

For pupils who do not have the phonic knowledge and skills they need for year 2, teachers should use the year 1 programmes of study for word reading and spelling so that pupils' word reading skills catch up. However, teachers should use the year 2 programme of study for comprehension so that these pupils hear and talk about new books, poems, other writing, and vocabulary with the rest of the class.

Year 2 programme of study

Reading – word reading

Statutory requirements

Pupils should be taught to:

- continue to apply phonic knowledge and skills as the route to decode words until automatic decoding has become embedded and reading is fluent
- read accurately by blending the sounds in words that contain the graphemes taught so far, especially recognising alternative sounds for graphemes

- read accurately words of two or more syllables that contain the same graphemes as above
- read words containing common suffixes
- read further common exception words, noting unusual correspondences between spelling and sound and where these occur in the word
- read most words quickly and accurately, without overt sounding and blending, when they have been frequently encountered
- read aloud books closely matched to their improving phonic knowledge, sounding out unfamiliar words accurately, automatically and without undue hesitation
- re-read these books to build up their fluency and confidence in word reading.

Notes and guidance (non-statutory)

Pupils should revise and consolidate the GPCs and the common exception words taught in year 1. The exception words taught will vary slightly, depending on the phonics programme being used. As soon as pupils can read words comprising the year 2 GPCs accurately and speedily, they should move on to the years 3 and 4 programme of study for word reading.

When pupils are taught how to read longer words, they should be shown syllable boundaries and how to read each syllable separately before they combine them to read the word.

Pupils should be taught how to read suffixes by building on the root words that they have already learnt. The whole suffix should be taught as well as the letters that make it up.

Pupils who are still at the early stages of learning to read should have ample practice in reading books that are closely matched to their developing phonic knowledge and knowledge of common exception words. As soon as the decoding of most regular words and common exception words is embedded fully, the range of books that pupils can read independently will expand rapidly. Pupils should have opportunities to exercise choice in selecting books and be taught how to do so.

Reading – comprehension

Statutory requirements

Pupils should be taught to:

- develop pleasure in reading, motivation to read, vocabulary and understanding by:
  - listening to, discussing and expressing views about a wide range of contemporary and classic poetry, stories and non-fiction at a level beyond that at which they can read independently
  - discussing the sequence of events in books and how items of information are related
  - becoming increasingly familiar with and retelling a wider range of stories, fairy stories and traditional tales

(Continued)

(Continued)

- o being introduced to non-fiction books that are structured in different ways
- o recognising simple recurring literary language in stories and poetry
- o discussing and clarifying the meanings of words, linking new meanings to known vocabulary
- o discussing their favourite words and phrases
- o continuing to build up a repertoire of poems learnt by heart, appreciating these and reciting some, with appropriate intonation to make the meaning clear

- understand both the books that they can already read accurately and fluently and those that they listen to by:

  - o drawing on what they already know or on background information and vocabulary provided by the teacher
  - o checking that the text makes sense to them as they read and correcting inaccurate reading
  - o making inferences on the basis of what is being said and done
  - o answering and asking questions
  - o predicting what might happen on the basis of what has been read so far

- participate in discussion about books, poems and other works that are read to them and those that they can read for themselves, taking turns and listening to what others say
- explain and discuss their understanding of books, poems and other material, both those that they listen to and those that they read for themselves.

Notes and guidance (non-statutory)

Pupils should be encouraged to read all the words in a sentence and to do this accurately, so that their understanding of what they read is not hindered by imprecise decoding [for example, by reading 'place' instead of 'palace'].

Pupils should monitor what they read, checking that the word they have decoded fits in with what else they have read and makes sense in the context of what they already know about the topic.

The meaning of new words should be explained to pupils within the context of what they are reading, and they should be encouraged to use morphology (such as prefixes) to work out unknown words.

Pupils should learn about cause and effect in both narrative and non-fiction (for example, what has prompted a character's behaviour in a story; why certain dates are commemorated annually). 'Thinking aloud' when reading to pupils may help them to understand what skilled readers do.

Deliberate steps should be taken to increase pupils' vocabulary and their awareness of grammar so that they continue to understand the differences between spoken and written language.

Discussion should be demonstrated to pupils. They should be guided to participate in it and they should be helped to consider the opinions of others. They should receive feedback on their discussions.

Role-play and other drama techniques can help pupils to identify with and explore characters. In these ways, they extend their understanding of what they read and have opportunities to try out the language they have listened to.

Writing – transcription

Statutory requirements

Spelling (see English Appendix 1)

Pupils should be taught to:

- spell by:
  - o segmenting spoken words into phonemes and representing these by graphemes, spelling many correctly
  - o learning new ways of spelling phonemes for which one or more spellings are already known, and learn some words with each spelling, including a few common homophones
  - o learning to spell common exception words
  - o learning to spell more words with contracted forms
  - o learning the possessive apostrophe (singular) [for example, the girl's book]
  - o distinguishing between homophones and near-homophones
- add suffixes to spell longer words, including –ment, –ness, –ful, –less, –ly
- apply spelling rules and guidance, as listed in English Appendix 1
- write from memory simple sentences dictated by the teacher that include words using the GPCs, common exception words and punctuation taught so far.

Notes and guidance (non-statutory)

In year 2, pupils move towards more word-specific knowledge of spelling, including homophones. The process of spelling should be emphasised: that is, that spelling involves segmenting spoken words into phonemes and then representing all the phonemes by graphemes in the right order. Pupils should do this both for single-syllable and multi-syllabic words.

At this stage children's spelling should be phonically plausible, even if not always correct. Misspellings of words that pupils have been taught to spell should be corrected; other misspelt words can be used as an opportunity to teach pupils about alternative ways of representing those sounds.

Pupils should be encouraged to apply their knowledge of suffixes from their word reading to their spelling. They should also draw from and apply their growing knowledge of word and spelling structure, as well as their knowledge of root words.

Statutory requirements

Handwriting

Pupils should be taught to:

- form lower-case letters of the correct size relative to one another
- start using some of the diagonal and horizontal strokes needed to join letters and understand which letters, when adjacent to one another, are best left unjoined
- write capital letters and digits of the correct size, orientation and relationship to one another and to lower case letters
- use spacing between words that reflects the size of the letters.

Notes and guidance (non-statutory)

Pupils should revise and practise correct letter formation frequently. They should be taught to write with a joined style as soon as they can form letters securely with the correct orientation.

Writing – composition

Statutory requirements

Pupils should be taught to:

- develop positive attitudes towards and stamina for writing by:
  - writing narratives about personal experiences and those of others (real and fictional)
  - writing about real events
  - writing poetry
  - writing for different purposes

- consider what they are going to write before beginning by:
  - planning or saying out loud what they are going to write about
  - writing down ideas and/or key words, including new vocabulary
  - encapsulating what they want to say, sentence by sentence

- make simple additions, revisions and corrections to their own writing by:
  - evaluating their writing with the teacher and other pupils
  - re-reading to check that their writing makes sense and that verbs to indicate time are used correctly and consistently, including verbs in the continuous form
  - proof-reading to check for errors in spelling, grammar and punctuation [for example, ends of sentences punctuated correctly]

- read aloud what they have written with appropriate intonation to make the meaning clear.

Notes and guidance (non-statutory)

Reading and listening to whole books, not simply extracts, helps pupils to increase their vocabulary and grammatical knowledge, including their knowledge of the vocabulary and grammar of Standard English. These activities also help them to understand how different types of writing, including narratives, are structured. All these can be drawn on for their writing.

Pupils should understand, through being shown these, the skills and processes essential to writing: that is, thinking aloud as they collect ideas, drafting, and re-reading to check their meaning is clear.

Drama and role-play can contribute to the quality of pupils' writing by providing opportunities for pupils to develop and order their ideas through playing roles and improvising scenes in various settings.

Pupils might draw on and use new vocabulary from their reading, their discussions about it (one-to-one and as a whole class) and from their wider experiences.

Writing – vocabulary, grammar and punctuation

Statutory requirements

Pupils should be taught to:

- develop their understanding of the concepts set out in **English Appendix 2** by:
  - learning how to use both familiar and new punctuation correctly (see English Appendix 2), including full stops, capital letters, exclamation marks, question marks, commas for lists and apostrophes for contracted forms and the possessive (singular)

- learn how to use:
  - sentences with different forms: statement, question, exclamation, command
  - expanded noun phrases to describe and specify [for example, the blue butterfly]
  - the present and past tenses correctly and consistently including the progressive form
  - subordination (using when, if, that, or because) and co-ordination (using or, and, or but)
  - the grammar for year 2 in English Appendix 2
  - some features of written Standard English

- use and understand the grammatical terminology in English Appendix 2 in discussing their writing.

Notes and guidance (non-statutory)

The terms for discussing language should be embedded for pupils in the course of discussing their writing with them. Their attention should be drawn to the technical terms they need to learn.

Lower key stage 2 – years 3 and 4

By the beginning of year 3, pupils should be able to read books written at an age-appropriate interest level. They should be able to read them accurately and at a speed that is sufficient for them to focus on understanding what they read rather than on decoding individual words. They should be able to decode most new words outside their spoken vocabulary, making a good approximation to the word's pronunciation. As their decoding skills become increasingly secure, teaching should be directed more towards developing their vocabulary and the breadth and depth of their reading, making sure that they become independent, fluent and enthusiastic readers who read widely and frequently. They should be developing their understanding and enjoyment of stories, poetry, plays and non-fiction, and learning to read silently. They should also be developing their knowledge and skills in reading non-fiction about a wide range of subjects. They should be learning to justify their views about what they have read: with support at the start of year 3 and increasingly independently by the end of year 4.

Pupils should be able to write down their ideas with a reasonable degree of accuracy and with good sentence punctuation. Teachers should therefore be consolidating pupils' writing skills, their vocabulary, their grasp of sentence structure and their knowledge of linguistic terminology. Teaching them to develop as writers involves teaching them to enhance the effectiveness of what they write as well as increasing their competence. Teachers should

make sure that pupils build on what they have learnt, particularly in terms of the range of their writing and the more varied grammar, vocabulary and narrative structures from which they can draw to express their ideas. Pupils should be beginning to understand how writing can be different from speech. Joined handwriting should be the norm; pupils should be able to use it fast enough to keep pace with what they want to say.

Pupils' spelling of common words should be correct, including common exception words and other words that they have learnt (see **English Appendix 1**). Pupils should spell words as accurately as possible using their phonic knowledge and other knowledge of spelling, such as morphology and etymology.

Most pupils will not need further direct teaching of word reading skills: they are able to decode unfamiliar words accurately, and need very few repeated experiences of this before the word is stored in such a way that they can read it without overt sound-blending. They should demonstrate understanding of figurative language, distinguish shades of meaning among related words and use age-appropriate, academic vocabulary.

As in key stage 1, however, pupils who are still struggling to decode need to be taught to do this urgently through a rigorous and systematic phonics programme so that they catch up rapidly with their peers. If they cannot decode independently and fluently, they will find it increasingly difficult to understand what they read and to write down what they want to say. As far as possible, however, these pupils should follow the year 3 and 4 programme of study in terms of listening to new books, hearing and learning new vocabulary and grammatical structures, and discussing these.

Specific requirements for pupils to discuss what they are learning and to develop their wider skills in spoken language form part of this programme of study. In years 3 and 4, pupils should become more familiar with and confident in using language in a greater variety of situations, for a variety of audiences and purposes, including through drama, formal presentations and debate.

Years 3 and 4 programme of study

Reading – word reading

Statutory requirements

Pupils should be taught to:

- apply their growing knowledge of root words, prefixes and suffixes (etymology and morphology) as listed in **English Appendix 1**, both to read aloud and to understand the meaning of new words they meet
- read further exception words, noting the unusual correspondences between spelling and sound, and where these occur in the word.

Notes and guidance (non-statutory)

At this stage, teaching comprehension should be taking precedence over teaching word reading directly. Any focus on word reading should support the development of vocabulary.

When pupils are taught to read longer words, they should be supported to test out different pronunciations. They will attempt to match what they decode to words they may have already heard but may not have seen in print [for example, in reading 'technical', the pronunciation /tɛtʃnɪkəl/ ('tetchnical') might not sound familiar, but /tɛknɪkəl/ ('teknical') should].

Reading – comprehension

Statutory requirements

Pupils should be taught to:

- develop positive attitudes to reading and understanding of what they read by:
  - listening to and discussing a wide range of fiction, poetry, plays, non-fiction and reference books or textbooks
  - reading books that are structured in different ways and reading for a range of purposes
  - using dictionaries to check the meaning of words that they have read
  - increasing their familiarity with a wide range of books, including fairy stories, myths and legends, and retelling some of these orally
  - identifying themes and conventions in a wide range of books
  - preparing poems and play scripts to read aloud and to perform, showing understanding through intonation, tone, volume and action
  - discussing words and phrases that capture the reader's interest and imagination
  - recognising some different forms of poetry [for example, free verse, narrative poetry]

- understand what they read, in books they can read independently, by:
  - checking that the text makes sense to them, discussing their understanding and explaining the meaning of words in context
  - asking questions to improve their understanding of a text
  - drawing inferences such as inferring characters' feelings, thoughts and motives from their actions, and justifying inferences with evidence
  - predicting what might happen from details stated and implied
  - identifying main ideas drawn from more than one paragraph and summarising these
  - identifying how language, structure, and presentation contribute to meaning

- retrieve and record information from non-fiction
- participate in discussion about both books that are read to them and those they can read for themselves, taking turns and listening to what others say.

Notes and guidance (non-statutory)

The focus should continue to be on pupils' comprehension as a primary element in reading. The knowledge and skills that pupils need in order to comprehend are very similar at different ages. This is why the programmes of study for comprehension in years 3 and 4 and years 5 and 6 are similar: the complexity of the writing increases the level of challenge.

Pupils should be taught to recognise themes in what they read, such as the triumph of good over evil or the use of magical devices in fairy stories and folk tales.

They should also learn the conventions of different types of writing (for example, the greeting in letters, a diary written in the first person or the use of presentational devices such as numbering and headings in instructions).

Pupils should be taught to use the skills they have learnt earlier and continue to apply these skills to read for different reasons, including for pleasure, or to find out information and the meaning of new words.

Pupils should continue to have opportunities to listen frequently to stories, poems, non-fiction and other writing, including whole books and not just extracts, so that they build on what was taught previously. In this way, they also meet books and authors that they might not choose themselves. Pupils should also have opportunities to exercise choice in selecting books and be taught how to do so, with teachers making use of any library services and expertise to support this.

(Continued)

(Continued)

Reading, re-reading, and rehearsing poems and plays for presentation and performance give pupils opportunities to discuss language, including vocabulary, extending their interest in the meaning and origin of words. Pupils should be encouraged to use drama approaches to understand how to perform plays and poems to support their understanding of the meaning. These activities also provide them with an incentive to find out what expression is required, so feeding into comprehension.

In using non-fiction, pupils should know what information they need to look for before they begin and be clear about the task. They should be shown how to use contents pages and indexes to locate information.

Pupils should have guidance about the kinds of explanations and questions that are expected from them. They should help to develop, agree on, and evaluate rules for effective discussion. The expectation should be that all pupils take part.

Writing – transcription

Statutory requirements

Spelling (see English Appendix 1)

Pupils should be taught to:

- use further prefixes and suffixes and understand how to add them (English Appendix 1)
- spell further homophones
- spell words that are often misspelt (English Appendix 1)
- place the possessive apostrophe accurately in words with regular plurals [for example, girls', boys'] and in words with irregular plurals [for example, children's]
- use the first two or three letters of a word to check its spelling in a dictionary
- write from memory simple sentences, dictated by the teacher, that include words and punctuation taught so far.

Notes and guidance (non-statutory)

Pupils should learn to spell new words correctly and have plenty of practice in spelling them.

As in years 1 and 2, pupils should continue to be supported in understanding and applying the concepts of word structure (see English Appendix 2).

Pupils need sufficient knowledge of spelling in order to use dictionaries efficiently.

Statutory requirements

Handwriting

Pupils should be taught to:

- use the diagonal and horizontal strokes that are needed to join letters and understand which letters, when adjacent to one another, are best left unjoined
- increase the legibility, consistency and quality of their handwriting [for example, by ensuring that the downstrokes of letters are parallel and equidistant; that lines of writing are spaced sufficiently so that the ascenders and descenders of letters do not touch].

Notes and guidance (non-statutory)

Pupils should be using joined handwriting throughout their independent writing. Handwriting should continue to be taught, with the aim of increasing the fluency with which pupils are able to write down what they want to say. This, in turn, will support their composition and spelling.

Writing – composition

Statutory requirements

Pupils should be taught to:

- plan their writing by:
  - discussing writing similar to that which they are planning to write in order to understand and learn from its structure, vocabulary and grammar
  - discussing and recording ideas
- draft and write by:
  - composing and rehearsing sentences orally (including dialogue), progressively building a varied and rich vocabulary and an increasing range of sentence structures (English Appendix 2)
  - organising paragraphs around a theme
  - in narratives, creating settings, characters and plot
  - in non-narrative material, using simple organisational devices [for example, headings and sub-headings]
- evaluate and edit by:
  - assessing the effectiveness of their own and others' writing and suggesting improvements
  - proposing changes to grammar and vocabulary to improve consistency, including the accurate use of pronouns in sentences
- proof-read for spelling and punctuation errors
- read aloud their own writing, to a group or the whole class, using appropriate intonation and controlling the tone and volume so that the meaning is clear.

Notes and guidance (non-statutory)

Pupils should continue to have opportunities to write for a range of real purposes and audiences as part of their work across the curriculum. These purposes and audiences should underpin the decisions about the form the writing should take, such as a narrative, an explanation or a description.

Pupils should understand, through being shown these, the skills and processes that are essential for writing: that is, thinking aloud to explore and collect ideas, drafting, and re-reading to check their meaning is clear, including doing so as the writing develops. Pupils should be taught to monitor whether their own writing makes sense in the same way that they monitor their reading, checking at different levels.

Writing – vocabulary, grammar and punctuation

Statutory requirements

Pupils should be taught to:

- develop their understanding of the concepts set out in **English Appendix 2** by:

  - extending the range of sentences with more than one clause by using a wider range of conjunctions, including when, if, because, although
  - using the present perfect form of verbs in contrast to the past tense
  - choosing nouns or pronouns appropriately for clarity and cohesion and to avoid repetition
  - using conjunctions, adverbs and prepositions to express time and cause
  - using fronted adverbials
  - learning the grammar for years 3 and 4 in English Appendix 2

- indicate grammatical and other features by:

  - using commas after fronted adverbials
  - indicating possession by using the possessive apostrophe with plural nouns
  - using and punctuating direct speech

- use and understand the grammatical terminology in English Appendix 2 accurately and appropriately when discussing their writing and reading.

Notes and guidance (non-statutory)

Grammar should be taught explicitly: pupils should be taught the terminology and concepts set out in English Appendix 2, and be able to apply them correctly to examples of real language, such as their own writing or books that they have read.

At this stage, pupils should start to learn about some of the differences between Standard English and non-Standard English and begin to apply what they have learnt [for example, in writing dialogue for characters].

Upper key stage 2 – years 5 and 6

By the beginning of year 5, pupils should be able to read aloud a wider range of poetry and books written at an age-appropriate interest level with accuracy and at a reasonable speaking pace. They should be able to read most words effortlessly and to work out how to pronounce unfamiliar written words with increasing automaticity. If the pronunciation sounds unfamiliar, they should ask for help in determining both the meaning of the word and how to pronounce it correctly.

They should be able to prepare readings, with appropriate intonation to show their understanding, and should be able to summarise and present a familiar story in their own words. They should be reading widely and frequently, outside as well as in school, for pleasure and information. They should be able to read silently, with good understanding, inferring the meanings of unfamiliar words, and then discuss what they have read.

Pupils should be able to write down their ideas quickly. Their grammar and punctuation should be broadly accurate. Pupils' spelling of most words taught so far should be accurate and they should be able to spell words that they have not yet been taught by using what they have learnt about how spelling works in English.

During years 5 and 6, teachers should continue to emphasise pupils' enjoyment and understanding of language, especially vocabulary, to support their reading and writing. Pupils' knowledge of language, gained from stories, plays, poetry, non-fiction and text-books, will support their increasing fluency as readers, their facility as writers, and their comprehension. As in years 3 and 4, pupils should be taught to enhance the effectiveness of their writing as well as their competence.

It is essential that pupils whose decoding skills are poor are taught through a rigorous and systematic phonics programme so that they catch up rapidly with their peers in terms of their decoding and spelling. However, as far as possible, these pupils should follow the upper key stage 2 programme of study in terms of listening to books and other writing that they have not come across before, hearing and learning new vocabulary and grammatical structures, and having a chance to talk about all of these.

By the end of year 6, pupils' reading and writing should be sufficiently fluent and effort-less for them to manage the general demands of the curriculum in year 7, across all subjects and not just in English, but there will continue to be a need for pupils to learn subject-specific vocabulary. They should be able to reflect their understanding of the audience for and purpose of their writing by selecting appropriate vocabulary and grammar. Teachers should prepare pupils for secondary education by ensuring that they can consciously control sentence struc-ture in their writing and understand why sentences are constructed as they are. Pupils should understand nuances in vocabulary choice and age-appropriate, academic vocabulary. This involves consolidation, practice and discussion of language.

Specific requirements for pupils to discuss what they are learning and to develop their wider skills in spoken language form part of this programme of study. In years 5 and 6, pupils' confidence, enjoyment and mastery of language should be extended through public speak-ing, performance and debate.

Years 5 and 6 programme of study

Reading – word reading

Statutory requirements

Pupils should be taught to:

- apply their growing knowledge of root words, prefixes and suffixes (morphology and etymology), as listed in English Appendix 1, both to read aloud and to under-stand the meaning of new words that they meet.

Notes and guidance (non-statutory)

At this stage, there should be no need for further direct teaching of word reading skills for almost all pupils. If pupils are struggling or failing in this, the reasons for this should be investigated. It is imperative that pupils are taught to read during their last two years at primary school if they enter year 5 not being able to do so.

Pupils should be encouraged to work out any unfamiliar word. They should focus on all the letters in a word so that they do not, for example, read 'invitation' for 'imitation' simply because they might be more familiar with the first word. Accurate reading of individual words, which might be key to the meaning of a sentence or paragraph, improves comprehension.

When teachers are reading with or to pupils, attention should be paid to new vocabulary – both a word's meaning(s) and its correct pronunciation.

Reading – comprehension

Statutory requirements

Pupils should be taught to:

- maintain positive attitudes to reading and understanding of what they read by:
  - continuing to read and discuss an increasingly wide range of fiction, poetry, plays, non-fiction and reference books or textbooks
  - reading books that are structured in different ways and reading for a range of purposes
  - increasing their familiarity with a wide range of books, including myths, legends and traditional stories, modern fiction, fiction from our literary heritage, and books from other cultures and traditions
  - recommending books that they have read to their peers, giving reasons for their choices
  - identifying and discussing themes and conventions in and across a wide range of writing
  - making comparisons within and across books
  - learning a wider range of poetry by heart
  - preparing poems and plays to read aloud and to perform, showing understanding through intonation, tone and volume so that the meaning is clear to an audience

- understand what they read by:
  - checking that the book makes sense to them, discussing their understanding and exploring the meaning of words in context
  - asking questions to improve their understanding
  - drawing inferences such as inferring characters' feelings, thoughts and motives from their actions, and justifying inferences with evidence
  - predicting what might happen from details stated and implied
  - summarising the main ideas drawn from more than one paragraph, identifying key details that support the main ideas
  - identifying how language, structure and presentation contribute to meaning

- discuss and evaluate how authors use language, including figurative language, considering the impact on the reader
- distinguish between statements of fact and opinion
- retrieve, record and present information from non-fiction
- participate in discussions about books that are read to them and those they can read for themselves, building on their own and others' ideas and challenging views courteously
- explain and discuss their understanding of what they have read, including through formal presentations and debates, maintaining a focus on the topic and using notes where necessary
- provide reasoned justifications for their views.

Notes and guidance (non-statutory)

Even though pupils can now read independently, reading aloud to them should include whole books so that they meet books and authors that they might not choose to read themselves.

The knowledge and skills that pupils need in order to comprehend are very similar at different ages. Pupils should continue to apply what they have already learnt to more complex writing.

Pupils should be taught to recognise themes in what they read, such as loss or heroism. They should have opportunities to compare characters, consider different accounts of the same event and discuss viewpoints (both of authors and of fictional characters), within a text and across more than one text.

They should continue to learn the conventions of different types of writing, such as the use of the first person in writing diaries and autobiographies.

Pupils should be taught the technical and other terms needed for discussing what they hear and read, such as metaphor, simile, analogy, imagery, style and effect.

In using reference books, pupils need to know what information they need to look for before they begin and need to understand the task. They should be shown how to use contents pages and indexes to locate information.

The skills of information retrieval that are taught should be applied, for example, in reading history, geography and science textbooks, and in contexts where pupils are genuinely motivated to find out information, for example, reading information leaflets before a gallery or museum visit or reading a theatre programme or review. Teachers should consider making use of any library services and expertise to support this.

Pupils should have guidance about and feedback on the quality of their explanations and contributions to discussions.

Pupils should be shown how to compare characters, settings, themes and other aspects of what they read.

Writing – transcription

Statutory requirements

Spelling (see English Appendix 1)

Pupils should be taught to:

- use further prefixes and suffixes and understand the guidance for adding them
- spell some words with 'silent' letters [for example, knight, psalm, solemn]
- continue to distinguish between homophones and other words which are often confused
- use knowledge of morphology and etymology in spelling and understand that the spelling of some words needs to be learnt specifically, as listed in English Appendix 1
- use dictionaries to check the spelling and meaning of words
- use the first three or four letters of a word to check spelling, meaning or both of these in a dictionary
- use a thesaurus.

Notes and guidance (non-statutory)

As in earlier years, pupils should continue to be taught to understand and apply the concepts of word structure so that they can draw on their knowledge of morphology and etymology to spell correctly.

Statutory requirements

Handwriting and presentation

Pupils should be taught to:

- write legibly, fluently and with increasing speed by:
  - choosing which shape of a letter to use when given choices and deciding whether or not to join specific letters
  - choosing the writing implement that is best suited for a task.

Notes and guidance (non-statutory)

Pupils should continue to practise handwriting and be encouraged to increase the speed of it, so that problems with forming letters do not get in the way of their writing down what they want to say. They should be clear about what standard of handwriting is appropriate for a particular task, for example, quick notes or a final handwritten version. They should also be taught to use an unjoined style, for example, for labelling a diagram or data, writing an email address, or for algebra and capital letters, for example, for filling in a form.

Writing – composition

Statutory requirements

Pupils should be taught to:

- plan their writing by:
  - identifying the audience for and purpose of the writing, selecting the appropriate form and using other similar writing as models for their own
  - noting and developing initial ideas, drawing on reading and research where necessary
  - in writing narratives, considering how authors have developed characters and settings in what pupils have read, listened to or seen performed

- draft and write by:
  - selecting appropriate grammar and vocabulary, understanding how such choices can change and enhance meaning
  - in narratives, describing settings, characters and atmosphere and integrating dialogue to convey character and advance the action
  - précising longer passages
  - using a wide range of devices to build cohesion within and across paragraphs
  - using further organisational and presentational devices to structure text and to guide the reader [for example, headings, bullet points, underlining]

- evaluate and edit by:
  - assessing the effectiveness of their own and others' writing
  - proposing changes to vocabulary, grammar and punctuation to enhance effects and clarify meaning

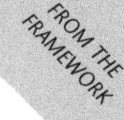

> - o ensuring the consistent and correct use of tense throughout a piece of writing
> - o ensuring correct subject and verb agreement when using singular and plural, distinguishing between the language of speech and writing and choosing the appropriate register
> - proof-read for spelling and punctuation errors
> - perform their own compositions, using appropriate intonation, volume, and movement so that meaning is clear.

Notes and guidance (non-statutory)

Pupils should understand, through being shown, the skills and processes essential for writing: that is, thinking aloud to generate ideas, drafting, and re-reading to check that the meaning is clear.

Writing – vocabulary, grammar and punctuation

Statutory requirements

Pupils should be taught to:

- develop their understanding of the concepts set out in English Appendix 2 by:
  - o recognising vocabulary and structures that are appropriate for formal speech and writing, including subjunctive forms
  - o using passive verbs to affect the presentation of information in a sentence
  - o using the perfect form of verbs to mark relationships of time and cause
  - o using expanded noun phrases to convey complicated information concisely
  - o using modal verbs or adverbs to indicate degrees of possibility
  - o using relative clauses beginning with who, which, where, when, whose, that or with an implied (i.e. omitted) relative pronoun
  - o learning the grammar for years 5 and 6 in English Appendix 2

- indicate grammatical and other features by:
  - o using commas to clarify meaning or avoid ambiguity in writing
  - o using hyphens to avoid ambiguity
  - o using brackets, dashes or commas to indicate parenthesis
  - o using semi-colons, colons or dashes to mark boundaries between independent clauses
  - o using a colon to introduce a list
  - o punctuating bullet points consistently

- use and understand the grammatical terminology in English Appendix 2 accurately and appropriately in discussing their writing and reading.

Notes and guidance (non-statutory)

Pupils should continue to add to their knowledge of linguistic terms, including those to describe grammar, so that they can discuss their writing and reading.

English Appendix 1: Spelling

Most people read words more accurately than they spell them. The younger pupils are, the truer this is.

By the end of year 1, pupils should be able to read a large number of different words containing the GPCs that they have learnt, whether or not they have seen these words before. Spelling, however, is a very different matter. Once pupils have learnt more than one way of spelling particular sounds, choosing the right letter or letters depends on their either having made a conscious effort to learn the words or having absorbed them less consciously through their reading. Younger pupils have not had enough time to learn or absorb the accurate spelling of all the words that they may want to write.

This appendix provides examples of words embodying each pattern which is taught. Many of the words listed as 'example words' for years 1 and 2, including almost all those listed as 'exception words', are used frequently in pupils' writing, and therefore it is worth pupils learning the correct spelling. The 'exception words' contain GPCs which have not yet been taught as widely applicable, but this may be because they are applicable in very few age-appropriate words rather than because they are rare in English words in general.

The word-lists for years 3 and 4 and years 5 and 6 are statutory. The lists are a mixture of words pupils frequently use in their writing and those which they often misspell. Some of the listed words may be thought of as quite challenging, but the 100 words in each list can easily be taught within the four years of key stage 2 alongside other words that teachers consider appropriate.

The rules and guidance are intended to support the teaching of spelling. Phonic knowledge should continue to underpin spelling after key stage 1; teachers should still draw pupils' attention to GPCs that do and do not fit in with what has been taught so far. Increasingly, however, pupils also need to understand the role of morphology and etymology. Although particular GPCs in root words simply have to be learnt, teachers can help pupils to understand relationships between meaning and spelling where these are relevant. For example, understanding the relationship between *medical* and *medicine* may help pupils to spell the /s/ sound in *medicine* with the letter 'c'. Pupils can also be helped to spell words with prefixes and suffixes correctly if they understand some general principles for adding them. Teachers should be familiar with what pupils have been taught about spelling in earlier years, such as which rules pupils have been taught for adding prefixes and suffixes.

In this spelling appendix, the left-hand column is statutory; the middle and right-hand columns are non-statutory guidance.

The International Phonetic Alphabet (IPA) is used to represent sounds (phonemes). A table showing the IPA is provided in this document.

Spelling – work for year 1

Revision of reception work

Statutory requirements

The boundary between revision of work covered in Reception and the introduction of new work may vary according to the programme used, but basic revision should include:

- all letters of the alphabet and the sounds which they most commonly represent
- consonant digraphs which have been taught and the sounds which they represent

- vowel digraphs which have been taught and the sounds which they represent
- the process of segmenting spoken words into sounds before choosing graphemes to represent the sounds
- words with adjacent consonants
- guidance and rules which have been taught

Statutory requirements	Rules and guidance (non-statutory)	Example words (non-statutory)
The sounds /f/, /l/, /s/, /z/ and /k/ spelt ff, ll, ss, zz and ck	The /f/, /l/, /s/, /z/ and /k/ sounds are usually spelt as **ff, ll, ss, zz** and **ck** if they come straight after a single vowel letter in short words. **Exceptions**: if, pal, us, bus, yes.	off, well, miss, buzz, back
The /ŋ/ sound spelt n before k		bank, think, honk, sunk
Division of words into syllables	Each syllable is like a 'beat' in the spoken word. Words of more than one syllable often have an unstressed syllable in which the vowel sound is unclear.	pocket, rabbit, carrot, thunder, sunset
-tch	The /tʃ/ sound is usually spelt as **tch** if it comes straight after a single vowel letter. **Exceptions**: rich, which, much, such.	catch, fetch, kitchen, notch, hutch
The /v/ sound at the end of words	English words hardly ever end with the letter **v**, so if a word ends with a /v/ sound, the letter **e** usually needs to be added after the 'v'.	have, live, give
Adding s and es to words (plural of nouns and the third person singular of verbs)	If the ending sounds like /s/ or /z/, it is spelt as –**s**. If the ending sounds like /ɪz/ and forms an extra syllable or 'beat' in the word, it is spelt as –**es**.	cats, dogs, spends, rocks, thanks, catches
Adding the endings –ing, –ed and –er to verbs where no change is needed to the root word	–**ing** and –**er** always add an extra syllable to the word and –**ed** sometimes does. The past tense of some verbs may sound as if it ends in /ɪd/ (extra syllable), /d/ or /t/ (no extra syllable), but all these endings are spelt –**ed**. If the verb ends in two consonant letters (the same or different), the ending is simply added on.	hunting, hunted, hunter, buzzing, buzzed, buzzer, jumping, jumped, jumper
Adding –er and –est to adjectives where no change is needed to the root word	As with verbs (see above), if the adjective ends in two consonant letters (the same or different), the ending is simply added on.	grander, grandest, fresher, freshest, quicker, quickest

Vowel digraphs and trigraphs

Some may already be known, depending on the programmes used in Reception, but some will be new.

Vowel digraphs and trigraphs	Rules and guidance (non-statutory)	Example words (non-statutory)
ai, oi	The digraphs ai and oi are virtually never used at the end of English words.	rain, wait, train, paid, afraid oil, join, coin, point, soil
ay, oy	**ay** and **oy** are used for those sounds at the end of words and at the end of syllables.	day, play, say, way, stay boy, toy, enjoy, annoy
a–e		made, came, same, take, safe
e–e		these, theme, complete
i–e		five, ride, like, time, side
o–e		home, those, woke, hope, hole
u–e	Both the /u:/ and /ju:/ ('oo' and 'yoo') sounds can be spelt as **u–e**.	June, rule, rude, use, tube, tune
ar		car, start, park, arm, garden
ee		see, tree, green, meet, week
ea (/iː/)		sea, dream, meat, each, read (present tense)
ea (/ɛ/)		head, bread, meant, instead, read (past tense)
er (/ɜː/)		(stressed sound): her, term, verb, person
er (/ə/)		(unstressed *schwa* sound): better, under, summer, winter, sister
ir		girl, bird, shirt, first, third
ur		turn, hurt, church, burst, Thursday
oo (/uː/)	Very few words end with the letters **oo**, although the few that do are often words that primary children in year 1 will encounter, for example, *zoo*	food, pool, moon, zoo, soon

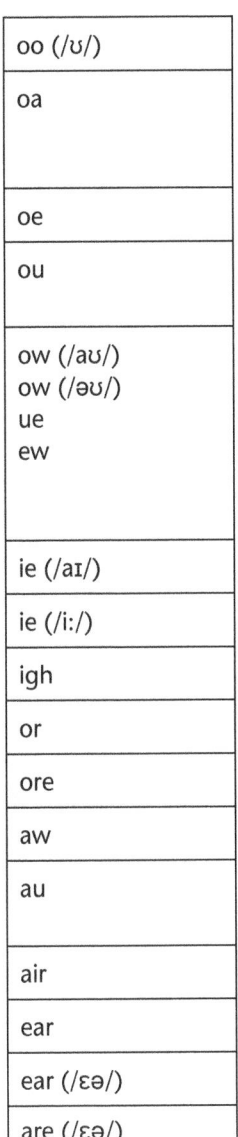

		book, took, foot, wood, good
oo (/ʊ/)		
oa	The digraph **oa** is very rare at the end of an English word.	boat, coat, road, coach, goal
oe		toe, goes
ou	The only common English word ending in **ou** is *you*.	out, about, mouth, around, sound
ow (/aʊ/) ow (/əʊ/) ue ew	Both the /u:/ and /ju:/ ('oo' and 'yoo') sounds can be spelt as **u–e**, **ue** and **ew**. If words end in the /oo/ sound, **ue** and **ew** are more common spellings than **oo**.	now, how, brown, down, town own, blow, snow, grow, show blue, clue, true, rescue, Tuesday new, few, grew, flew, drew, threw
ie (/aɪ/)		lie, tie, pie, cried, tried, dried
ie (/i:/)		chief, field, thief
igh		high, night, light, bright, right
or		for, short, born, horse, morning
ore		more, score, before, wore, shore
aw		saw, draw, yawn, crawl
au		author, August, dinosaur, astronaut
air		air, fair, pair, hair, chair
ear		dear, hear, beard, near, year
ear (/ɛə/)		bear, pear, wear
are (/ɛə/)		bare, dare, care, share, scared

Statutory requirements	Rules and guidance (non-statutory)	Example words (non-statutory)
Words ending –y (/i:/ or /ɪ/)		very, happy, funny, party, family
New consonant spellings ph and wh	The /f/ sound is not usually spelt as **ph** in short everyday words (e.g. *fat, fill, fun*).	dolphin, alphabet, phonics, elephant when, where, which, wheel, while
Using k for the /k/ sound	The /k/ sound is spelt as **k** rather than as **c** before **e**, **i** and **y**.	Kent, sketch, kit, skin, frisky

Statutory requirements	Rules and guidance (non-statutory)	Example words (non-statutory)
Adding the prefix –un	The prefix **un–** is added to the beginning of a word without any change to the spelling of the root word.	unhappy, undo, unload, unfair, unlock
Compound words	Compound words are two words joined together. Each part of the longer word is spelt as it would be if it were on its own.	football, playground, farmyard, bedroom, blackberry
Common exception words	Pupils' attention should be drawn to the grapheme-phoneme correspondences that do and do not fit in with what has been taught so far.	the, a, do, to, today, of, said, says, are, were, was, is, his, has, I, you, your, they, be, he, me, she, we, no, go, so, by, my, here, there, where, love, come, some, one, once, ask, friend, school, put, push, pull, full, house, our – and/or others, according to the programme used

Spelling – work for year 2

Revision of work from year 1

As words with new GPCs are introduced, many previously-taught GPCs can be revised at the same time as these words will usually contain them.

New work for year 2

Statutory requirements	Rules and guidance (non-statutory)	Example words (non-statutory)
The /dʒ/ sound spelt as ge and dge at the end of words, and sometimes spelt as g elsewhere in words before e, i and y	The letter j is never used for the /dʒ/ sound at the end of English words.	
	At the end of a word, the /dʒ/ sound is spelt –**dge** straight after the /æ/, /ɛ/, /ɪ/, /ɒ/, /ʌ/ and /ʊ/ sounds (sometimes called 'short' vowels).	badge, edge, bridge, dodge, fudge
	After all other sounds, whether vowels or consonants, the /dʒ/ sound is spelt as –**ge** at the end of a word.	age, huge, change, charge, bulge, village
	In other positions in words, the /dʒ/ sound is often (but not always) spelt as g before e, i, and y. The /dʒ/ sound is always spelt as j before a, o and u.	gem, giant, magic, giraffe, energy jacket, jar, jog, join, adjust

The /s/ sound spelt c before e, i and y		race, ice, cell, city, fancy
The /n/ sound spelt kn and (less often) gn at the beginning of words	The 'k' and 'g' at the beginning of these words was sounded hundreds of years ago.	knock, know, knee, gnat, gnaw
The /r/ sound spelt wr at the beginning of words	This spelling probably also reflects an old pronunciation.	write, written, wrote, wrong, wrap
The /l/ or /əl/ sound spelt –le at the end of words	The –**le** spelling is the most common spelling for this sound at the end of words.	table, apple, bottle, little, middle
The /l/ or /əl/ sound spelt –el at the end of words	The –**el** spelling is much less common than –**le**. The –**el** spelling is used after **m, n, r, s, v, w** and more often than not after **s**.	camel, tunnel, squirrel, travel, towel, tinsel
The /l/ or /əl/ sound spelt –al at the end of words	Not many nouns end in –**al**, but many adjectives do.	metal, pedal, capital, hospital, animal
Words ending –il	There are not many of these words.	pencil, fossil, nostril
The /aɪ/ sound spelt –y at the end of words	This is by far the most common spelling for this sound at the end of words.	cry, fly, dry, try, reply, July
Adding –es to nouns and verbs ending in –y	The **y** is changed to **i** before –**es** is added.	flies, tries, replies, copies, babies, carries
Adding –ed, –ing, –er and –est to a root word ending in –y with a consonant before it	The **y** is changed to **i** before –**ed**, –**er** and –**est** are added, but not before –**ing** as this would result in **ii**. The only ordinary words with **ii** are *skiing* and *taxiing*.	copied, copier, happier, happiest, cried, replied . . . **but** copying, crying, replying
Adding the endings –ing, –ed, –er, –est and –y to words ending in –e with a consonant before it	The –**e** at the end of the root word is dropped before –**ing**, –**ed**, –**er**, –**est**, –**y** or any other suffix beginning with a vowel letter is added. **Exception**: *being*.	hiking, hiked, hiker, nicer, nicest, shiny

Statutory requirements	Rules and guidance (non-statutory)	Example words (non-statutory)
Adding –ing, –ed, –er, –est and –y to words of one syllable ending in a single consonant letter after a single vowel letter	The last consonant letter of the root word is doubled to keep the /æ/, /ɛ/, /ɪ/, /ɒ/ and /ʌ/ sound (i.e. to keep the vowel 'short'). **Exception:** The letter 'x' is never doubled: *mixing, mixed, boxer, sixes.*	patting, patted, humming, hummed, dropping, dropped, sadder, saddest, fatter, fattest, runner, runny
The /ɔː/ sound spelt a before l and ll	The /ɔː/ sound ('or') is usually spelt as **a** before **l** and **ll**.	all, ball, call, walk, talk, always
The /ʌ/ sound spelt o		other, mother, brother, nothing, Monday
The /iː/ sound spelt –ey	The plural of these words is formed by the addition of –s (*donkeys, monkeys,* etc.).	key, donkey, monkey, chimney, valley
The /ɒ/ sound spelt a after w and qu	**a** is the most common spelling for the /ɒ/ ('h<u>o</u>t') sound after **w** and **qu**.	want, watch, wander, quantity, squash
The /ɜː/ sound spelt or after w	There are not many of these words.	word, work, worm, world, worth
The /ɔː/ sound spelt ar after w	There are not many of these words.	war, warm, towards
The /ʒ/ sound spelt s		television, treasure, usual
The suffixes –ment, –ness, –ful, –less and –ly	If a suffix starts with a consonant letter, it is added straight on to most root words without any change to the last letter of those words. **Exceptions:** (1) *argument* (2) root words ending in –**y** with a consonant before it but only if the root word has more than one syllable.	enjoyment, sadness, careful, playful, hopeless, plainness (plain + ness), badly merriment, happiness, plentiful, penniless, happily
Contractions	In contractions, the apostrophe shows where a letter or letters would be if the words were written in full (e.g. *can't – cannot*). *It's* means *it is* (e.g. *It's* raining) or sometimes *it has* (e.g. *It's* been raining), but *it's* is never used for the possessive.	can't, didn't, hasn't, couldn't, it's, I'll

The possessive apostrophe (singular nouns)		Megan's, Ravi's, the girl's, the child's, the man's
Words ending in –tion		station, fiction, motion, national, section
Homophones and near-homophones	It is important to know the difference in meaning between homophones.	there/their/they're, here/hear, quite/quiet, see/sea, bare/bear, one/won, sun/son, to/too/two, be/bee, blue/blew, night/knight
Common exception words	Some words are exceptions in some accents but not in others – e.g. *past, last, fast, path* and *bath* are not exceptions in accents where the **a** in these words is pronounced /æ/, as in *cat*. *Great, break* and *steak* are the only common words where the /eɪ/ sound is spelt **ea**.	door, floor, poor, because, find, kind, mind, behind, child, children*, wild, climb, most, only, both, old, cold, gold, hold, told, every, everybody, even, great, break, steak, pretty, beautiful, after, fast, last, past, father, class, grass, pass, plant, path, bath, hour, move, prove, improve, sure, sugar, eye, could, should, would, who, whole, any, many, clothes, busy, people, water, again, half, money, Mr, Mrs, parents, Christmas – and/or others according to programme used. **Note:** 'children' is not an exception to what has been taught so far but is included because of its relationship with 'child'.

Spelling – work for years 3 and 4

Revision of work from years 1 and 2

Pay special attention to the rules for adding suffixes.

New work for years 3 and 4

Statutory requirements	Rules and guidance (non-statutory)	Example words (non-statutory)
Adding suffixes beginning with vowel letters to words of more than one syllable	If the last syllable of a word is stressed and ends with one consonant letter which has just one vowel letter before it, the final consonant letter is doubled before any ending beginning with a vowel letter is added. The consonant letter is not doubled if the syllable is unstressed.	forgetting, forgotten, beginning, beginner, prefer, preferred gardening, gardener, limiting, limited, limitation

Statutory requirements	Rules and guidance (non-statutory)	Example words (non-statutory)
The /ɪ/ sound spelt y elsewhere than at the end of words	These words should be learnt as needed.	myth, gym, Egypt, pyramid, mystery
The /ʌ/ sound spelt ou	These words should be learnt as needed.	young, touch, double, trouble, country
More prefixes	Most prefixes are added to the beginning of root words without any changes in spelling, but see **in**– below. Like **un**–, the prefixes **dis**– and **mis**– have negative meanings.	**dis**–: disappoint, disagree, disobey **mis**–: misbehave, mislead, misspell (mis + spell)
	The prefix **in**– can mean both 'not' and 'in'/'into'. In the words given here it means 'not'.	**in**–: inactive, incorrect
	Before a root word starting with **l**, **in**– becomes **il**.	illegal, illegible
	Before a root word starting with **m** or **p**, **in**– becomes **im**–.	immature, immortal, impossible, impatient, imperfect
	Before a root word starting with **r**, **in**– becomes **ir**–.	irregular, irrelevant, irresponsible
	re– means 'again' or 'back'.	**re**–: redo, refresh, return, reappear, redecorate
	sub– means 'under'.	**sub**–: subdivide, subheading, submarine, submerge
	inter– means 'between' or 'among'.	**inter**–: interact, intercity, international, interrelated (inter + related)
	super– means 'above'.	**super**–: supermarket, superman, superstar
	anti– means 'against'.	**anti**–: antiseptic, anti-clockwise, antisocial
	auto– means 'self' or 'own'.	**auto**–: autobiography, autograph

The suffix –ation	The suffix –**ation** is added to verbs to form nouns. The rules already learnt still apply.	information, adoration, sensation, preparation, admiration
The suffix –ly	The suffix –**ly** is added to an adjective to form an adverb. The rules already learnt still apply. The suffix –**ly** starts with a consonant letter, so it is added straight on to most root words.	sadly, completely, usually (usual + ly), finally (final + ly), comically (comical + ly)
	Exceptions: (1) If the root word ends in –y with a consonant letter before it, the **y** is changed to **i**, but only if the root word has more than one syllable.	happily, angrily
	(2) If the root word ends with –**le**, the –**le** is changed to –**ly**.	gently, simply, humbly, nobly
	(3) If the root word ends with –**ic**, –**ally** is added rather than just –**ly**, except in the word *publicly*.	basically, frantically, dramatically
	(4) The words *truly, duly, wholly*.	
Words with endings sounding like /ʒə/ or /tʃə/	The ending sounding like /ʒə/ is always spelt –**sure**. The ending sounding like /tʃə/ is often spelt –**ture**, but check that the word is not a root word ending in **(t)ch** with an **er** ending – e.g. *teacher, catcher, richer, stretcher.*	measure, treasure, pleasure, enclosure creature, furniture, picture, nature, adventure
Endings which sound like /ʒən/	If the ending sounds like /ʒən/, it is spelt as –**sion**.	division, invasion, confusion, decision, collision, television
The suffix –ous	Sometimes the root word is obvious and the usual rules apply for adding suffixes beginning with vowel letters. Sometimes there is no obvious root word. –**our** is changed to –**or** before –**ous** is added. A final 'e' of the root word must be kept if the /dʒ/ sound of 'g' is to be kept. If there is an /iː/ sound before the –**ous** ending, it is usually spelt as **i**, but a few words have **e**.	poisonous, dangerous, mountainous, famous, various tremendous, enormous, jealous humorous, glamorous, vigorous courageous, outrageous serious, obvious, curious hideous, spontaneous, courteous

Statutory requirements	Rules and guidance (non-statutory)	Example words (non-statutory)
Endings which sound like /ʃən/, spelt –tion, –sion, –ssion, –cian	Strictly speaking, the suffixes are –**ion** and –**ian**. Clues about whether to put **t**, **s**, **ss** or **c** before these suffixes often come from the last letter or letters of the root word.	
	–**tion** is the most common spelling. It is used if the root word ends in **t** or **te**.	invention, injection, action, hesitation, completion
	–**ssion** is used if the root word ends in **ss** or –**mit**.	expression, discussion, confession, permission, admission
	–**sion** is used if the root word ends in **d** or **se**. **Exceptions:** *attend – attention, intend – intention.*	expansion, extension, comprehension, tension
	–**cian** is used if the root word ends in **c** or **cs**.	musician, electrician, magician, politician, mathematician
Words with the /k/ sound spelt ch (Greek in origin)		scheme, chorus, chemist, echo, character
Words with the /ʃ/ sound spelt ch (mostly French in origin)		chef, chalet, machine, brochure
Words ending with the /g/ sound spelt –gue and the /k/ sound spelt –que (French in origin)		league, tongue, antique, unique
Words with the /s/ sound spelt sc (Latin in origin)	In the Latin words from which these words come, the Romans probably pronounced the **c** and the **k** as two sounds rather than one – /s/ /k/.	science, scene, discipline, fascinate, crescent
Words with the /eɪ/ sound spelt ei, eigh, or ey		vein, weigh, eight, neighbour, they, obey
Possessive apostrophe with plural words	The apostrophe is placed after the plural form of the word; –s is not added if the plural already ends in –s, but *is* added if the plural does not end in –s (i.e. is an irregular plural – e.g. *children's*).	girls', boys', babies', children's, men's, mice's (**Note:** singular proper nouns ending in an *s* use the 's suffix e.g. Cyprus's population)

Homophones and near-homophones		accept/except, affect/effect, ball/bawl, berry/bury, brake/break, fair/fare, grate/great, groan/grown, here/hear, heel/heal/he'll, knot/not, mail/male, main/mane, meat/meet, medal/meddle, missed/mist, peace/piece, plain/plane, rain/rein/reign, scene/seen, weather/whether, whose/who's

Word list – years 3 and 4

accident(ally)	disappear	interest	pressure
actual(ly)	early	island	probably
address	earth	knowledge	promise
answer	eight/eighth	learn	purpose
appear	enough	length	quarter
arrive	exercise	library	question
believe	experience	material	recent
bicycle	experiment	medicine	regular
breath	extreme	mention	reign
breathe	famous	minute	remember
build	favourite	natural	sentence
busy/business	February	naughty	separate
calendar	forward(s)	notice	special
caught	fruit	occasion(ally)	straight
centre	grammar	often	strange
century	group	opposite	strength
certain	guard	ordinary	suppose
circle	guide	particular	surprise
complete	heard	peculiar	therefore
consider	heart	perhaps	though/although
continue	height	popular	thought
decide	history	position	through
describe	imagine	possess(ion)	various
different	increase	possible	weight
difficult	important	potatoes	woman/women

Notes and guidance (non-statutory)

Teachers should continue to emphasise to pupils the relationships between sounds and letters, even when the relationships are unusual. Once root words are learnt in this way, longer words can be spelt correctly, if the rules and guidance for adding prefixes and suffixes are also known.

(Continued)

(Continued)

Examples:

business: once busy is learnt, with due attention to the unusual spelling of the /i/ sound as 'u', business can then be spelt as **busy + ness**, with the **y** of **busy** changed to **i** according to the rule.

disappear: the root word *appear* contains sounds which can be spelt in more than one way so it needs to be learnt, but the prefix **dis–** is then simply added to **appear**.

Understanding the relationships between words can also help with spelling. Examples:

- *bicycle* is *cycle* (from the Greek for *wheel*) with **bi–** (meaning 'two') before it.
- *medicine* is related to *medical* so the /s/ sound is spelt as **c**.
- *opposite* is related to *oppose*, so the schwa sound in *opposite* is spelt as **o**.

Spelling – years 5 and 6

Revise work done in previous years

New work for years 5 and 6

Statutory requirements	Rules and guidance (non-statutory)	Example words (non-statutory)
Endings which sound like /ʃəs/ spelt –cious or –tious	Not many common words end like this. If the root word ends in **–ce**, the /ʃ/ sound is usually spelt as **c** – e.g. *vice – vicious, grace – gracious, space – spacious, malice – malicious*. **Exception**: *anxious*.	vicious, precious, conscious, delicious, malicious, suspicious ambitious, cautious, fictitious, infectious, nutritious
Endings which sound like /ʃəl/	**–cial** is common after a vowel letter and **–tial** after a consonant letter, but there are some exceptions. **Exceptions**: initial, financial, commercial, provincial (the spelling of the last three is clearly related to *finance, commerce* and *province*).	official, special, artificial, partial, confidential, essential
Words ending in –ant, –ance/–ancy, –ent, –ence/–ency	Use **–ant** and **–ance/–ancy** if there is a related word with a /æ/ or /eɪ/ sound in the right position; **–ation** endings are often a clue.	observant, observance, (observation), expectant (expectation), hesitant, hesitancy (hesitation), tolerant, tolerance (toleration), substance (substantial)

	Use –ent and –ence/–ency after soft c (/s/ sound), soft g (/dʒ/ sound) and qu, or if there is a related word with a clear /ε/ sound in the right position.	innocent, innocence, decent, decency, frequent, frequency, confident, confidence (confidential)
	There are many words, however, where the above guidance does not help. These words just have to be learnt.	assistant, assistance, obedient, obedience, independent, independence
Words ending in –able and –ible Words ending in –ably and –ibly	The –able/–ably endings are far more common than the –ible/–ibly endings. As with –ant and –ance/–ancy, the –able ending is used if there is a related word ending in –ation.	adorable/adorably (adoration), applicable/ applicably (application), considerable/considerably (consideration), tolerable/ tolerably (toleration)
	If the –able ending is added to a word ending in –ce or –ge, the e after the c or g must be kept as those letters would otherwise have their 'hard' sounds (as in cap and gap) before the a of the –able ending.	changeable, noticeable, forcible, legible
	The –able ending is usually but not always used if a complete root word can be heard before it, even if there is no related word ending in –ation. The first five examples opposite are obvious; in reliable, the complete word rely is heard, but the y changes to i in accordance with the rule.	dependable, comfortable, understandable, reasonable, enjoyable, reliable
	The –ible ending is common if a complete root word can't be heard before it but it also sometimes occurs when a complete word can be heard (e.g. sensible).	possible/possibly, horrible/ horribly, terrible/terribly, visible/visibly, incredible/ incredibly, sensible/sensibly
Adding suffixes beginning with vowel letters to words ending in –fer	The r is doubled if the –fer is still stressed when the ending is added.	referring, referred, referral, preferring, preferred, transferring, transferred
	The r is not doubled if the –fer is no longer stressed.	reference, referee, preference, transference
Use of the hyphen	Hyphens can be used to join a prefix to a root word, especially if the prefix ends in a vowel letter and the root word also begins with one.	co-ordinate, re-enter, co-operate, co-own

Statutory requirements	Rules and guidance (non-statutory)	Example words (non-statutory)
Words with the /i:/ sound spelt ei after c	The 'i before e except after c' rule applies to words where the sound spelt by **ei** is /i:/. **Exceptions**: *protein, caffeine, seize* (and *either* and *neither* if pronounced with an initial /i:/ sound).	deceive, conceive, receive, perceive, ceiling
Words containing the letter-string ough	**ough** is one of the trickiest spellings in English – it can be used to spell a number of different sounds.	ought, bought, thought, nought, brought, fought rough, tough, enough cough though, although, dough through thorough, borough plough, bough
Words with 'silent' letters (i.e. letters whose presence cannot be predicted from the pronunciation of the word)	Some letters which are no longer sounded used to be sounded hundreds of years ago: e.g. in *knight*, there was a /k/ sound before the /n/, and the **gh** used to represent the sound that 'ch' now represents in the Scottish word *loch*.	doubt, island, lamb, solemn, thistle, knight
Homophones and other words that are often confused	In the pairs of words opposite, nouns end **–ce** and verbs end **–se**. *Advice* and *advise* provide a useful clue as the word *advise* (verb) is pronounced with a /z/ sound – which could not be spelt **c**. More examples: aisle: a gangway between seats (in a church, train, plane). isle: an island. aloud: out loud. allowed: permitted. affect: usually a verb (e.g. *The weather may affect our plans*). effect: usually a noun (e.g. *It may have an effect on our plans*). If a verb, it means 'bring about' (e.g. *He will effect changes in the running of the business*).	advice/advise device/devise licence/license practice/practise prophecy/prophesy farther: further father: a male parent guessed: past tense of the verb *guess* guest: visitor heard: past tense of the verb *hear* herd: a group of animals led: past tense of the verb *lead*

altar: a table-like piece of furniture in a church.
alter: to change.

ascent: the act of ascending (going up).
assent: to agree/agreement (verb and noun).

bridal: to do with a bride at a wedding.
bridle: reins etc. for controlling a horse.

cereal: made from grain (e.g. breakfast cereal).
serial: adjective from the noun *series* – a succession of things one after the other.

compliment: to make nice remarks about someone (verb) or the remark that is made (noun).
complement: related to the word *complete* – to make something complete or more complete (e.g. *her scarf complemented her outfit*).

descent: the act of descending (going down).
dissent: to disagree/disagreement (verb and noun).

desert: as a noun – a barren place (stress on first syllable); as a verb – to abandon (stress on second syllable)
dessert: (stress on second syllable) a sweet course after the main course of a meal.

draft: noun – a first attempt at writing something; verb – to make the first attempt; also, to draw in someone (e.g. *to draft in extra help*)
draught: a current of air.

lead: present tense of that verb, or else the metal which is very heavy (*as heavy as lead*)

morning: before noon
mourning: grieving for someone who has died

past: noun or adjective referring to a previous time (e.g. *In the past*) or preposition or adverb showing place (e.g. *he walked past me*)
passed: past tense of the verb 'pass' (e.g. *I passed him in the road*)

precede: go in front of or before
proceed: go on

principal: adjective – most important (e.g. *principal ballerina*) noun – important person (e.g. *principal of a college*)
principle: basic truth or belief

profit: money that is made in selling things
prophet: someone who foretells the future

stationary: not moving
stationery: paper, envelopes etc.

steal: take something that does not belong to you
steel: metal

wary: cautious
weary: tired

who's: contraction of *who is* or *who has*
whose: belonging to someone (e.g. *Whose jacket is that?*)

Word list – years 5 and 6

accommodate	correspond	identity	queue
accompany	criticise (critic + ise)	immediate(ly)	recognise
according	curiosity	individual	recommend
achieve	definite	interfere	relevant
aggressive	desperate	interrupt	restaurant
amateur	determined	language	rhyme
ancient	develop	leisure	rhythm
apparent	dictionary	lightning	sacrifice
appreciate	disastrous	marvellous	secretary
attached	embarrass	mischievous	shoulder
available	environment	muscle	signature
average	equip (–ped, –ment)	necessary	sincere(ly)
awkward	especially	neighbour	soldier
bargain	exaggerate	nuisance	stomach
bruise	excellent	occupy	sufficient
category	existence	occur	suggest
cemetery	explanation	opportunity	symbol
committee	familiar	parliament	system
communicate	foreign	persuade	temperature
community	forty	physical	thorough
competition	frequently	prejudice	twelfth
conscience	government	privilege	variety
conscious	guarantee	profession	vegetable
controversy	harass	programme	vehicle
convenience	hindrance	pronunciation	yacht

Notes and guidance (non-statutory)

Teachers should continue to emphasis to pupils the relationships between sounds and letters, even when the relationships are unusual. Once root words are learnt in this way, longer words can be spelt correctly if the rules and guidance for adding prefixes and suffixes are also known. Many of the words in the list above can be used for practice in adding suffixes.

Understanding the history of words and relationships between them can also help with spelling.

Examples:

- *Conscience* and *conscious* are related to *science: conscience* is simply *science* with the prefix *con-* added. These words come from the Latin word *scio* meaning *I know.*
- The word *desperate*, meaning 'without hope', is often pronounced in English as *desp'rate*, but the *–sper-* part comes from the Latin *spero,* meaning 'I hope', in which the **e** was clearly sounded.
- *Familiar* is related to *family,* so the /ə/ sound in the first syllable of *familiar* is spelt as **a**.

International Phonetic Alphabet (non-statutory)

The table below shows each symbol of the International Phonetic Alphabet (IPA) and provides examples of the associated grapheme(s).[1] The table is not a comprehensive alphabetic code chart; it is intended simply as guidance for teachers in understanding the IPA symbols used in the spelling appendix (**English Appendix 1**). The pronunciations in the table are, by convention, based on Received Pronunciation and could be significantly different in other accents.

Consonants	
/b/	bad
/d/	dog
/ð/	this
/dʒ/	gem, jug
/f/	if, puff, photo
/g/	gum
/h/	how
/j/	yes
/k/	cat, check, key, school
/l/	leg, hill
/m/	man
/n/	man
/ŋ/	sing
/θ/	both
/p/	pet
/r/	red
/s/	sit, miss, cell
/ʃ/	she, chef
/t/	tea
/tʃ/	check
/v/	vet
/w/	wet, when
/z/	zip, hens, buzz
/ʒ/	pleasure

Vowels	
/ɑ:/	father, arm
/ɒ/	hot
/æ/	cat
/aɪ/	mind, fine, pie, high
/aʊ/	out, cow
/ɛ/	hen, head
/eɪ/	say, came, bait
/ɛə/	air
/əʊ/	cold, boat, cone, blow
/ɪ/	hit
/ɪə/	beer
/i:/	she, bead, see, scheme, chief
/ɔ:/	launch, raw, born
/ɔɪ/	coin, boy
/ʊ/	book
/ʊə/	tour
/u:/	room, you, blue, brute
/ʌ/	cup
/ɜ:/	fern, turn, girl
/ə/	farmer

---

[1] This chart is adapted slightly from the version provided on the DfE's website to support the Year 1 phonics screening check.

English Appendix 2: Vocabulary, grammar and punctuation

The grammar of our first language is learnt naturally and implicitly through interactions with other speakers and from reading. Explicit knowledge of grammar is, however, very important, as it gives us more conscious control and choice in our language. Building this knowledge is best achieved through a focus on grammar within the teaching of reading, writing and speaking. Once pupils are familiar with a grammatical concept [for example 'modal verb'], they should be encouraged to apply and explore this concept in the grammar of their own speech and writing and to note where it is used by others. Young pupils, in particular, use more complex language in speech than in writing, and teachers should build on this, aiming for a smooth transition to sophisticated writing.

The table below focuses on Standard English and should be read in conjunction with the programmes of study as it sets out the statutory requirements. The table shows when concepts should be introduced first, not necessarily when they should be completely understood. It is very important, therefore, that the content in earlier years be revisited in subsequent years to consolidate knowledge and build on pupils' understanding. Teachers should also go beyond the content set out here if they feel it is appropriate.

The grammatical terms that pupils should learn are labelled as 'terminology for pupils'. They should learn to recognise and use the terminology through discussion and practice. All terms in **bold** should be understood with the meanings set out in the Glossary.

Vocabulary, grammar and punctuation – Years 1 to 6

Year 1: Detail of content to be introduced (statutory requirement)	
Word	Regular **plural noun suffixes** –s or –es [for example, *dog, dogs; wish, wishes*], including the effects of these suffixes on the meaning of the noun
	Suffixes that can be added to **verbs** where no change is needed in the spelling of root words (e.g. *helping, helped, helper*)
	How the **prefix** *un–* changes the meaning of **verbs** and **adjectives** [negation, for example, *unkind*, or *undoing*: *untie the boat*]
Sentence	How **words** can combine to make **sentences**
	Joining **words** and joining **clauses** using *and*
Text	Sequencing **sentences** to form short narratives
Punctuation	Separation of **words** with spaces
	Introduction to capital letters, full stops, question marks and exclamation marks to demarcate **sentences**
	Capital letters for names and for the personal **pronoun** *I*
Terminology for pupils	letter, capital letter
	word, singular, plural
	sentence
	punctuation, full stop, question mark, exclamation mark

Year 2: Detail of content to be introduced (statutory requirement)	
Word	Formation of **nouns** using **suffixes** such as –*ness*, –*er* and by compounding [for example, *whiteboard, superman*]
	Formation of **adjectives** using **suffixes** such as –*ful*, –*less*
	(A fuller list of **suffixes** can be found on **page 66** in the year 2 spelling section in English Appendix 1)
	Use of the **suffixes** –*er*, –*est* in **adjectives** and the use of –ly in Standard English to turn adjectives into **adverbs**
Sentence	**Subordination** (using *when, if, that, because*) and **co-ordination** (using *or, and, but*)
	Expanded **noun phrases** for description and specification [for example, *the blue butterfly, plain flour, the man in the moon*]
	How the grammatical patterns in a sentence indicate its function as a statement, question, exclamation or command
Text	Correct choice and consistent use of **present tense** and **past tense** throughout writing
	Use of the **progressive** form of **verbs** in the **present** and **past tense** to mark actions in progress [for example, *she is drumming, he was shouting*]
Punctuation	Use of capital letters, full stops, question marks and exclamation marks to demarcate **sentences**
	Commas to separate items in a list
	Apostrophes to mark where letters are missing in spelling and to mark singular possession in nouns [for example, *the girl's name*]
Terminology for pupils	noun, noun phrase
	statement, question, exclamation, command
	compound, suffix
	adjective, adverb, verb
	tense (past, present)
	apostrophe, comma

Year 3: Detail of content to be introduced (statutory requirement)	
Word	Formation of **nouns** using a range of **prefixes** [for example *super–, anti–, auto–*]
	Use of the **forms** *a* or *an* according to whether the next **word** begins with a **consonant** or a **vowel** [for example, *a rock, an open box*]
	Word families based on common **words**, showing how words are related in form and meaning [for example, *solve, solution, solver, dissolve, insoluble*]
Sentence	Expressing time, place and cause using **conjunctions** [for example, *when, before, after, while, so, because*], **adverbs** [for example, *then, next, soon, therefore*], or **prepositions** [for example, *before, after, during, in, because of*]

Year 3: Detail of content to be introduced (statutory requirement)	
Text	Introduction to paragraphs as a way to group related material
	Headings and sub-headings to aid presentation
	Use of the **present perfect** form of **verbs** instead of the simple past [for example, *He has gone out to play* contrasted with *He went out to play*]
Punctuation	Introduction to inverted commas to **punctuate** direct speech
Terminology for pupils	preposition, conjunction
	word family, prefix
	clause, subordinate clause
	direct speech
	consonant, consonant letter vowel, vowel letter
	inverted commas (or 'speech marks')

Year 4: Detail of content to be introduced (statutory requirement)	
Word	The grammatical difference between **plural** and **possessive** *–s*
	Standard English forms for **verb inflections** instead of local spoken forms [for example, *we were* instead of *we was*, or *I did* instead of *I done*]
Sentence	Noun phrases expanded by the addition of modifying adjectives, nouns and preposition phrases (e.g. *the teacher* expanded to: *the strict maths teacher with curly hair*)
	Fronted adverbials [for example, <u>*Later that day*</u>, *I heard the bad news.*]
Text	Use of paragraphs to organise ideas around a theme
	Appropriate choice of **pronoun** or **noun** within and across **sentences** to aid **cohesion** and avoid repetition
Punctuation	Use of inverted commas and other **punctuation** to indicate direct speech [for example, a comma after the reporting clause; end punctuation within inverted commas: *The conductor shouted, "Sit down!"*]
	Apostrophes to mark **plural** possession [for example, *the girl's name, the girls' names*]
	Use of commas after **fronted adverbials**
Terminology for pupils	determiner
	pronoun, possessive pronoun
	adverbial

Year 5: Detail of content to be introduced (statutory requirement)	
Word	Converting **nouns** or **adjectives** into **verbs** using **suffixes** [for example, *–ate; –ise; –ify*]
	Verb prefixes [for example, *dis–, de–, mis–, over–* and *re–*]

Sentence	**Relative clauses** beginning with *who, which, where, when, whose, that,* or an omitted relative pronoun Indicating degrees of possibility using **adverbs** [for example, *perhaps, surely*] or **modal verbs** [for example, *might, should, will, must*]
Text	Devices to build **cohesion** within a paragraph [for example, *then, after that, this, firstly*] Linking ideas across paragraphs using **adverbials** of time [for example, *later*], place [for example, *nearby*] and number [for example, *secondly*] or tense choices [for example, he *had* seen her before]
Punctuation	Brackets, dashes or commas to indicate parenthesis Use of commas to clarify meaning or avoid ambiguity
Terminology for pupils	modal verb, relative pronoun relative clause parenthesis, bracket, dash cohesion, ambiguity

Year 6: Detail of content to be introduced (statutory requirement)	
Word	The difference between vocabulary typical of informal speech and vocabulary appropriate for formal speech and writing [for example, *find out – discover; ask for – request; go in – enter*] How words are related by meaning as synonyms and antonyms [for example, *big, large, little*].
Sentence	Use of the **passive** to affect the presentation of information in a **sentence** [for example, *I broke the window in the greenhouse* versus *The window in the greenhouse was broken (by me)*]. The difference between structures typical of informal speech and structures appropriate for formal speech and writing [for example, the use of question tags: *He's your friend, isn't he?*, or the use of **subjunctive** forms such as *If I were* or *Were they to come* in some very formal writing and speech]
Text	Linking ideas across paragraphs using a wider range of **cohesive devices**: repetition of a **word** or phrase, grammatical connections [for example, the use of **adverbials** such as *on the other hand, in contrast,* or *as a consequence*], and **ellipsis** Layout devices [for example, headings, sub-headings, columns, bullets, or tables, to structure text]
Punctuation	Use of the semi-colon, colon and dash to mark the boundary between independent **clauses** [for example, *It's raining; I'm fed up*] Use of the colon to introduce a list and use of semi-colons within lists **Punctuation** of bullet points to list information How hyphens can be used to avoid ambiguity [for example, *man eating shark* versus *man-eating shark*, or *recover* versus *re-cover*]

Year 6: Detail of content to be introduced (statutory requirement)	
Terminology for pupils	subject, object
	active, passive
	synonym, antonym
	ellipsis, hyphen, colon, semi-colon, bullet points

Glossary for the programmes of study for English (non-statutory)

The following glossary includes all the technical grammatical terms used in the programmes of study for English, as well as others that might be useful. It is intended as an aid for teachers, not as the body of knowledge that should be learnt by pupils. Apart from a few which are used only in schools (for example, *root word*), the terms below are used with the meanings defined here in most modern books on English grammar. It is recognised that there are different schools of thought on grammar, but the terms defined here clarify those being used in the programmes of study. For further details, teachers should consult the many books that are available.

Terms in definitions

As in any tightly structured area of knowledge, grammar, vocabulary and spelling involve a network of technical concepts that help to define each other. Consequently, the definition of one concept builds on other concepts that are equally technical. Concepts that are defined elsewhere in the glossary are bold. For some concepts, the technical definition may be slightly different from the meaning that some teachers may have learnt at school or may have been using with their own pupils; in these cases, the more familiar meaning is also discussed.

Term	Guidance	Example
active voice	An active **verb** has its usual pattern of **subject** and **object** (in contrast with the **passive**).	Active: *The school arranged a visit.* Passive: *A visit was arranged* by the school.
adjective	The surest way to identify adjectives is by the ways they can be used: • before a noun, to make the noun's meaning more specific (i.e. to **modify** the noun), or • after the verb *be*, as its **complement**. Adjectives cannot be modified by other adjectives. This distinguishes them from **nouns**, which can be. Adjectives are sometimes called 'describing words' because they pick out single characteristics such as size or colour. This is	*The pupils did some really good work.* [adjective used before a noun, to modify it] *Their work was good.* [adjective used after the verb *be*, as its complement] Not adjectives: *The lamp glowed.* [verb] *It was such a bright red!* [noun] *He spoke loudly.* [adverb] *It was a French grammar book.* [noun]

	often true, but it doesn't help to distinguish adjectives from other word classes, because **verbs**, **nouns** and **adverbs** can do the same thing.	
adverb	The surest way to identify adverbs is by the ways they can be used: they can **modify a verb**, an **adjective**, another adverb or even a whole clause. Adverbs are sometimes said to describe manner or time. This is often true, but it doesn't help to distinguish adverbs from other word classes that can be used as **adverbials**, such as **preposition phrases**, **noun phrases** and **subordinate clauses**.	*Usha <u>soon</u> started snoring <u>loudly</u>.* [adverbs modifying the verbs *started* and *snoring*] *That match was <u>really</u> exciting!* [adverb modifying the adjective *exciting*] *We don't get to play games <u>very often</u>.* [adverb modifying the other adverb, *often*] *<u>Fortunately,</u> it didn't rain.* [adverb modifying the whole clause 'it didn't rain' by commenting on it] Not adverbs: • *Usha went <u>up the stairs</u>.* [preposition phrase used as adverbial] • *She finished her work <u>this evening</u>.* [noun phrase used as adverbial] • *She finished <u>when the teacher got cross</u>.* [subordinate clause used as adverbial]
adverbial	An adverbial is a word or phrase that is used, like an adverb, to modify a verb or clause. Of course, **adverbs** can be used as adverbials, but many other types of words and phrases can be used this way, including **preposition phrases** and **subordinate clauses**.	*The bus leaves <u>in five minutes</u>.* [preposition phrase as adverbial: modifies *leaves*] *She promised to see him <u>last night</u>.* [noun phrase modifying either *promised* or *see*, according to the intended meaning] *She worked <u>until she had finished</u>.* [subordinate clause as adverbial]
antonym	Two words are antonyms if their meanings are opposites.	*hot – cold* *light – dark* *light – heavy*
apostrophe	Apostrophes have two completely different uses: • showing the place of missing letters (e.g. *I'm* for *I am*) • marking **possessives** (e.g. *Hannah's mother*).	*<u>I'm</u> going out and I <u>won't</u> be long.* [showing missing letters] *<u>Hannah's</u> mother went to town in <u>Justin's</u> car.* [marking possessives]
article	The articles *the* (definite) and *a* or *an* (indefinite) are the most common type of **determiner**.	*<u>The</u> dog found <u>a</u> bone in <u>an</u> old box.*

Term	Guidance	Example
auxiliary verb	The auxiliary **verbs** are: *be, have, do* and the **modal verbs**. They can be used to make questions and negative statements. In addition: • *be* is used in the **progressive** and **passive** • *have* is used in the **perfect** • *do* is used to form questions and negative statements if no other auxiliary verb is present	*They <u>are</u> winning the match.* [*be* used in the progressive] *<u>Have</u> you finished your picture?* [*have* used to make a question, and the perfect] *No, I <u>don't</u> know him.* [*do* used to make a negative; no other auxiliary is present] *<u>Will</u> you come with me or not?* [modal verb *will* used to make a question about the other person's willingness]
clause	A clause is a special type of **phrase** whose **head** is a **verb**. Clauses can sometimes be complete sentences. Clauses may be **main** or **subordinate**. Traditionally, a clause had to have a **finite verb**, but most modern grammarians also recognise non-finite clauses.	*It was raining.* [single-clause sentence] *It was raining but we were indoors.* [two finite clauses] *<u>If you are coming to the party</u>, please let us know.* [finite subordinate clause inside a finite main clause] *Usha went upstairs <u>to play on her computer</u>.* [non-finite clause]
cohesion	A text has cohesion if it is clear how the meanings of its parts fit together. **Cohesive devices** can help to do this. In the example, there are repeated references to the same thing (shown by the different style pairings), and the logical relations, such as time and cause, between different parts are clear.	**A visit** has been arranged for *<u>Year 6</u>*, to the <u>Mountain Peaks Field Study Centre</u>, leaving school at 9.30am. **This** is **an overnight visit.** <u>The centre</u> has beautiful grounds and *a nature trail*. During the afternoon, *<u>the children</u>* will follow *the trail*.
cohesive device	Cohesive devices are words used to show how the different parts of a text fit together. In other words, they create **cohesion**. Some examples of cohesive devices are: • **determiners** and **pronouns**, which can refer back to earlier words • **conjunctions** and **adverbs**, which can make relations between words clear • **ellipsis** of expected words.	*Julia's dad bought her a football. <u>The</u> football was expensive!* [determiner; refers us back to a particular football] *Joe was given a bike for Christmas. <u>He</u> liked <u>it</u> very much.* [the pronouns refer back to Joe and the bike] *We'll be going shopping <u>before</u> we go to the park.* [**conjunction**; makes a relationship of time clear] *I'm afraid we're going to have to wait for the next train. <u>Meanwhile</u>, we could have a cup of tea.* [**adverb**; refers back to the time of waiting]

		Where are you going? [_] To school! [ellipsis of the expected words *I'm going*; links the answer back to the question]
complement	A verb's subject complement adds more information about its **subject**, and its object complement does the same for its **object**. Unlike the verb's object, its complement may be an adjective. The verb *be* normally has a complement.	*She is <u>our teacher</u>.* [adds more information about the subject, *she*] *They seem <u>very competent</u>.* [adds more information about the subject, *they*] *Learning makes me <u>happy</u>.* [adds more information about the object, *me*]
compound, compounding	A compound word contains at least two **root words** in its **morphology**; e.g. *whiteboard, superman*. Compounding is very important in English.	*blackbird, blow-dry, bookshop, ice-cream, English teacher, inkjet, one-eyed, bone-dry, baby-sit, daydream, outgrow*
conjunction	A conjunction links two words or phrases together. There are two main types of conjunctions: • **co-ordinating** conjunctions (e.g. *and*) link two words or phrases together as an equal pair • subordinating conjunctions (e.g. *when*) introduce a **subordinate clause**.	*James bought a bat <u>and</u> ball.* [links the words *bat* and *ball* as an equal pair] *Kylie is young <u>but</u> she can kick the ball hard.* [links two clauses as an equal pair] *Everyone watches <u>when</u> Kyle does back-flips.* [introduces a subordinate clause] *Joe can't practise kicking <u>because</u> he's injured.* [introduces a subordinate clause]
consonant	A sound which is produced when the speaker closes off or obstructs the flow of air through the vocal tract, usually using lips, tongue or teeth. Most of the letters of the alphabet represent consonants. Only the letters *a, e, i, o, u* and *y* can represent **vowel** sounds.	/p/ [flow of air stopped by the lips, then released] /t/ [flow of air stopped by the tongue touching the roof of the mouth, then released] /f/ [flow of air obstructed by the bottom lip touching the top teeth] /s/ [flow of air obstructed by the tip of the tongue touching the gum line]
continuous	See **progressive**	
co-ordinate, co-ordination	Words or phrases are co-ordinated if they are linked as an equal pair by a co-ordinating **conjunction** (i.e. *and, but, or*).	***Susan <u>and</u> Amra** met in a café.* [links the words *Susan* and *Amra* as an equal pair] ***They talked <u>and</u> drank tea** for an hour.* [links two clauses as an equal pair]

Term	Guidance	Example
	In the examples on the right, the co-ordinated elements are shown in bold, and the conjunction is underlined. The difference between co-ordination and **subordination** is that, in subordination, the two linked elements are not equal.	***Susan got a bus*** <u>*but*</u> ***Amra walked***. [links two clauses as an equal pair] Not co-ordination: *They ate <u>before</u> they met.* [*before* introduces a subordinate clause]
determiner	A determiner specifies a noun as known or unknown, and it goes before any modifiers (e.g. adjectives or other nouns). Some examples of determiners are: • **articles** (*the*, *a* or *an*) • demonstratives (e.g. *this, those*) • **possessives** (e.g. *my, your*) • quantifiers (e.g. *some, every*).	<u>*the*</u> *home team* [article, specifies the team as known] <u>*a*</u> *good team* [article, specifies the team as unknown] <u>*that*</u> *pupil* [demonstrative, known] <u>*Julia's*</u> *parents* [possessive, known] <u>*some*</u> *big boys* [quantifier, unknown] Contrast: *home* <u>*the*</u> *team, big* <u>*some*</u> *boys* [both incorrect, because the determiner should come before other modifiers]
digraph	A type of **grapheme** where two letters represent one **phoneme**. Sometimes, these two letters are not next to one another; this is called a split digraph.	The digraph <u>*ea*</u> in *ea̲ch* is pronounced /iː/. The digraph <u>*sh*</u> in *s̲h̲ed* is pronounced /ʃ/. The split digraph <u>*i–e*</u> in *li̲ne̲* is pronounced /aɪ/.
ellipsis	Ellipsis is the omission of a word or phrase which is expected and predictable.	*Frankie waved to Ivana and* <u>~~she~~</u> *watched her drive away.* *She did it because she wanted to* ~~*do it*~~.
etymology	A word's etymology is its history: its origins in earlier forms of English or other languages, and how its form and meaning have changed. Many words in English have come from Greek, Latin or French.	The word *school* was borrowed from a Greek word σχολή (*skholē*) meaning 'leisure'. The word *verb* comes from Latin *verbum*, meaning 'word'. The word *mutton* comes from French *mouton*, meaning 'sheep'.
finite verb	Every sentence typically has at least one verb which is either past or present tense. Such verbs are called 'finite'. The imperative verb in a command is also finite.	*Lizzie* <u>*does*</u> *the dishes every day.* [**present tense**] *Even Hana* <u>*did*</u> *the dishes yesterday.* [**past tense**] <u>*Do*</u> *the dishes, Naser!* [imperative]

	Verbs that are not finite, such as participles or infinitives, cannot stand on their own: they are linked to another verb in the sentence.	Not finite verbs: • *I have done them.* [combined with the finite verb *have*] • *I will do them.* [combined with the finite verb *will*] • *I want to do them!* [combined with the finite verb *want*]
fronting, fronted	A word or phrase that normally comes after the **verb** may be moved before the verb: when this happens, we say it has been 'fronted'. For example, a fronted adverbial is an **adverbial** which has been moved before the verb. When writing fronted phrases, we often follow them with a comma.	*Before we begin, make sure you've got a pencil.* [Without fronting: *Make sure you've got a pencil before we begin.*] *The day after tomorrow, I'm visiting my granddad.* [Without fronting: *I'm visiting my granddad the day after tomorrow.*]
future	Reference to future time can be marked in a number of different ways in English. All these ways involve the use of a **present-tense verb**. See also **tense**. Unlike many other languages (such as French, Spanish or Italian), English has no distinct 'future tense' form of the verb comparable with its **present** and **past** tenses.	*He will leave tomorrow.* [present-tense *will* followed by infinitive *leave*] *He may leave tomorrow.* [present-tense *may* followed by infinitive *leave*] *He leaves tomorrow.* [present-tense *leaves*] *He is going to leave tomorrow.* [present tense *is* followed by *going to* plus the infinitive *leave*]
GPC	See **grapheme-phoneme correspondences**.	
grapheme	A letter, or combination of letters, that corresponds to a single **phoneme** within a word.	The grapheme *t* in the words *ten*, *bet* and *ate* corresponds to the phoneme /t/. The grapheme *ph* in the word *dolphin* corresponds to the phoneme /f/.
grapheme-phoneme correspondences	The links between letters, or combinations of letters (**graphemes**) and the speech sounds (**phonemes**) that they represent. In the English writing system, graphemes may correspond to different phonemes in different words.	The grapheme *s* corresponds to the phoneme /s/ in the word *see*, but . . . . . . it corresponds to the phoneme /z/ in the word *easy*.

Term	Guidance	Example
head	See **phrase**.	
homonym	Two different words are homonyms if they both look exactly the same when written, and sound exactly the same when pronounced.	*Has he <u>left</u> yet? Yes – he went through the door on the <u>left</u>.* *The noise a dog makes is called a <u>bark</u>. Trees have <u>bark</u>.*
homophone	Two different words are homophones if they sound exactly the same when pronounced.	*<u>hear</u>, <u>here</u>* *<u>some</u>, <u>sum</u>*
infinitive	A verb's infinitive is the basic form used as the head-word in a dictionary (e.g. *walk, be*). Infinitives are often used: • after *to* • after **modal verbs**.	*I want to <u>walk</u>.* *I will <u>be</u> quiet.*
inflection	When we add *-ed* to *walk*, or change *mouse* to *mice*, this change of **morphology** produces an inflection ('bending') of the basic word which has special grammar (e.g. **past tense** or **plural**). In contrast, adding *-er* to *walk* produces a completely different word, *walker*, which is part of the same **word family**. Inflection is sometimes thought of as merely a change of ending, but, in fact, some words change completely when inflected.	*dogs* is an inflection of *dog*. *went* is an inflection of *go*. *better* is an inflection of *good*.
intransitive verb	A verb which does not need an object in a sentence to complete its meaning is described as intransitive. See **'transitive verb'**.	*We all <u>laughed</u>.* *We would like to stay longer, but we must <u>leave</u>.*
main clause	A **sentence** contains at least one **clause** which is not a **subordinate clause**; such a clause is a main clause. A main clause may contain any number of subordinate clauses.	*It was raining but <u>the sun was shining</u>.* [two main clauses] *<u>The man **who wrote it** told me **that it was true**</u>.* [one main clause containing two subordinate clauses.] *She said, "It rained all day."* [one main clause containing another.]

modal verb	Modal verbs are used to change the meaning of other **verbs**. They can express meanings such as certainty, ability, or obligation. The main modal verbs are *will, would, can, could, may, might, shall, should, must* and *ought*. A modal verb only has **finite** forms and has no **suffixes** (e.g. *I sing – he sings*, but not *I must – he musts*).	*I <u>can</u> do this maths work by myself.* *This ride <u>may</u> be too scary for you!* *You <u>should</u> help your little brother.* *Is it going to rain? Yes, it <u>might</u>.* *Canning swim is important.* [not possible because *can* must be finite; contrast: *Being able to swim is important*, where *being* is not a modal verb]
modify, modifier	One word or phrase modifies another by making its meaning more specific. Because the two words make a **phrase**, the 'modifier' is normally close to the modified word.	In the phrase *primary-school teacher*: • *teacher* is modified by *primary-school* (to mean a specific kind of teacher) • *school* is modified by *primary* (to mean a specific kind of school).
morphology	A word's morphology is its internal make-up in terms of **root words** and **suffixes** or **prefixes**, as well as other kinds of change such as the change of *mouse* to *mice*. Morphology may be used to produce different **inflections** of the same word (e.g. *boy – boys*), or entirely new words (e.g. *boy – boyish*) belonging to the same **word family**. A word that contains two or more root words is a **compound** (e.g. *news+paper, ice+cream*).	*dogs* has the morphological make-up: *dog + s*. *unhelpfulness* has the morphological make-up: *unhelpful + ness* • where *unhelpful = un + helpful* • and *helpful = help + ful*
noun	The surest way to identify nouns is by the ways they can be used after **determiners** such as *the*: for example, most nouns will fit into the frame "The __ matters/ matter." Nouns are sometimes called 'naming words' because they name people, places and 'things'; this is often true, but it doesn't help to distinguish nouns from other **word classes**. For example, **prepositions** can name places	*Our <u>dog</u> bit the <u>burglar</u> on his <u>behind</u>!* *My big <u>brother</u> did an amazing <u>jump</u> on his <u>skateboard</u>.* *<u>Actions</u> speak louder than <u>words</u>.* Not nouns: • *He's <u>behind</u> you!* [this names a place, but is a preposition, not a noun] • *She can <u>jump</u> so high!* [this names an action, but is a verb, not a noun]

Term	Guidance	Example
	and **verbs** can name 'things' such as actions. Nouns may be classified as **common** (e.g. *boy, day*) or **proper** (e.g. *Ivan, Wednesday*), and also as **countable** (e.g. *thing, boy*) or **non-countable** (e.g. *stuff, money*). These classes can be recognised by the determiners they combine with.	common, countable: *a book, books,* two *chocolates,* one *day,* fewer *ideas* common, non-countable: *money, some chocolate, less imagination* proper, countable: *Marilyn, London, Wednesday*
noun phrase	A noun phrase is a **phrase** with a noun as its **head**, e.g. *some foxes, foxes with bushy tails.* Some grammarians recognise one-word phrases, so that *foxes are multiplying* would contain the noun *foxes* acting as the head of the noun phrase *foxes.*	*Adult foxes can jump.* [*adult* modifies *foxes,* so *adult* belongs to the noun phrase] *Almost all healthy adult foxes in this area can jump.* [all the other words help to modify *foxes,* so they all belong to the noun phrase]
object	An object is normally a **noun**, **pronoun** or **noun phrase** that comes straight after the **verb**, and shows what the verb is acting upon. Objects can be turned into the **subject** of a **passive** verb, and cannot be **adjectives** (contrast with **complements**).	*Year 2 designed puppets.* [noun acting as object] *I like that.* [pronoun acting as object] *Some people suggested a pretty display.* [noun phrase acting as object] Contrast: • *A display was suggested.* [object of active verb becomes the subject of the passive verb] • *Year 2 designed pretty.* [incorrect, because adjectives cannot be objects]
participle	Verbs in English have two participles, called 'present participle' (e.g. *walking, taking*) and 'past participle' (e.g. *walked, taken*). Unfortunately, these terms can be confusing to learners, because: • they don't necessarily have anything to do with present or past time • although past participles are used as **perfects** (e.g. *has eaten*) they are also used as **passives** (e.g. *was eaten*).	*He is walking to school.* [present participle in a **progressive**] *He has taken the bus to school.* [past participle in a **perfect**] *The photo was taken in the rain.* [past participle in a **passive**]

passive	The sentence *It was eaten by our dog* is the passive of *Our dog ate it.* A passive is recognisable from: • the past **participle** form *eaten* • the normal **object** (*it*) turned into the **subject** • the normal subject (*our dog*) turned into an optional **preposition phrase** with *by* as its **head** • the verb *be* (*was*), or some other verb such as *get*. Contrast **active**. A verb is not 'passive' just because it has a passive meaning: it must be the passive version of an active verb.	*A visit was <u>arranged</u> by the school.* *Our cat got <u>run</u> over by a bus.* Active versions: • *The school arranged a visit.* • *A bus ran over our cat.* Not passive: • *He received a warning.* [past tense, active *received*] • *We had an accident.* [past tense, active *had*]
past tense	Verbs in the past tense are commonly used to: • talk about the past • talk about imagined situations • make a request sound more polite. Most verbs take a suffix *–ed*, to form their past tense, but many commonly-used verbs are irregular. See also **tense**.	*Tom and Chris <u>showed</u> me their new TV.* [names an event in the past] *Antonio <u>went</u> on holiday to Brazil.* [names an event in the past; irregular past of *go*] *I wish I <u>had</u> a puppy.* [names an imagined situation, not a situation in the past] *I <u>was</u> hoping you'd help tomorrow.* [makes an implied request sound more polite]
perfect	The perfect form of a <u>verb</u> generally calls attention to the consequences of a prior event; for example, *he has gone to lunch* implies that he is still away, in contrast with *he went to lunch.* 'Had gone to lunch' takes a past time point (i.e. when we arrived) as its reference point and is another way of establishing time relations in a text. The perfect tense is formed by: • turning the verb into its past **participle inflection** • adding a form of the verb *have* before it.	*She <u>has downloaded</u> some songs.* [present perfect; now she has some songs] *I <u>had eaten</u> lunch when you came.* [past perfect; I wasn't hungry when you came]

Term	Guidance	Example
	It can also be combined with the **progressive** (e.g. *he has been going*).	
phoneme	A phoneme is the smallest unit of sound that signals a distinct, contrasting meaning. For example: • /t/ contrasts with /k/ to signal the difference between *tap* and *cap* • /t/ contrasts with /l/ to signal the difference between *bought* and *ball*. It is this contrast in meaning that tells us there are two distinct phonemes at work. There are around 44 phonemes in English; the exact number depends on regional accents. A single phoneme may be represented in writing by one, two, three or four letters constituting a single **grapheme**.	The word *cat* has three letters and three phonemes: /kæt/ The word *catch* has five letters and three phonemes: /katʃ/ The word *caught* has six letters and three phonemes: /kɔːt/
phrase	A phrase is a group of words that are grammatically connected so that they stay together, and that expand a single word, called the 'head'. The phrase is a **noun phrase** if its head is a noun, a **preposition phrase** if its head is a preposition, and so on; but if the head is a **verb**, the phrase is called a **clause**. Phrases can be made up of other phrases.	*She waved to <u>her mother</u>.* [a noun phrase, with the noun *mother* as its head] *She waved <u>to her mother</u>.* [a preposition phrase, with the preposition *to* as its head] *<u>She waved to her mother</u>.* [a clause, with the verb *waved* as its head]
plural	A plural **noun** normally has a **suffix** –*s* or –*es* and means 'more than one'. There are a few nouns with different **morphology** in the plural (e.g. *mice, formulae*).	<u>*dogs*</u> [more than one dog]; <u>*boxes*</u> [more than one box] <u>*mice*</u> [more than one mouse]
possessive	A possessive can be: • a **noun** followed by an **apostrophe**, with or without *s* • a possessive **pronoun**.	*<u>Tariq's</u> book* [Tariq has the book] *The <u>boys'</u> arrival* [the boys arrive] *<u>His</u> obituary* [the obituary is about him]

	The relation expressed by a possessive goes well beyond ordinary ideas of 'possession'. A possessive may act as a **determiner**.	*That essay is <u>mine</u>.* [I wrote the essay]
prefix	A prefix is added at the beginning of a **word** in order to turn it into another word. Contrast **suffix**.	<u>*over*</u>*take,* <u>*dis*</u>*appear*
preposition	A preposition links a following **noun**, **pronoun** or **noun phrase** to some other word in the sentence. Prepositions often describe locations or directions, but can describe other things, such as relations of time. Words like *before* or *since* can act either as prepositions or as **conjunctions**.	*Tom waved goodbye <u>to</u> Christy. She'll be back <u>from</u> Australia <u>in</u> two weeks.* *I haven't seen my dog <u>since</u> this morning.* Contrast: *I'm going, <u>since</u> no-one wants me here!* [conjunction: links two clauses]
preposition phrase	A preposition phrase has a preposition as its head followed by a noun, pronoun or noun phrase.	*He was <u>in bed</u>.* *I met them <u>after the party</u>.*
present tense	**Verbs** in the present tense are commonly used to: • talk about the present • talk about the **future**. They may take a suffix *–s* (depending on the **subject**). See also **tense**.	*Jamal <u>goes</u> to the pool every day.* [describes a habit that exists now] *He <u>can</u> swim.* [describes a state that is true now] *The bus <u>arrives</u> at three.* [scheduled now] *My friends <u>are</u> coming to play.* [describes a plan in progress now]
progressive	The progressive (also known as the 'continuous') form of a **verb** generally describes events in progress. It is formed by combining the verb's present **participle** (e.g. *singing*) with a form of the verb *be* (e.g. *he was singing*). The progressive can also be combined with the **perfect** (e.g. *he has been singing*).	*Michael <u>is singing</u> in the store room.* [present progressive] *Amanda <u>was making</u> a patchwork quilt.* [past progressive] *Usha <u>had been practising</u> for an hour when I called.* [past perfect progressive]
pronoun	Pronouns are normally used like **nouns**, except that: • they are grammatically more specialised • it is harder to **modify** them	***Amanda** waved to **Michael**.* *<u>**She**</u> waved to <u>**him**</u>.* ***John's** mother is over there. <u>**His**</u> mother is over there.*

FROM THE FRAMEWORK

Term	Guidance	Example
	In the examples, each sentence is written twice: once with nouns, and once with pronouns (underlined). Where the same thing is being talked about, the words are shown in bold.	*The **visit** will be an overnight **visit**.* ***This** will be an overnight **visit**.* ***Simon** is the person: **Simon** broke it*. ***He** is the one **who** broke it.*
punctuation	Punctuation includes any conventional features of writing other than spelling and general layout: the standard punctuation marks . , ; : ? ! - – ( ) " " ' ' , and also word-spaces, capital letters, apostrophes, paragraph breaks and bullet points. One important role of punctuation is to indicate **sentence** boundaries.	*"I'm going out, Usha, and I won't be long," Mum said.*
Received Pronunciation	Received Pronunciation (often abbreviated to RP) is an accent which is used only by a small minority of English speakers in England. It is not associated with any one region. Because of its regional neutrality, it is the accent which is generally shown in dictionaries in the UK (but not, of course, in the USA). RP has no special status in the national curriculum.	
register	Classroom lessons, football commentaries and novels use different registers of the same language, recognised by differences of vocabulary and grammar. Registers are 'varieties' of a language which are each tied to a range of uses, in contrast with dialects, which are tied to groups of users.	*I regret to inform you that Mr Joseph Smith has passed away.* [formal letter] *Have you heard that Joe has died?* [casual speech] *Joe falls down and dies, centre stage.* [stage direction]
relative clause	A relative clause is a special type of **subordinate clause** that modifies a **noun**. It often does this by using a relative **pronoun** such as *who* or *that* to refer back to that noun, though the relative pronoun *that* is often omitted.	*That's the **boy** <u>who lives near school</u>.* [who refers back to *boy*] *The **prize** <u>**that** I won</u> was a book.* [*that* refers back to *prize*] *The **prize** <u>I won</u> was a book.* [the pronoun *that* is omitted] ***Tom broke the game**, <u>**which** annoyed Ali</u>.* [*which* refers back to the whole clause]

	A relative clause may also be attached to a **clause**. In that case, the pronoun refers back to the whole clause, rather than referring back to a noun.	
	In the examples, the relative clauses are underlined, and both the pronouns and the words they refer back to are in bold.	
root word	**Morphology** breaks words down into root words, which can stand alone, and **suffixes** or **prefixes** which can't. For example, *help* is the root word for other words in its **word family** such as *helpful* and *helpless*, and also for its **inflections** such as *helping*. **Compound** words (e.g. *help-desk*) contain two or more root words. When looking in a dictionary, we sometimes have to look for the root word (or words) of the word we are interested in.	*pla**y**ed* [the root word is *play*] *un**fair*** [the root word is *fair*] *football* [the root words are *foot* and *ball*]
schwa	The name of a vowel sound that is found only in unstressed positions in English. It is the most common vowel sound in English. It is written as /ə/ in the International Phonetic Alphabet. In the English writing system, it can be written in many different ways.	/əlɒŋ/ [*a*long] /bʌtə/ [*butter*] /dɒktə/ [*doctor*]
sentence	A sentence is a group of **words** which are grammatically connected to each other but not to any words outside the sentence. The form of a sentence's main clause shows whether it is being used as a statement, a question, a command or an exclamation. A sentence may consist of a single clause or it may contain several clauses held together by subordination or co-ordination. Classifying sentences as 'simple', 'complex' or 'compound' can be confusing, because a 'simple'	*John went to his friend's house. He stayed there till tea-time.* *John went to his friend's house, he stayed there till tea-time.* [This is a 'comma splice', a common error in which a comma is used where either a full stop or a semi-colon is needed to indicate the lack of any grammatical connection between the two clauses.] *You are my friend.* [statement] *Are you my friend?* [question] *Be my friend!* [command] *What a good friend you are!* [exclamation]

Term	Guidance	Example
	sentence may be complicated, and a 'complex' one may be straightforward. The terms **'single-clause sentence'** and **'multi-clause sentence'** may be more helpful.	*Ali went home on his bike to his goldfish and his current library book about pets.* [single-clause sentence] *She went shopping but took back everything she had bought because she didn't like any of it.* [multi-clause sentence]
split digraph	See **digraph**.	
Standard English	Standard English can be recognised by the use of a very small range of forms such as *those books, I did it* and *I wasn't doing anything* (rather than their non-Standard equivalents); it is not limited to any particular accent. It is the variety of English which is used, with only minor variation, as a major world language. Some people use Standard English all the time, in all situations from the most casual to the most formal, so it covers most **registers**. The aim of the national curriculum is that everyone should be able to use Standard English as needed in writing and in relatively formal speaking.	*I did it because they were not willing to undertake any more work on those houses.* [formal Standard English] *I did it cos they wouldn't do any more work on those houses.* [casual Standard English] *I done it cos they wouldn't do no more work on them houses.* [casual non-Standard English]
stress	A **syllable** is stressed if it is pronounced more forcefully than the syllables next to it. The other syllables are unstressed.	a<u>bout</u> <u>vi</u>sit
subject	The subject of a verb is normally the **noun**, **noun phrase** or **pronoun** that names the 'do-er' or 'be-er'. The subject's normal position is: • just before the **verb** in a statement • just after the **auxiliary verb**, in a question. Unlike the verb's **object** and **complement**, the subject can determine the form of the verb (e.g. *I am, you are*).	<u>*Rula's mother*</u> *went out.* <u>*That*</u> *is uncertain.* <u>*The children*</u> *will study the animals.* *Will* <u>*the children*</u> *study the animals?*

subjunctive	In some languages, the **inflections** of a **verb** include a large range of special forms which are used typically in **subordinate clauses**, and are called 'subjunctives'. English has very few such forms and those it has tend to be used in rather formal styles.	*The school requires that all pupils <u>be</u> honest.* *The school rules demand that pupils not <u>enter</u> the gym at lunchtime.* *If Zoë <u>were</u> the class president, things would be much better.*
subordinate, subordination	A subordinate word or phrase tells us more about the meaning of the word it is subordinate to. Subordination can be thought of as an unequal relationship between a subordinate word and a main word. For example: • an adjective is subordinate to the noun it **modifies** • **subjects** and **objects** are subordinate to their **verbs**. Subordination is much more common than the equal relationship of **co-ordination**. See also **subordinate clause**.	*<u>big</u> dogs* [*big* is subordinate to *dogs*] *<u>Big dogs</u> need <u>long walks</u>.* [*big dogs* and *long walks* are subordinate to *need*] *We can watch TV <u>when we've finished</u>.* [*when we've finished* is subordinate to *watch*]
subordinate clause	A clause which is **subordinate** to some other part of the same **sentence** is a subordinate clause; for example, in *The apple that I ate was sour*, the clause *that I ate* is subordinate to *apple* (which it **modifies**). Subordinate clauses contrast with **co-ordinate** clauses as in *It was sour but looked very tasty*. (Contrast: **main clause**) However, clauses that are directly quoted as direct speech are not subordinate clauses.	*That's the street <u>where Ben lives</u>.* [**relative clause**; modifies *street*] *He watched her <u>as she disappeared</u>.* [**adverbial**; modifies *watched*] *<u>What you said</u> was very nice.* [acts as **subject** of *was*] *She noticed <u>an hour had passed</u>.* [acts as **object** of *noticed*] Not subordinate: *He shouted, "<u>Look out!</u>"*
suffix	A suffix is an 'ending', used at the end of one word to turn it into another word. Unlike **root words**, suffixes cannot stand on their own as a complete word. Contrast **prefix**.	*call – call<u>ed</u>* *teach – teach<u>er</u>* [turns a **verb** into a **noun**] *terror – terror<u>ise</u>* [turns a noun into a verb] *green – green<u>ish</u>* [leaves **word class** unchanged]

Term	Guidance	Example
syllable	A syllable sounds like a beat in a **word**. Syllables consist of at least one **vowel**, and possibly one or more **consonants**.	*Cat* has one syllable. *Fairy* has two syllables. *Hippopotamus* has five syllables.
synonym	Two words are synonyms if they have the same meaning, or similar meanings. Contrast **antonym**.	*talk – speak* *old – elderly*
tense	In English, tense is the choice between **present** and **past verbs**, which is special because it is signalled by **inflections** and normally indicates differences of time. In contrast, languages like French, Spanish and Italian, have three or more distinct tense forms, including a future tense. (See also: **future**.) The simple tenses (present and past) may be combined in English with the **perfect** and **progressive**.	*He <u>studies</u>.* [present tense – present time] *He <u>studied</u> yesterday.* [past tense – past time] *He <u>studies</u> tomorrow, or else!* [present tense – future time] *He <u>may study</u> tomorrow.* [present tense + infinitive – future time] *He <u>plans</u> to <u>study</u> tomorrow.* [present tense + infinitive – future time] *If he <u>studied</u> tomorrow, he'd see the difference!* [past tense – imagined future] Contrast three distinct tense forms in Spanish: • *Estudia.* [present tense] • *Estudió.* [past tense] • *Estudiará.* [future tense]
transitive verb	A transitive verb takes at least one object in a sentence to complete its meaning, in contrast to an **intransitive verb**, which does not.	*He <u>loves</u> Juliet.* *She <u>understands</u> English grammar.*
trigraph	A type of **grapheme** where three letters represent one **phoneme**.	*H<u>igh</u>, p<u>ure</u>, pa<u>tch</u>, he<u>dge</u>*
unstressed	See **stressed**.	
verb	The surest way to identify verbs is by the ways they can be used: they can usually have a **tense**, either **present** or **past** (see also **future**). Verbs are sometimes called 'doing words' because many verbs name an action that someone does; while this can be a way of recognising verbs, it doesn't distinguish verbs from **nouns** (which can also name actions). Moreover many verbs name states or feelings rather than actions.	*He <u>lives</u> in Birmingham.* [present tense] *The teacher <u>wrote</u> a song for the class.* [past tense] *He <u>likes</u> chocolate.* [present tense; not an action] *He <u>knew</u> my father.* [past tense; not an action] Not verbs: • *The <u>walk</u> to Halina's house will take an hour.* [noun] • *All that <u>surfing</u> makes Morwenna so sleepy!* [noun]

	Verbs can be classified in various ways: for example, as **auxiliary**, or **modal**; as **transitive** or **intransitive**; and as states or events.	
vowel	A vowel is a speech sound which is produced without any closure or obstruction of the vocal tract. Vowels can form **syllables** by themselves, or they may combine with **consonants**. In the English writing system, the letters *a*, *e*, *i*, *o*, *u* and *y* can represent vowels.	
word	A word is a unit of grammar: it can be selected and moved around relatively independently, but cannot easily be split. In punctuation, words are normally separated by word spaces. Sometimes, a sequence that appears grammatically to be two words is collapsed into a single written word, indicated with a hyphen or apostrophe (e.g. *well-built, he's*).	*headteacher* or *head teacher* [can be written with or without a space] *I'm* going out. *9.30 am*
word class	Every **word** belongs to a word class which summarises the ways in which it can be used in grammar. The major word classes for English are: **noun**, **verb**, **adjective**, **adverb**, **preposition**, **determiner**, **pronoun**, **conjunction**. Word classes are sometimes called 'parts of speech'.	
word family	The **words** in a word family are normally related to each other by a combination of **morphology**, grammar and meaning.	*teach – teacher* *extend – extent – extensive* *grammar – grammatical – grammarian*

5 Mathematics

Planning mathematics in the national curriculum

Sam Parkes

Mathematics 1 Principles of planning

This section looks at the key factors which are specific to planning effective mathematics lessons. It builds on the generic factors for planning found in Chapter 1 and should be read in conjunction with these ideas.

Working mathematically

> Math makes sense of the world. Math is the vocabulary for your own intuition.

(Meyer, 2010)

I offer the quote above, and a recommendation that you watch the associated TED talk (the link is included in the further reading section) as providing a solid starting point from which to build all of your mathematics teaching. In essence, when getting to grips with the many challenges and complexities inherent in planning for mathematics lessons, I suggest you begin by asking yourself this: 'how can I best support my learners to *make sense* of this piece of mathematics?'

If you begin with 'making sense' of what your intended learning is, then you are rooting your teaching in many of the core principles for developing children who work, and therefore think, like mathematicians. The following questions and prompts (adapted from Jeffcoat et al., 2004) provide a useful starting point alongside the national curriculum programmes of study (PoS) statements when planning. They highlight and develop fundamentally mathematical behaviours like using pattern spotting and an exploration of the structure of mathematics to underpin key concepts such as proof, generalising, specialising and equivalence.

- How do you see this?
- What do you know that is like this?
- What is the same and different about . . .?
- How do you know . . .?
- Explain why . . .
- Is this sometimes/always/never true?

- What do you notice?
- Can you see a pattern?
- Can you give me an example of . . .?
- Can you show/draw/describe . . .?

For example, when starting with the year 3 PoS statement 'count from 0 in multiples of 4', you might begin a lesson by showing the sequence 0, 4, 8, 12, 20, 24 and ask questions such as 'What do you notice?', 'How do you see this?', 'Could you draw/ build something that shows this?', 'Can you give me an example of another number that would belong in this sequence? Where? Why?', 'If we keep going, can you spot/ describe a pattern?', 'Is it like anything else/can you see any other patterns hidden in the sequence?' and so on. Note I have deliberately left out 16; I want to see if any-one can spot that something is wrong, and explain why – thus *making sense* of the mathematics they are learning. The National Centre for Excellence in the Teaching of Mathematics (NCETM) has produced a very useful document which takes each of the PoS statements and suggests question-based starting points for learning rooted in the mathematical reasoning as exemplified above (see further reading section).

We can see this emphasis on working mathematically embodied in the national curriculum's three aims for all pupils that they *become fluent . . . reason mathemati-cally (and) can solve problems*. Each of these aims can be seen to be rooted in the need to make connections within and across mathematics, other curriculum subjects and the wider world beyond school. While the cross-curricular potential of mathematics is touched on in Chapter 15, there are some core teaching strategies that should be included in daily mathematics planning to support children to make connections, most notably opportunities for dialogue, the use of a range of representations and the application of learning in a meaningful context.

Dialogue and vocabulary

The type of classroom dialogue generated by the questions suggested above and the incorporation of opportunities for children to talk and listen to each other in mathematics is coming to the fore currently with particular regard to 'number talks' (Parrish, 2011) and a focus on the necessity of 'number sense' (Boaler, 2014) as the most effective foundation on which to build fluency. In essence, 'number talk' is the opportunity to articulate and share strategies, and effective mathematics planning should make daily provision for this. For example, in teaching children to 'recall multiplication and division facts for multiplication tables up to 12 × 12' (year 4 PoS), you might start with 6 × 8, 8 × 7 or 7 × 6 (allegedly the three hardest 'times table' facts to remember) and encourage discussion about the variety of ways that children see them or 'work them out'. This can be made even more interesting by starting with a calculation that could involve these facts but is outside the usual 12 × 12 list, such as 24 × 8. The quality of learning that will take place as a result of this is extremely valuable and provides excellent opportunities for formative assessment – more on that later.

It is also important to immerse yourself and your learners in the world of math-ematical vocabulary. One of the most comprehensive vocabulary lists was produced by the National Numeracy Strategy (NNS) (1999), and also includes some very good examples of questioning. The variety of different words that mean the same thing in mathematics (e.g. add, combine, total, sum) as well as words that have a differ-ent meaning in mathematics to their use in a linguistic context (e.g. difference,

product, negative) can make for a confusing time in the classroom. However, a focus on learning the correct words and accurately using them is imperative from the very beginning. We have a tendency, as early years practitioners and primary teachers, to try to simplify the language used or favour a small variety of words because we feel we are helping children access the mathematics more easily. It is worth watching the Teachers TV programme *Primary Maths: How They Do It in Hungary* for some excellent examples of effective modelling and use of mathematical vocabulary with children aged five upwards. In the short term, including how you will introduce and reinforce the use of the correct mathematical vocabulary in each of your lessons is key, while the longer-term use of 'working walls' and the creation of a 'class maths dictionary' can also be effective.

Resources

Resources (sometimes called manipulatives) for mathematics are wide-ranging and have a variety of uses. For example:

- rulers, balance and weighing scales and coins have a very practical, real-life application;
- bead strings, Numicon, Cuisenaire rods and Dienes equipment support developing understanding of the number system;
- fraction walls, pattern blocks and pretend food pieces illustrate the concept of fractions;
- Clixi, Polydron and solid shapes support learning about 3D shape;
- there's a vast array of games and puzzles, including ICT-based programmes and online resources.

When planning a mathematics lesson it can seem overwhelming to be faced with such a range of materials, but the key to their effective use lies in being clear yourself on how they support children to make sense of what they are learning. Importantly, remember that the resource does not make learning happen by itself.

Enactive representation

In order to understand mathematics it is vital that learners have experience of a concept at three levels of representation: enactive, iconic and symbolic (Bruner, 1966). This provides a secure foundation upon which to build your mathematics planning. The manipulatives listed above provide the enactive (sometimes called concrete) representation that enables children to *feel* the mathematics. This is particularly important when working with number; children need to develop a feel for the 'five-ness' of 5, or the 'seventy-two-ness' of 72, or the 'three-thousand-and-forty-one-ness' of 3041 and all the component, flexible parts that can make up such a quantity.

Iconic representation

The second level of experience, iconic (sometimes called representational), refers to the need for visual representations of the mathematical idea being taught. Visual representations, or models, include anything that represents a mathematical

concept pictorially or as a diagram and might include arrays, drawings of sets of objects, pictures of a whole shape split into sections, and images which expose the structure of the number system such as number lines and hundred squares. When planning, it can be useful to ask yourself: 'How could I draw this?', 'Is there another way to see it?' and 'Does this really show the mathematics I am teaching?'

Symbolic representation

The final level of representation is the symbolic (sometimes called abstract) and refers largely to the digits, words and algorithms that we associate with mathematical areas. It is worth noting here that number lines and hundred squares are both iconic and symbolic, and they are useful representations in that they reveal the structure of the number system to learners. It is important that children are exposed to the symbolic representations in your lessons but these need to be strongly connected to the enactive and iconic representations to ensure they carry deep meaning and understanding built in a solid foundation. For example, when understanding the process of exchanging in formal written subtraction, you might physically break up a ten into ten ones and calculate the units' column accordingly. Some of the most useful materials that exemplify this combining of representations are found in a series of videos to support the implementation of the national curriculum on the NCETM website (see further reading at the end of this chapter).

Using Information and communications technology (ICT) in mathematics

As with concrete mathematical resources, the use of ICT, in the form of an interactive whiteboard, can help to support understanding, largely through the demonstration of and interaction with visual models of mathematical ideas. There is a wide variety of software available to support mathematics teaching and, just as with any other resource, it is vital that you develop your ability to critique these examples by asking, 'How does this help to *make sense* of this mathematics?' The 'interactive teaching programmes' (ITPs) developed by the NNS are a particularly good resource for exemplifying many of the statements in the PoS, as is the National Library of Virtual Manipulatives (see further reading). While calculators are no longer an encouraged curriculum resource until near the end of key stage 2, it is worth considering their use beyond simply generating an answer to a calculation. For example, when finding 10 or 100 more or less than any given number (year 3 PoS), inputting any number and repeatedly adding 10 (or 100) and articulating what you notice happening can support mental calculation when crossing hundred and thousand boundaries.

Relevance

The relevance of mathematics is undeniable and is well articulated in the national curriculum's purpose of study statement. In terms of supporting learners to make sense of mathematics, connections need to be made through the application of mathematical learning in a meaningful context. What is meant by a 'meaningful context' depends on the mathematical idea and the reason it is being taught, and will often, though not always, be provided through enabling the children to find relevance in what they are learning to their own lives and experiences. However, it

is worth noting here that meaningful contexts in mathematics can involve learning and using transferable problem solving or thinking skills. For example, investigating the area of different rectangles does not necessarily need to be dressed up in terms of chocolate bars to make it relevant.

The mathematical tasks you choose when planning will greatly influence the quality of and opportunities for learning in your classroom (Hiebert et al., 1997) and the 'richer' the task, the better. The following useful set of criteria for identifying a 'rich mathematical activity' suggests that it:

- must be accessible to everyone at the start;
- needs to allow further challenges and be extendable;
- should invite learners to make decisions;
- should involve learners in speculating, hypothesis making and testing, proving or explaining, reflecting and interpreting;
- should not restrict learners from searching in other directions;
- should promote discussion and communication;
- should encourage originality and invention;
- should encourage 'what if?' and 'what if not?' questions;
- should have an element of surprise;
- should be enjoyable.

(Adapted from Ahmed, 1987, page 20)

Of the criteria above, the accessibility and potential for extension that a chosen task includes will be key factors in how the learning can be differentiated to ensure that all children learn during the lesson. Nrich uses the term 'low threshold, high ceiling' to describe such tasks and its website **www.nrich.org** is a goldmine of games, activities and questions for use when planning. Nrich has also produced a planning grid that matches many of the PoS statements to specific activities (see further reading). Additionally, NCETM has created a national curriculum for mathematics resource tool which suggests appropriate activities (plus related information on subject knowledge, making connections, articles, exemplifications and videos) for the teaching of each PoS statement.

Misconceptions

A mathematical misconception is different to an error or mistake in that it is likely to show repeatedly in a child's thinking and work as a piece of knowledge they hold to be true that goes against what is known and understood about mathematics (Barmby, 2009). Hansen (2014) provides many examples of common misconceptions, such as a learner writing the number fourteen as 41, and offers suggestions as to why these misconceptions occur. In this example, it could be that the child hears the word 'four-teen' and is writing the digits left to right in the order that represents the word, with the 4 first.

The ability to deal with misconceptions in mathematics relies on the ongoing development of your subject knowledge of mathematics. By this I mean your knowledge of the relevant mathematical subject matter (content), knowledge of appropriate pedagogical strategies for mathematical learning and knowledge of the curriculum resources that can support your teaching (Shulman, 1986). When planning the first of a sequence of lessons, it is important to ask yourself, 'What is it that makes this

mathematics easy/difficult to understand?' and, as you become more experienced, 'What mistakes and misconceptions are likely to arise?' You can then choose your questions, representations and tasks to develop a logical sequence of learning that can help to avoid such misconceptions being formed. (See further reading for resources to support your developing subject knowledge, e.g. Haylock, 2014; Rickard, 2013; Mooney, 2007.)

When misconceptions come to light during a piece of teaching, as is far more often the case, it is important to get to the root of the problem and this can be done by having authentic conversations with children. Questions and statements such as 'How do you know that?' or 'Tell/show me why/what you mean' that come from a sincere desire to understand how they are thinking or seeing a piece of mathematics are crucial. Providing the opportunity for children to talk through and share their ideas, and having relevant manipulatives and visual models available to allow for well-timed illustration and explanation of the mathematics being learnt are also essential.

Assessment

All assessment, but particularly formative assessment that continually informs your planning, can be most effective when rooted in open-ended starting points and questioning to encourage dialogue. As the Spoken language section of the national curriculum says, children *must be assisted in making their thinking clear to themselves as well as others and teachers should ensure that pupils build secure foundations by using discussion to probe and remedy their misconceptions.* Therefore, much of your assessment information will be gathered from your conversations with children, and schools advocate a variety of methods for capturing this, such as notes taken during or soon after discussions by the teacher or teaching assistant, visual and audio recordings of group work, annotated planning, photographs and speech bubble messages written by the children. Some of these can also form part of a system of recorded dialogue between you and the learner in terms of academic guidance to enable and evidence progress. Written feedback in mathematics is most effective when it gives something for the learner to do in response. For example, when feeding back on a written record of number sequences where the intended learning was to 'count in multiples of 6, 7 and 9' you might write, 'Look at the numbers I have underlined (both correct and incorrect examples), how do you know these are right? Make any changes you think you need to. Create another sequence that shows counting in multiples of 12 (or 14 or 18), explain what you notice.' The opportunity for the child to spend time responding to your feedback then needs to be included in your subsequent planning.

The information gathered through formative assessment also impacts on how you may choose to plan for differentiation. While the most common method of differentiation in mathematics lessons is to have 'table groups' based on attainment data, there are alternatives that allow for all pupils to learn at an appropriate challenge level and give more detailed and meaningful assessment information. These might include the use of flexible grouping based on ongoing formative assessment, open questions, common tasks with multiple variations or multiple entry points (Van de Walle, 2006) as well as differentiating according to Bruner's three levels of representation. There is a growing evidence base that planning for static groups has the potential to be damaging to the quality of learning and pupil progress in mathematics and, although this debate is wider than this chapter allows for, further reading of Boaler (2009) and Stripp (2014) is a good starting point.

The learning environment

When planning for mathematics lessons, it is worth thinking about the potential of the school building, outside spaces and the surrounding area as a stimulus for learning. Maths trails which focus on 'finding the maths' in architecture and playground design can be fertile starting points for learning about geometry, position direction and movement and measure. Many of the statistics PoS statements can be learnt by engaging in school issues and displaying the resulting data collections. A rich and positive learning environment rooted in a growth mindset (Dweck, 2012) about mathematics which includes displays that celebrate the process of learning and the inevitable challenge and 'stuckness' that is part of that, while demonstrating all of the connections the subject has across our lives, will help to develop a culture in which all the learners of mathematics in your classroom can thrive.

Further reading

Videos

Meyer, D. (2010) *Math Class Needs a Makeover*. [online] Available at: **www.ted.com/talks/ dan_meyer_math_curriculum_makeover?language=en**

Number Talks: Building Numerical Reasoning. [online] Available at: **www.youtube.com/watch? v=twGipANcIqg**

Primary Maths: How They Do It in Hungary. [online] Available at: **www.youtube.com/watch? v=w_hs5PpySJo**

Planning resources

Interactive Teaching Programmes. [online] Available at: **www.taw.org.uk/lic/itp**

Jeffcoat, M., Jones, M., Mansergh, J., Mason, J., Sewell, H. and Watson, A. (2004) *Primary Questions and Prompts*. Derby: ATM.

National Library of Virtual Manipulatives. [online] Available at: **http://nlvm.usu.edu/en/ nav/vlibrary.html**

National Numeracy Strategy vocabulary book (1999). [online] Available at: **http:// webarchive.nationalarchives.gov.uk/20110202093118/http:/nationalstrategies. standards.dcsf.gov.uk/node/84996**

*NCETM The national curriculum for mathematics – resource tool. [online] Available at: **www.ncetm.org.uk/resources/41211#previewanchor**

*NCETM Achieving the aims of the new national curriculum: Developing opportunities and ensuring progression in the development of reasoning skills. [online] Available at: **www. ncetm.org.uk/resources/44672**

*NCETM Video material to support the implementation of the national curriculum. [online] Available at: **www.ncetm.org.uk/resources/40529**

Nrich Stage 1 and 2 Curriculum. [online] Available at: **www.nrich.maths.org/8935**

*Note: In order to access the NCETM materials you will need to become a member. It is free and highly recommended.

Texts and articles

Ahmed, A. (1987) *Better Mathematics: A Curriculum Development Study: Based on the Low Attainers in Mathematics Project* (carried out at the Mathematics Centre, West Sussex Institute of Higher Education in conjunction with Dorset, East Sussex, Hampshire, Isle of Wight, Surrey and West Sussex Local Education Authorities). London: HMSO.

Barmby, P. (2009) *Primary Mathematics: Teaching for Understanding*. Maidenhead: Open University Press.

Boaler, J. (2009) *The Elephant in the Classroom: Helping Children Learn and Love Maths*. London: Souvenir Press.

Boaler, J. (2014) Fluency without fear. [online] Available at: **http://youcubed.stanford.edu/ fluency-without-fear**

Bruner, J. (1966) *Toward a Theory of Instruction*. Cambridge, MA: Belkapp Press.

Dweck, C. (2012) *Mindset: How You Can Fulfill Your Potential*. New York: Robinson.

Hansen, A. (ed.) (2014) *Children's Errors in Mathematics*. London: Sage.

Haylock, D. (2014) *Mathematics Explained for Primary Teachers* (5th edition). London: Sage.

Hiebert, J., Carpenter, T., Fennema, E., Fuson, K., Wearne, D., Murray, H., Olivier, A. and Human, P. (1997) *Making Sense: Teaching and Learning Mathematics with Understanding*. Portsmouth: Heinemann.

McClure, L. (2014) Developing number fluency: What, why and how. [online] Available at: **www.nrich.maths.org/10624**

McClure, L. (2014) Using low threshold high ceiling tasks in ordinary classrooms. [online] Available at: **www.nrich.maths.org/7701**

Mooney, C. (2007) *Primary Mathematics: Knowledge and Understanding*. Exeter: Learning Matters.

Parrish, S. (2011) Number talks build numerical reasoning. [online] Available at: **www.math solutions.com/documents/NumberTalks_SParrish.pdf**

Rickard, C. (2013) *Essential Primary Mathematics*. Maidenhead: Open University Press.

Shulman, L. (1986) Those who understand: Knowledge growth in teaching. *Educational Researcher*, 15.2: 4–14.

Stripp, C. (2014) Mastery in mathematics: What it is and why we should be doing it. [online] Available at: **www.ncetm.org.uk/resources/45776**

Van De Walle, J. A. (2006) Creating an effective learning environment. [online] Available at: **www.lrt.ednet.ns.ca/PD/math7support/binder_resources/05_creating_effective_ environment_DI.pdf**

Mathematics 2 Examples of planning

The following three lesson plans are provided as examples of planning in mathematics. They do not contain the detail you will probably wish to have on your plans but do illustrate some of the points discussed previously.

Lesson One

Subject/topic: Number and place value	Date: 10/9/2016 Time: 11:00 a.m.	Teaching group/set: Year 4 No. of pupils: 30
Intended learning: Children will learn to: • recognise the place value of each digit in a four-digit number (thousands, hundreds, tens, and ones) • order and compare numbers beyond 1000 • identify and represent numbers using different representations.		**NC reference/context:** Y4 Number and place value PoS
Success criteria: All children will be able to: • recognise the place value of each digit in a four-digit number (thousands, hundreds, tens, and ones) • order and compare numbers beyond 1000 • identify and represent numbers using different representations. Some children will be able to • explain the effect of 0 as a place holder.		**Assessment strategy:** • Photographs of group number lines • Recordings of justifications on class list • 'I've learnt . . .' speech bubbles
Key vocabulary: units, ones, tens, hundreds, thousands, digit, four-digit number, place value, represents, greater than, more than, larger than, bigger than, less than, fewer than, smaller than, greatest, most, largest, biggest, least, fewest, smallest, compare, order, size, before, after, between		**Resources:** base 10 materials and/or whiteboards and pens for drawing if necessary digit cards 0–9 10 skipping ropes approx. 50 pegs

Time	Teacher focus	Pupil focus
15 mins	Show a number line with three 4-digit numbers on including a mistake. Are these in the right order? How do you know? Can you show how you know using base 10? Can you match a base 10 representation (manipulative or drawing) of a 4-digit number with a number? Q: How do you see this? Can you show/draw/describe . . .? What is the same and different about . . . ? How do you know . . . ? Explain why . . .	Discussing with a partner to justify and prove their understanding. One child makes a 4-digit number from base 10; the other writes the number that matches it. Swop and repeat.

All discussion points in these plans are intended for use within a 'lolly stick' culture where all children know they could be asked to share their thinking

25 mins	Monitor group working, continue to use the above questions to probe understanding and encourage use of materials where needed. Extend thinking by suggesting 4-digit numbers that include one or two zeros or repeated digits. Record each group's work in a photograph.	In groups of 3/4, children create 4-digit numbers by turning over four random 0–9 digit cards. They record the number on a piece of paper/card and peg it to the skipping rope number line. They then repeat this process and have to discuss and agree where each of the newly generated numbers should go. All children need to be able to explain how they know they are right, using visual or concrete representations as appropriate.
15 mins	Split the class in two. Play one of the 'nice or nasty' dice games **www.nrich.maths.org/6605** and note children's comments.	Discussing and justifying decisions and explaining their thinking.
5 mins	Assist with recording for those who need support with sentence writing.	Children complete individual 'I've learnt . . .' speech bubbles

All pairings and groups in these plans are intended to be based on a combination of personalities that have the ability to collaborate OR AfL evidence, NOT a preconception about mathematical 'ability'

Differentiation through support with visualisation and addressing potential misconception of the use of 0 with an expectation that some children can articulate the effect of 0 as a place holder

Lesson Two

Subject/topic: Number and place value	Date: 11/9/2016 Time: 11:00 a.m.	Teaching group/set: Y4 No. of pupils: 30
Intended learning: Children will learn to: • recognise and write decimal equivalents of any number of tenths • round decimals with one decimal place to the nearest whole number • identify and represent numbers using different representations.		**NC reference/context:** Y4 Number and place value PoS
Success criteria: All children will be able to: • recognise and write decimal equivalents of any number of tenths • round decimals with one decimal place to the nearest whole number • identify and represent numbers using different representations. Some children will be able to: • generalise a rule about which decimal numbers round to the left and which to the right on a number line.		**Assessment strategy:** • Answers to problem recorded individually in books • Formative assessment throughout lesson to respond to need for support or further challenge

Key vocabulary:		Resources:
tenths, whole number, unit, decimal, decimal place, decimal point, digit, place value, represents, between, half-way between, too many, too few, enough, not enough, round (up or down), nearest		tape measures
		bead bar initially labelled 0–10
		bead strings

	Time	Teacher focus	Pupil focus
Differentiation through open ended starting point and opportunity for discussion	20 mins	**If a number with one decimal place rounds to 3, what could the number be?** Make sense of the problem as a class. Structure discussion with Qs such as: What does one decimal place mean? What do you all know about decimals? What do decimals show? Create class mind map about decimal knowledge. Take suggestions of answers.	Discuss prior knowledge of decimals in pairs (different partners to yesterday); record on whiteboard
		Tie together suggestions from children, noting misconceptions and guiding towards connecting tenths with one decimal place.	Children to suggest numbers that have one decimal place, i.e. 6.3 etc. and point to where this would sit on the bead bar.
		Use the bead bar to demonstrate ten divisions between each whole number (tenths) and discuss where each of the children's suggestions would sit.	Justify why.
Depending on what you've chosen!		Use a ruler to measure the height of a small toy. Problem: It's 4.7 cm tall (connect to bead bar – where would 4.7 be?) and we don't talk about people's height in decimals (we say 'I'm 153 cm tall'), so what's the closest unit/whole number to 4.7 on our bead bar?	Discuss with partner and justify answer of 5 cm.
Linking concept of rounding to practical application	10 mins	**Can you say your height, and your partner's height in cm to the nearest whole cm?** What was the height said as a decimal? How do you know which whole cm it rounds to?	In pairs use a tape measure to measure each child's height.
	5 mins	Did anyone get a height that was .5? What do you think we should do with a .5 number when rounding to the nearest whole number? Why? Explain mathematical convention that this would 'round to the nearest whole number to the right' on the number line.	Discuss and be prepared to share ideas.
Differentiation through open ended starting point and opportunity for discussion	20 mins	Can you use what you know to answer our problem and explain how you know you are right? **If a number with one decimal place rounds to 3, what could the number be? Can you use a number line or a bead string to show how you know?**	Individually record a list of numbers in answer to the problem in books. Draw a number line or use a bead string to show how they know they are right.

	Circulate as children work. Record those who have achieved the success criteria and set extension question: What if the number rounds to 12? What do you notice about the two lists of numbers you have made? Would the pattern continue with any rounded number? Gather those who need further support and work through problem as a group using the bead bar to support their thinking.	
5 mins	Show a pre-prepared table of height measurements with one decimal place. What would these be rounded to the nearest whole cm?	Discussing and justifying decisions and explaining their thinking.

Use of 'what if' question to extend and consolidate thinking

Encourages pattern spotting and transferable understanding

Generalising

Lesson Three

Subject/topic: Number and place value	Date: 12/9/2016 Time: 11:00 a.m.	Teaching group/set: Y4 No. of pupils: 30

Intended learning:	NC reference/context:
Children will learn to: • recognise and write decimal equivalents of any number of tenths or hundredths • compare numbers with the same number of decimal places up to two decimal places • identify and represent numbers using different representations.	Y4 Number and place value PoS
Success criteria:	Assessment strategy:
All children will be able to: • recognise and write decimal equivalents of any number of tenths or hundredths • compare numbers with the same number of decimal places up to two decimal places • identify and represent numbers using different representations. Some children will be able to: • create their own 'spiralling decimals' game with different start and end points and explain the relative difficulty of the numbers they have chosen.	• Recordings of game • Class observation notes
Key vocabulary:	Resources:
tenths, hundredths, units, ones, tens, place value, represents, greater than, more than, larger than, bigger than, less than, fewer than, smaller than, greatest, most, largest, biggest, least, fewest, smallest, compare, order, size, before, after, between, decimal, decimal point, decimal place	bead bar labelled 0–100 or interactive resource ITP 'Counting' £10 notes, £1, 10p and 1p coins

Avoid other denominations of coins for this lesson as the focus is place value

Linking two decimal places to money is a strong practical application

Encourage the comparison of the quantity of £10, £1, 10p and 1p

Differentiation through choice of resources, what if questions suggested in the activity and the potential to create their own version

Addresses common misconception that the more digits = the bigger number

Time	Teacher focus	Pupil focus
15 mins	Would you rather have £4.34 or £4.43? Why? How do you know which is more? Can you show these amounts using notes and coins or a bead bar? What do you notice?	Work with a partner (different to the previous two days) and justify reasoning. Draw connections between the different representations of the same amount of money.
30 mins	Introduce Spiralling Decimals game: model how to play **www.nrich.maths.org/10326** Ensure concrete representations are available to support understanding where needed and address mistakes and misconceptions as necessary.	In pairs, play game as per instructions using materials/ drawings as needed to justify decisions. Move on to challenge in agreement with partner.
15 mins	Which is bigger, 36.06 or 36.6? How do you know? Can you represent both numbers on the bead bar?	Discussing and justifying decisions and explaining their thinking.

Mathematics 3 The framework for mathematics

Purpose of study

Mathematics is a creative and highly inter-connected discipline that has been developed over centuries, providing the solution to some of history's most intriguing problems. It is essential to everyday life, critical to science, technology and engineering, and necessary for financial literacy and most forms of employment. A high-quality mathematics education therefore provides a foundation for understanding the world, the ability to reason mathematically, an appreciation of the beauty and power of mathematics, and a sense of enjoyment and curiosity about the subject.

Aims

The national curriculum for mathematics aims to ensure that all pupils:

- become **fluent** in the fundamentals of mathematics, including through varied and frequent practice with increasingly complex problems over time, so that pupils develop conceptual understanding and the ability to recall and apply knowledge rapidly and accurately;
- **reason mathematically** by following a line of enquiry, conjecturing relationships and generalisations, and developing an argument, justification or proof using mathematical language;
- can **solve problems** by applying their mathematics to a variety of routine and non-routine problems with increasing sophistication, including breaking down problems into a series of simpler steps and persevering in seeking solutions.

Mathematics is an interconnected subject in which pupils need to be able to move fluently between representations of mathematical ideas. The programmes of study are, by necessity, organised into apparently distinct domains, but pupils should make rich connections across mathematical ideas to develop fluency, mathematical reasoning and competence in solving increasingly sophisticated problems. They should also apply their mathematical knowledge to science and other subjects.

The expectation is that the majority of pupils will move through the programmes of study at broadly the same pace. However, decisions about when to progress should always be based on the security of pupils' understanding and their readiness to progress to the next stage. Pupils who grasp concepts rapidly should be challenged through being offered rich and sophisticated problems before any acceleration through new content. Those who are not sufficiently fluent with earlier material should consolidate their understanding, including through additional practice, before moving on.

Information and communication technology (ICT)

Calculators should not be used as a substitute for good written and mental arithmetic. They should therefore only be introduced near the end of key stage 2 to support pupils' conceptual understanding and exploration of more complex

number problems, if written and mental arithmetic are secure. In both primary and secondary schools, teachers should use their judgement about when ICT tools should be used.

Spoken language

The national curriculum for mathematics reflects the importance of spoken language in pupils' development across the whole curriculum – cognitively, socially and linguistically. The quality and variety of language that pupils hear and speak are key factors in developing their mathematical vocabulary and presenting a mathematical justification, argument or proof. They must be assisted in making their thinking clear to themselves as well as others and teachers should ensure that pupils build secure foundations by using discussion to probe and remedy their misconceptions.

School curriculum

The programmes of study for mathematics are set out year-by-year for key stages 1 and 2. Schools are, however, only required to teach the relevant programme of study by the end of the key stage. Within each key stage, schools therefore have the flexibility to introduce content earlier or later than set out in the programme of study. In addition, schools can introduce key stage content during an earlier key stage, if appropriate. All schools are also required to set out their school curriculum for mathematics on a year-by-year basis and make this information available online.

Attainment targets

By the end of each key stage, pupils are expected to know, apply and understand the matters, skills and processes specified in the relevant programme of study.

Schools are not required by law to teach the example content in [square brackets] or the content indicated as being 'non-statutory'.

Key stage 1 – years 1 and 2

The principal focus of mathematics teaching in key stage 1 is to ensure that pupils develop confidence and mental fluency with whole numbers, counting and place value. This should involve working with numerals, words and the four operations, including with practical resources [for example, concrete objects and measuring tools].

At this stage, pupils should develop their ability to recognise, describe, draw, compare and sort different shapes and use the related vocabulary. Teaching should also involve using a range of measures to describe and compare different quantities such as length, mass, capacity/volume, time and money.

By the end of year 2, pupils should know the number bonds to 20 and be precise in using and understanding place value. An emphasis on practice at this early stage will aid fluency.

Pupils should read and spell mathematical vocabulary, at a level consistent with their increasing word reading and spelling knowledge at key stage 1.

Year 1 programme of study

Number – number and place value

Statutory requirements

Pupils should be taught to:

- count to and across 100, forwards and backwards, beginning with 0 or 1, or from any given number
- count, read and write numbers to 100 in numerals; count in multiples of twos, fives and tens
- given a number, identify one more and one less
- identify and represent numbers using objects and pictorial representations including the number line, and use the language of: equal to, more than, less than (fewer), most, least
- read and write numbers from 1 to 20 in numerals and words.

Notes and guidance (non-statutory)

Pupils practise counting (1, 2, 3 . . .), ordering (for example, first, second, third . . .), and to indicate a quantity (for example, 3 apples, 2 centimetres), including solving simple concrete problems, until they are fluent.

Pupils begin to recognise place value in numbers beyond 20 by reading, writing, counting and comparing numbers up to 100, supported by objects and pictorial representations.

They practise counting as reciting numbers and counting as enumerating objects, and counting in twos, fives and tens from different multiples to develop their recognition of patterns in the number system (for example, odd and even numbers), including varied and frequent practice through increasingly complex questions.

They recognise and create repeating patterns with objects and with shapes.

Number – addition and subtraction

Statutory requirements

Pupils should be taught to:

- read, write and interpret mathematical statements involving addition (+), subtraction (–) and equals (=) signs
- represent and use number bonds and related subtraction facts within 20
- add and subtract one-digit and two-digit numbers to 20, including zero
- solve one-step problems that involve addition and subtraction, using concrete objects and pictorial representations, and missing number problems such as $7 = \square - 9$.

Notes and guidance (non-statutory)

Pupils memorise and reason with number bonds to 10 and 20 in several forms (for example, 9 + 7 = 16; 16 − 7 = 9; 7 = 16 − 9). They should realise the effect of adding or subtracting zero. This establishes addition and subtraction as related operations.

Pupils combine and increase numbers, counting forwards and backwards.

They discuss and solve problems in familiar practical contexts, including using quantities. Problems should include the terms: put together, add, altogether, total, take away, distance between, difference between, more than and less than, so that pupils develop the concept of addition and subtraction and are enabled to use these operations flexibly.

Number – multiplication and division

Statutory requirements

Pupils should be taught to:

- solve one-step problems involving multiplication and division, by calculating the answer using concrete objects, pictorial representations and arrays with the support of the teacher.

Notes and guidance (non-statutory)

Through grouping and sharing small quantities, pupils begin to understand: multiplication and division; doubling numbers and quantities; and finding simple fractions of objects, numbers and quantities.

They make connections between arrays, number patterns, and counting in twos, fives and tens.

Number – fractions

Statutory requirements

Pupils should be taught to:

- recognise, find and name a half as one of two equal parts of an object, shape or quantity
- recognise, find and name a quarter as one of four equal parts of an object, shape or quantity.

Notes and guidance (non-statutory)

Pupils are taught half and quarter as 'fractions of' discrete and continuous quantities by solving problems using shapes, objects and quantities. For example, they could recognise and find half a length, quantity, set of objects or shape. Pupils connect halves and quarters to the equal sharing and grouping of sets of objects and to measures, as well as recognising and combining halves and quarters as parts of a whole.

Measurement

Statutory requirements

Pupils should be taught to:

- compare, describe and solve practical problems for:

  - lengths and heights [for example, long/short, longer/shorter, tall/short, double/half]
  - mass/weight [for example, heavy/light, heavier than, lighter than]
  - capacity and volume [for example, full/empty, more than, less than, half, half full, quarter]
  - time [for example, quicker, slower, earlier, later]

- measure and begin to record the following:

  - lengths and heights
  - mass/weight
  - capacity and volume
  - time (hours, minutes, seconds)

- recognise and know the value of different denominations of coins and notes
- sequence events in chronological order using language [for example, before and after, next, first, today, yesterday, tomorrow, morning, afternoon and evening]
- recognise and use language relating to dates, including days of the week, weeks, months and years
- tell the time to the hour and half past the hour and draw the hands on a clock face to show these times.

Notes and guidance (non-statutory)

The pairs of terms: mass and weight, volume and capacity, are used interchangeably at this stage.

Pupils move from using and comparing different types of quantities and measures using non-standard units, including discrete (for example, counting) and continuous (for example, liquid) measurement, to using manageable common standard units.

In order to become familiar with standard measures, pupils begin to use measuring tools such as a ruler, weighing scales and containers.

Pupils use the language of time, including telling the time throughout the day, first using o'clock and then half past.

Geometry – properties of shapes

Statutory requirements

Pupils should be taught to:

- recognise and name common 2-D and 3-D shapes, including:

  - 2-D shapes [for example, rectangles (including squares), circles and triangles]
  - 3-D shapes [for example, cuboids (including cubes), pyramids and spheres].

Notes and guidance (non-statutory)

Pupils handle common 2-D and 3-D shapes, naming these and related everyday objects fluently. They recognise these shapes in different orientations and sizes, and know that rectangles, triangles, cuboids and pyramids are not always similar to each other.

Geometry – position and direction

Statutory requirements

Pupils should be taught to:

- describe position, direction and movement, including whole, half, quarter and three-quarter turns.

Notes and guidance (non-statutory)

Pupils use the language of position, direction and motion, including: left and right, top, middle and bottom, on top of, in front of, above, between, around, near, close and far, up and down, forwards and backwards, inside and outside.

Pupils make whole, half, quarter and three-quarter turns in both directions and connect turning clockwise with movement on a clock face.

Year 2 programme of study

Number – number and place value

Statutory requirements

Pupils should be taught to:

- count in steps of 2, 3, and 5 from 0, and in tens from any number, forward and backward
- recognise the place value of each digit in a two-digit number (tens, ones)
- identify, represent and estimate numbers using different representations, including the number line
- compare and order numbers from 0 up to 100; use <, > and = signs
- read and write numbers to at least 100 in numerals and in words
- use place value and number facts to solve problems.

Notes and guidance (non-statutory)

Using materials and a range of representations, pupils practise counting, reading, writing and comparing numbers to at least 100 and solving a variety of related problems to

develop fluency. They count in multiples of three to support their later understanding of a third.

As they become more confident with numbers up to 100, pupils are introduced to larger numbers to develop further their recognition of patterns within the number system and represent them in different ways, including spatial representations.

Pupils should partition numbers in different ways (for example, 23 = 20 + 3 and 23 = 10 + 13) to support subtraction. They become fluent and apply their knowledge of numbers to reason with, discuss and solve problems that emphasise the value of each digit in two-digit numbers. They begin to understand zero as a place holder.

Number – addition and subtraction

Statutory requirements

Pupils should be taught to:

- solve problems with addition and subtraction:

  o using concrete objects and pictorial representations, including those involving numbers, quantities and measures
  o applying their increasing knowledge of mental and written methods

- recall and use addition and subtraction facts to 20 fluently, and derive and use related facts up to 100
- add and subtract numbers using concrete objects, pictorial representations, and mentally, including:

  o a two-digit number and ones
  o a two-digit number and tens
  o two two-digit numbers
  o adding three one-digit numbers

- show that addition of two numbers can be done in any order (commutative) and subtraction of one number from another cannot
- recognise and use the inverse relationship between addition and subtraction and use this to check calculations and solve missing number problems.

Notes and guidance (non-statutory)

Pupils extend their understanding of the language of addition and subtraction to include sum and difference.

Pupils practise addition and subtraction to 20 to become increasingly fluent in deriving facts such as using 3 + 7 = 10; 10 – 7 = 3 and 7 = 10 – 3 to calculate 30 + 70 = 100; 100 – 70 = 30 and 70 = 100 – 30. They check their calculations, including by adding to check subtraction and adding numbers in a different order to check addition (for example, 5 + 2 + 1 = 1 + 5 + 2 = 1 + 2 + 5). This establishes commutativity and associativity of addition.

Recording addition and subtraction in columns supports place value and prepares for formal written methods with larger numbers.

Number – multiplication and division

Statutory requirements

Pupils should be taught to:

- recall and use multiplication and division facts for the 2, 5 and 10 multiplication tables, including recognising odd and even numbers
- calculate mathematical statements for multiplication and division within the multiplication tables and write them using the multiplication (×), division (÷) and equals (=) signs
- show that multiplication of two numbers can be done in any order (commutative) and division of one number by another cannot
- solve problems involving multiplication and division, using materials, arrays, repeated addition, mental methods, and multiplication and division facts, including problems in contexts.

Notes and guidance (non-statutory)

Pupils use a variety of language to describe multiplication and division.

Pupils are introduced to the multiplication tables. They practise to become fluent in the 2, 5 and 10 multiplication tables and connect them to each other. They connect the 10 multiplication table to place value, and the 5 multiplication table to the divisions on the clock face. They begin to use other multiplication tables and recall multiplication facts, including using related division facts to perform written and mental calculations.

Pupils work with a range of materials and contexts in which multiplication and division relate to grouping and sharing discrete and continuous quantities, to arrays and to repeated addition. They begin to relate these to fractions and measures (for example, $40 \div 2 = 20$, 20 is a half of 40). They use commutativity and inverse relations to develop multiplicative reasoning (for example, $4 \times 5 = 20$ and $20 \div 5 = 4$).

Number – fractions

Statutory requirements

Pupils should be taught to:

- recognise, find, name and write fractions $\frac{1}{3}$, $\frac{1}{4}$, $\frac{2}{4}$ and $\frac{3}{4}$ of a length, shape, set of objects or quantity
- write simple fractions for example, $\frac{1}{2}$ of 6 = 3 and recognise the equivalence of $\frac{2}{4}$ and $\frac{1}{2}$.

Notes and guidance (non-statutory)

Pupils use fractions as 'fractions of' discrete and continuous quantities by solving problems using shapes, objects and quantities. They connect unit fractions to equal sharing and grouping, to numbers when they can be calculated, and to measures, finding fractions of lengths, quantities, sets of objects or shapes. They meet $\frac{3}{4}$ as the first example of a non-unit fraction.

FROM THE FRAMEWORK

Pupils should count in fractions up to 10, starting from any number and using the $\frac{1}{2}$ and $\frac{2}{4}$ equivalence on the number line (for example, $1\frac{1}{4}$, $1\frac{2}{4}$ (or $1\frac{1}{2}$), $1\frac{3}{4}$, 2). This reinforces the concept of fractions as numbers and that they can add up to more than one.

Measurement

Statutory requirements

Pupils should be taught to:

- choose and use appropriate standard units to estimate and measure length/height in any direction (m/cm); mass (kg/g); temperature (°C); capacity (litres/ml) to the nearest appropriate unit, using rulers, scales, thermometers and measuring vessels
- compare and order lengths, mass, volume/capacity and record the results using >, < and =
- recognise and use symbols for pounds (£) and pence (p); combine amounts to make a particular value
- find different combinations of coins that equal the same amounts of money
- solve simple problems in a practical context involving addition and subtraction of money of the same unit, including giving change
- compare and sequence intervals of time
- tell and write the time to five minutes, including quarter past/to the hour and draw the hands on a clock face to show these times
- know the number of minutes in an hour and the number of hours in a day.

Notes and guidance (non-statutory)

Pupils use standard units of measurement with increasing accuracy, using their knowledge of the number system. They use the appropriate language and record using standard abbreviations.

Comparing measures includes simple multiples such as 'half as high'; 'twice as wide'.

They become fluent in telling the time on analogue clocks and recording it.

Pupils become fluent in counting and recognising coins. They read and say amounts of money confidently and use the symbols £ and p accurately, recording pounds and pence separately.

Geometry – properties of shapes

Statutory requirements

Pupils should be taught to:

- identify and describe the properties of 2-D shapes, including the number of sides and line symmetry in a vertical line
- identify and describe the properties of 3-D shapes, including the number of edges, vertices and faces
- identify 2-D shapes on the surface of 3-D shapes [for example, a circle on a cylinder and a triangle on a pyramid]
- compare and sort common 2-D and 3-D shapes and everyday objects.

Notes and guidance (non-statutory)

Pupils handle and name a wide variety of common 2-D and 3-D shapes including: quadrilaterals and polygons, and cuboids, prisms and cones, and identify the properties of each shape (for example, number of sides, number of faces). Pupils identify, compare and sort shapes on the basis of their properties and use vocabulary precisely, such as sides, edges, vertices and faces.

Pupils read and write names for shapes that are appropriate for their word reading and spelling.

Pupils draw lines and shapes using a straight edge.

Geometry – position and direction

Statutory requirements

Pupils should be taught to:

- order and arrange combinations of mathematical objects in patterns and sequences
- use mathematical vocabulary to describe position, direction and movement, including movement in a straight line and distinguishing between rotation as a turn and in terms of right angles for quarter, half and three-quarter turns (clockwise and anti-clockwise).

Notes and guidance (non-statutory)

Pupils should work with patterns of shapes, including those in different orientations.

Pupils use the concept and language of angles to describe 'turn' by applying rotations, including in practical contexts (for example, pupils themselves moving in turns, giving instructions to other pupils to do so, and programming robots using instructions given in right angles).

Statistics

Statutory requirements

Pupils should be taught to:

- interpret and construct simple pictograms, tally charts, block diagrams and simple tables
- ask and answer simple questions by counting the number of objects in each category and sorting the categories by quantity
- ask and answer questions about totalling and comparing categorical data.

Notes and guidance (non-statutory)

Pupils record, interpret, collate, organise and compare information (for example, using many-to-one correspondence in pictograms with simple ratios 2, 5, 10).

Lower key stage 2 – years 3 and 4

The principal focus of mathematics teaching in lower key stage 2 is to ensure that pupils become increasingly fluent with whole numbers and the four operations, including number facts and the concept of place value. This should ensure that pupils develop efficient written and mental methods and perform calculations accurately with increasingly large whole numbers.

At this stage, pupils should develop their ability to solve a range of problems, including with simple fractions and decimal place value. Teaching should also ensure that pupils draw with increasing accuracy and develop mathematical reasoning so they can analyse shapes and their properties, and confidently describe the relationships between them. It should ensure that they can use measuring instruments with accuracy and make connections between measure and number.

By the end of year 4, pupils should have memorised their multiplication tables up to and including the 12 multiplication table and show precision and fluency in their work.

Pupils should read and spell mathematical vocabulary correctly and confidently, using their growing word reading knowledge and their knowledge of spelling.

Year 3 programme of study

Number – number and place value

Statutory requirements

Pupils should be taught to:

- count from 0 in multiples of 4, 8, 50 and 100; find 10 or 100 more or less than a given number
- recognise the place value of each digit in a three-digit number (hundreds, tens, ones)
- compare and order numbers up to 1000
- identify, represent and estimate numbers using different representations
- read and write numbers up to 1000 in numerals and in words
- solve number problems and practical problems involving these ideas.

Notes and guidance (non-statutory)

Pupils now use multiples of 2, 3, 4, 5, 8, 10, 50 and 100.

They use larger numbers to at least 1000, applying partitioning related to place value using varied and increasingly complex problems, building on work in year 2 (for example, 146 = 100 + 40 and 6, 146 = 130 + 16).

Using a variety of representations, including those related to measure, pupils continue to count in ones, tens and hundreds, so that they become fluent in the order and place value of numbers to 1000.

Number – addition and subtraction

Statutory requirements

Pupils should be taught to:

- add and subtract numbers mentally, including:
  - a three-digit number and ones
  - a three-digit number and tens
  - a three-digit number and hundreds
- add and subtract numbers with up to three digits, using formal written methods of columnar addition and subtraction
- estimate the answer to a calculation and use inverse operations to check answers
- solve problems, including missing number problems, using number facts, place value, and more complex addition and subtraction.

Notes and guidance (non-statutory)

Pupils practise solving varied addition and subtraction questions. For mental calculations with two-digit numbers, the answers could exceed 100.

Pupils use their understanding of place value and partitioning, and practise using columnar addition and subtraction with increasingly large numbers up to three digits to become fluent (see **Mathematics Appendix 1**).

Number – multiplication and division

Statutory requirements

Pupils should be taught to:

- recall and use multiplication and division facts for the 3, 4 and 8 multiplication tables
- write and calculate mathematical statements for multiplication and division using the multiplication tables that they know, including for two-digit numbers times one-digit numbers, using mental and progressing to formal written methods
- solve problems, including missing number problems, involving multiplication and division, including positive integer scaling problems and correspondence problems in which n objects are connected to m objects.

Notes and guidance (non-statutory)

Pupils continue to practise their mental recall of multiplication tables when they are calculating mathematical statements in order to improve fluency. Through doubling, they connect the 2, 4 and 8 multiplication tables.

Pupils develop efficient mental methods, for example, using commutativity and associativity (for example, $4 \times 12 \times 5 = 4 \times 5 \times 12 = 20 \times 12 = 240$) and multiplication and division facts (for example, using $3 \times 2 = 6$, $6 \div 3 = 2$ and $2 = 6 \div 3$) to derive related facts (for example, $30 \times 2 = 60$, $60 \div 3 = 20$ and $20 = 60 \div 3$).

Pupils develop reliable written methods for multiplication and division, starting with calculations of two-digit numbers by one-digit numbers and progressing to the formal written methods of short multiplication and division.

Pupils solve simple problems in contexts, deciding which of the four operations to use and why. These include measuring and scaling contexts, (for example, four times as high, eight times as long etc.) and correspondence problems in which m objects are connected to n objects (for example, 3 hats and 4 coats, how many different outfits?; 12 sweets shared equally between 4 children; 4 cakes shared equally between 8 children).

Number – fractions

Statutory requirements

Pupils should be taught to:

- count up and down in tenths; recognise that tenths arise from dividing an object into 10 equal parts and in dividing one-digit numbers or quantities by 10
- recognise, find and write fractions of a discrete set of objects: unit fractions and non-unit fractions with small denominators
- recognise and use fractions as numbers: unit fractions and non-unit fractions with small denominators
- recognise and show, using diagrams, equivalent fractions with small denominators
- add and subtract fractions with the same denominator within one whole [for example, $\frac{5}{7} + \frac{1}{7} = \frac{6}{7}$]
- compare and order unit fractions, and fractions with the same denominators
- solve problems that involve all of the above.

Notes and guidance (non-statutory)

Pupils connect tenths to place value, decimal measures and to division by 10.

They begin to understand unit and non-unit fractions as numbers on the number line, and deduce relations between them, such as size and equivalence. They should go beyond the [0, 1] interval, including relating this to measure.

Pupils understand the relation between unit fractions as operators (fractions of), and division by integers.

They continue to recognise fractions in the context of parts of a whole, numbers, measurements, a shape, and unit fractions as a division of a quantity.

Pupils practise adding and subtracting fractions with the same denominator through a variety of increasingly complex problems to improve fluency.

Measurement

Statutory requirements

Pupils should be taught to:

- measure, compare, add and subtract: lengths (m/cm/mm); mass (kg/g); volume/capacity (l/ml)
- measure the perimeter of simple 2-D shapes
- add and subtract amounts of money to give change, using both £ and p in practical contexts

(Continued)

(Continued)

- tell and write the time from an analogue clock, including using Roman numerals from I to XII, and 12-hour and 24-hour clocks
- estimate and read time with increasing accuracy to the nearest minute; record and compare time in terms of seconds, minutes and hours; use vocabulary such as o'clock, a.m./p.m., morning, afternoon, noon and midnight
- know the number of seconds in a minute and the number of days in each month, year and leap year
- compare durations of events [for example to calculate the time taken by particular events or tasks].

Notes and guidance (non-statutory)

Pupils continue to measure using the appropriate tools and units, progressing to using a wider range of measures, including comparing and using mixed units (for example, 1 kg and 200g) and simple equivalents of mixed units (for example, 5m = 500cm).

The comparison of measures includes simple scaling by integers (for example, a given quantity or measure is twice as long or five times as high) and this connects to multiplication.

Pupils continue to become fluent in recognising the value of coins, by adding and subtracting amounts, including mixed units, and giving change using manageable amounts. They record £ and p separately. The decimal recording of money is introduced formally in year 4.

Pupils use both analogue and digital 12-hour clocks and record their times. In this way they become fluent in and prepared for using digital 24-hour clocks in year 4.

Geometry – properties of shapes

Statutory requirements

Pupils should be taught to:

- draw 2-D shapes and make 3-D shapes using modelling materials; recognise 3-D shapes in different orientations and describe them
- recognise angles as a property of shape or a description of a turn
- identify right angles, recognise that two right angles make a half-turn, three make three quarters of a turn and four a complete turn; identify whether angles are greater than or less than a right angle
- identify horizontal and vertical lines and pairs of perpendicular and parallel lines.

Notes and guidance (non-statutory)

Pupils' knowledge of the properties of shapes is extended at this stage to symmetrical and non-symmetrical polygons and polyhedra. Pupils extend their use of the properties of shapes. They should be able to describe the properties of 2-D and 3-D shapes using accurate language, including lengths of lines and acute and obtuse for angles greater or lesser than a right angle.

Pupils connect decimals and rounding to drawing and measuring straight lines in centimetres, in a variety of contexts.

Statistics

Statutory requirements

Pupils should be taught to:

- interpret and present data using bar charts, pictograms and tables
- solve one-step and two-step questions [for example, 'How many more?' and 'How many fewer?'] using information presented in scaled bar charts and pictograms and tables.

Notes and guidance (non-statutory)

Pupils understand and use simple scales (for example, 2, 5, 10 units per cm) in pictograms and bar charts with increasing accuracy.

They continue to interpret data presented in many contexts.

Year 4 programme of study

Number – number and place value

Statutory requirements

Pupils should be taught to

- count in multiples of 6, 7, 9, 25 and 1000
- find 1000 more or less than a given number
- count backwards through zero to include negative numbers
- recognise the place value of each digit in a four-digit number (thousands, hundreds, tens, and ones)
- order and compare numbers beyond 1000
- identify, represent and estimate numbers using different representations
- round any number to the nearest 10, 100 or 1000
- solve number and practical problems that involve all of the above and with increasingly large positive numbers
- read Roman numerals to 100 (I to C) and know that over time, the numeral system changed to include the concept of zero and place value.

Notes and guidance (non-statutory)

Using a variety of representations, including measures, pupils become fluent in the order and place value of numbers beyond 1000, including counting in tens and hundreds, and maintaining fluency in other multiples through varied and frequent practice.

They begin to extend their knowledge of the number system to include the decimal numbers and fractions that they have met so far.

They connect estimation and rounding numbers to the use of measuring instruments.

Roman numerals should be put in their historical context so pupils understand that there have been different ways to write whole numbers and that the important concepts of zero and place value were introduced over a period of time.

Number – addition and subtraction

Statutory requirements

Pupils should be taught to:

- add and subtract numbers with up to 4 digits using the formal written methods of columnar addition and subtraction where appropriate
- estimate and use inverse operations to check answers to a calculation
- solve addition and subtraction two-step problems in contexts, deciding which operations and methods to use and why.

Notes and guidance (non-statutory)

Pupils continue to practise both mental methods and columnar addition and subtraction with increasingly large numbers to aid fluency (see **Mathematics Appendix 1**).

Number – multiplication and division

Statutory requirements

Pupils should be taught to:

- recall multiplication and division facts for multiplication tables up to 12×12
- use place value, known and derived facts to multiply and divide mentally, including: multiplying by 0 and 1; dividing by 1; multiplying together three numbers
- recognise and use factor pairs and commutativity in mental calculations
- multiply two-digit and three-digit numbers by a one-digit number using formal written layout
- solve problems involving multiplying and adding, including using the distributive law to multiply two-digit numbers by one digit, integer scaling problems and harder correspondence problems such as n objects are connected to m objects.

Notes and guidance (non-statutory)

Pupils continue to practise recalling and using multiplication tables and related division facts to aid fluency.

Pupils practise mental methods and extend this to three-digit numbers to derive facts (for example $600 \div 3 = 200$ can be derived from $2 \times 3 = 6$).

Pupils practise to become fluent in the formal written method of short multiplication and short division with exact answers (see **Mathematics Appendix 1**).

Pupils write statements about the equality of expressions (for example, use the distributive law $39 \times 7 = 30 \times 7 + 9 \times 7$ and associative law $(2 \times 3) \times 4 = 2 \times (3 \times 4)$). They combine their knowledge of number facts and rules of arithmetic to solve mental and written calculations for example, $2 \times 6 \times 5 = 10 \times 6 = 60$.

Pupils solve two-step problems in contexts, choosing the appropriate operation, working with increasingly harder numbers. This should include correspondence questions such as the numbers of choices of a meal on a menu, or three cakes shared equally between 10 children.

Number – fractions (including decimals)

Statutory requirements

Pupils should be taught to:

- recognise and show, using diagrams, families of common equivalent fractions
- count up and down in hundredths; recognise that hundredths arise when dividing an object by one hundred and dividing tenths by ten
- solve problems involving increasingly harder fractions to calculate quantities, and fractions to divide quantities, including non-unit fractions where the answer is a whole number
- add and subtract fractions with the same denominator
- recognise and write decimal equivalents of any number of tenths or hundredths
- recognise and write decimal equivalents to $\frac{1}{4}$, $\frac{1}{2}$, $\frac{3}{4}$
- find the effect of dividing a one- or two-digit number by 10 and 100, identifying the value of the digits in the answer as ones, tenths and hundredths
- round decimals with one decimal place to the nearest whole number
- compare numbers with the same number of decimal places up to two decimal places
- solve simple measure and money problems involving fractions and decimals to two decimal places.

Notes and guidance (non-statutory)

Pupils should connect hundredths to tenths and place value and decimal measure.

They extend the use of the number line to connect fractions, numbers and measures.

Pupils understand the relation between non-unit fractions and multiplication and division of quantities, with particular emphasis on tenths and hundredths.

Pupils make connections between fractions of a length, of a shape and as a representation of one whole or set of quantities. Pupils use factors and multiples to recognise equivalent fractions and simplify where appropriate (for example, $\frac{6}{9} = \frac{2}{3}$ or $\frac{1}{4} = \frac{2}{8}$).

Pupils continue to practise adding and subtracting fractions with the same denominator, to become fluent through a variety of increasingly complex problems beyond one whole.

Pupils are taught throughout that decimals and fractions are different ways of expressing numbers and proportions.

Pupils' understanding of the number system and decimal place value is extended at this stage to tenths and then hundredths. This includes relating the decimal notation to division of whole number by 10 and later 100.

They practise counting using simple fractions and decimals, both forwards and backwards.

Pupils learn decimal notation and the language associated with it, including in the context of measurements. They make comparisons and order decimal amounts and quantities that are expressed to the same number of decimal places. They should be able to represent numbers with one or two decimal places in several ways, such as on number lines.

Measurement

Statutory requirements

Pupils should be taught to:

- convert between different units of measure [for example, kilometre to metre; hour to minute]
- measure and calculate the perimeter of a rectilinear figure (including squares) in centimetres and metres
- find the area of rectilinear shapes by counting squares
- estimate, compare and calculate different measures, including money in pounds and pence
- read, write and convert time between analogue and digital 12- and 24-hour clocks
- solve problems involving converting from hours to minutes; minutes to seconds; years to months; weeks to days.

Notes and guidance (non-statutory)

Pupils build on their understanding of place value and decimal notation to record metric measures, including money.

They use multiplication to convert from larger to smaller units.

Perimeter can be expressed algebraically as $2(a + b)$ where a and b are the dimensions in the same unit.

They relate area to arrays and multiplication.

Geometry – properties of shapes

Statutory requirements

Pupils should be taught to:

- compare and classify geometric shapes, including quadrilaterals and triangles, based on their properties and sizes
- identify acute and obtuse angles and compare and order angles up to two right angles by size
- identify lines of symmetry in 2-D shapes presented in different orientations
- complete a simple symmetric figure with respect to a specific line of symmetry.

Notes and guidance (non-statutory)

Pupils continue to classify shapes using geometrical properties, extending to classifying different triangles (for example, isosceles, equilateral, scalene) and quadrilaterals (for example, parallelogram, rhombus, trapezium).

Pupils compare and order angles in preparation for using a protractor and compare lengths and angles to decide if a polygon is regular or irregular.

Pupils draw symmetric patterns using a variety of media to become familiar with different orientations of lines of symmetry; and recognise line symmetry in a variety of diagrams, including where the line of symmetry does not dissect the original shape.

Geometry – position and direction

Statutory requirements

Pupils should be taught to:

- describe positions on a 2-D grid as coordinates in the first quadrant
- describe movements between positions as translations of a given unit to the left/ right and up/down
- plot specified points and draw sides to complete a given polygon.

Notes and guidance (non-statutory)

Pupils draw a pair of axes in one quadrant, with equal scales and integer labels. They read, write and use pairs of coordinates, for example (2, 5), including using coordinate-plotting ICT tools.

Statistics

Statutory requirements

Pupils should be taught to:

- interpret and present discrete and continuous data using appropriate graphical methods, including bar charts and time graphs
- solve comparison, sum and difference problems using information presented in bar charts, pictograms, tables and other graphs.

Notes and guidance (non-statutory)

Pupils understand and use a greater range of scales in their representations.
  Pupils begin to relate the graphical representation of data to recording change over time.

Upper key stage 2 – years 5 and 6

The principal focus of mathematics teaching in upper key stage 2 is to ensure that pupils extend their understanding of the number system and place value to include larger integers. This should develop the connections that pupils make between multiplication and division with fractions, decimals, percentages and ratio.

At this stage, pupils should develop their ability to solve a wider range of problems, including increasingly complex properties of numbers and arithmetic, and problems demanding efficient written and mental methods of calculation. With this foundation in arithmetic, pupils are introduced to the language of algebra as a means for solving a variety of problems. Teaching in geometry and measures should consolidate and extend knowledge developed in number. Teaching should also ensure that pupils classify shapes with increasingly complex geometric properties and that they learn the vocabulary they need to describe them.

By the end of year 6, pupils should be fluent in written methods for all four operations, including long multiplication and division, and in working with fractions, decimals and percentages.

Pupils should read, spell and pronounce mathematical vocabulary correctly.

Year 5 programme of study

Number – number and place value

Statutory requirements

Pupils should be taught to:

- read, write, order and compare numbers to at least 1 000 000 and determine the value of each digit
- count forwards or backwards in steps of powers of 10 for any given number up to 1 000 000
- interpret negative numbers in context, count forwards and backwards with positive and negative whole numbers, including through zero
- round any number up to 1 000 000 to the nearest 10, 100, 1000, 10 000 and 100 000
- solve number problems and practical problems that involve all of the above
- read Roman numerals to 1000 (M) and recognise years written in Roman numerals.

Notes and guidance (non-statutory)

Pupils identify the place value in large whole numbers.

They continue to use number in context, including measurement. Pupils extend and apply their understanding of the number system to the decimal numbers and fractions that they have met so far.

They should recognise and describe linear number sequences, including those involving fractions and decimals, and find the term-to-term rule.

They should recognise and describe linear number sequences (for example, 3, $3\frac{1}{2}$, 4, $4\frac{1}{2}$ . . .), including those involving fractions and decimals, and find the term-to-term rule in words (for example, add $\frac{1}{2}$).

Number – addition and subtraction

Statutory requirements

Pupils should be taught to:

- add and subtract whole numbers with more than 4 digits, including using formal written methods (columnar addition and subtraction)
- add and subtract numbers mentally with increasingly large numbers
- use rounding to check answers to calculations and determine, in the context of a problem, levels of accuracy
- solve addition and subtraction multi-step problems in contexts, deciding which operations and methods to use and why.

Pupils practise using the formal written methods of columnar addition and subtraction with increasingly large numbers to aid fluency (see **Mathematics Appendix 1**).
    They practise mental calculations with increasingly large numbers to aid fluency (for example, 12 462 – 2300 = 10 162).

Number – multiplication and division

Statutory requirements

Pupils should be taught to:

- identify multiples and factors, including finding all factor pairs of a number, and common factors of two numbers
- know and use the vocabulary of prime numbers, prime factors and composite (non-prime) numbers
- establish whether a number up to 100 is prime and recall prime numbers up to 19
- multiply numbers up to 4 digits by a one- or two-digit number using a formal written method, including long multiplication for two-digit numbers
- multiply and divide numbers mentally drawing upon known facts
- divide numbers up to 4 digits by a one-digit number using the formal written method of short division and interpret remainders appropriately for the context
- multiply and divide whole numbers and those involving decimals by 10, 100 and 1000
- recognise and use square numbers and cube numbers, and the notation for squared (^{2}) and cubed (^{3})
- solve problems involving multiplication and division including using their knowledge of factors and multiples, squares and cubes
- solve problems involving addition, subtraction, multiplication and division and a combination of these, including understanding the meaning of the equals sign
- solve problems involving multiplication and division, including scaling by simple fractions and problems involving simple rates.

Notes and guidance (non-statutory)

Pupils practise and extend their use of the formal written methods of short multiplication and short division (see **Mathematics Appendix 1**). They apply all the multiplication tables and related division facts frequently, commit them to memory and use them confidently to make larger calculations.
    They use and understand the terms factor, multiple and prime, square and cube numbers.
    Pupils interpret non-integer answers to division by expressing results in different ways according to the context, including with remainders, as fractions, as decimals or by rounding (for example, $98 \div 4 = \frac{98}{4} = 24 \text{ r } 2 = 24\frac{1}{2} = 24.5 \approx 25$).

(Continued)

(Continued)

Pupils use multiplication and division as inverses to support the introduction of ratio in year 6, for example, by multiplying and dividing by powers of 10 in scale drawings or by multiplying and dividing by powers of a 1000 in converting between units such as kilometres and metres.

Distributivity can be expressed as $a(b + c) = ab + ac$.

They understand the terms factor, multiple and prime, square and cube numbers and use them to construct equivalence statements (for example, 4 x 35 = 2 x 2 x 35; 3 x 270 = 3 x 3 x 9 x 10 = 9^2 x 10).

Pupils use and explain the equals sign to indicate equivalence, including in missing number problems (for example, 13 + 24 = 12 + 25; 33 = 5 x ☐).

Number – fractions (including decimals and percentages)

Statutory requirements

Pupils should be taught to:

- compare and order fractions whose denominators are all multiples of the same number
- identify, name and write equivalent fractions of a given fraction, represented visually, including tenths and hundredths
- recognise mixed numbers and improper fractions and convert from one form to the other and write mathematical statements > 1 as a mixed number [for example, $\frac{2}{5} + \frac{4}{5} = \frac{6}{5} = 1\frac{1}{5}$]
- add and subtract fractions with the same denominator and denominators that are multiples of the same number
- multiply proper fractions and mixed numbers by whole numbers, supported by materials and diagrams
- read and write decimal numbers as fractions [for example, $0.71 = \frac{71}{100}$]
- recognise and use thousandths and relate them to tenths, hundredths and decimal equivalents
- round decimals with two decimal places to the nearest whole number and to one decimal place
- read, write, order and compare numbers with up to three decimal places
- solve problems involving number up to three decimal places
- recognise the per cent symbol (%) and understand that per cent relates to 'number of parts per hundred', and write percentages as a fraction with denominator 100, and as a decimal
- solve problems which require knowing percentage and decimal equivalents of $\frac{1}{2}, \frac{1}{4}, \frac{1}{5}, \frac{2}{5}, \frac{4}{5}$ and those fractions with a denominator of a multiple of 10 or 25.

Notes and guidance (non-statutory)

Pupils should be taught throughout that percentages, decimals and fractions are different ways of expressing proportions.

They extend their knowledge of fractions to thousandths and connect to decimals and measures.

Pupils connect equivalent fractions > 1 that simplify to integers with division and other fractions > 1 to division with remainders, using the number line and other models, and hence move from these to improper and mixed fractions.

Pupils connect multiplication by a fraction to using fractions as operators (fractions of), and to division, building on work from previous years. This relates to scaling by simple fractions, including fractions > 1.

Pupils practise adding and subtracting fractions to become fluent through a variety of increasingly complex problems. They extend their understanding of adding and subtracting fractions to calculations that exceed 1 as a mixed number.

Pupils continue to practise counting forwards and backwards in simple fractions.

Pupils continue to develop their understanding of fractions as numbers, measures and operators by finding fractions of numbers and quantities.

Pupils extend counting from year 4, using decimals and fractions including bridging zero, for example on a number line.

Pupils say, read and write decimal fractions and related tenths, hundredths and thousandths accurately and are confident in checking the reasonableness of their answers to problems.

They mentally add and subtract tenths, and one-digit whole numbers and tenths.

They practise adding and subtracting decimals, including a mix of whole numbers and decimals, decimals with different numbers of decimal places, and complements of 1 (for example, 0.83 + 0.17 = 1).

Pupils should go beyond the measurement and money models of decimals, for example, by solving puzzles involving decimals.

Pupils should make connections between percentages, fractions and decimals (for example, 100% represents a whole quantity and 1% is $\frac{1}{100}$, 50% is $\frac{50}{100}$, 25% is $\frac{25}{100}$) and relate this to finding 'fractions of'.

Measurement

Statutory requirements

Pupils should be taught to:

- convert between different units of metric measure (for example, kilometre and metre; centimetre and metre; centimetre and millimetre; gram and kilogram; litre and millilitre)
- understand and use approximate equivalences between metric units and common imperial units such as inches, pounds and pints
- measure and calculate the perimeter of composite rectilinear shapes in centimetres and metres
- calculate and compare the area of rectangles (including squares), and including using standard units, square centimetres (cm^2) and square metres (m^2) and estimate the area of irregular shapes
- estimate volume [for example, using 1 cm^3 blocks to build cuboids (including cubes)] and capacity [for example, using water]
- solve problems involving converting between units of time
- use all four operations to solve problems involving measure [for example, length, mass, volume, money] using decimal notation, including scaling.

Notes and guidance (non-statutory)

Pupils use their knowledge of place value and multiplication and division to convert between standard units.

Pupils calculate the perimeter of rectangles and related composite shapes, including using the relations of perimeter or area to find unknown lengths. Missing measures

(Continued)

(Continued)

questions such as these can be expressed algebraically, for example $4 + 2b = 20$ for a rectangle of sides 2 cm and b cm and perimeter of 20cm.

Pupils calculate the area from scale drawings using given measurements.

Pupils use all four operations in problems involving time and money, including conversions (for example, days to weeks, expressing the answer as weeks and days).

Geometry – properties of shapes

Statutory requirements

Pupils should be taught to:

- identify 3-D shapes, including cubes and other cuboids, from 2-D representations
- know angles are measured in degrees: estimate and compare acute, obtuse and reflex angles
- draw given angles, and measure them in degrees (°)
- identify:

  - angles at a point and one whole turn (total 360°)
  - angles at a point on a straight line and $\frac{1}{2}$ a turn (total 180°)
  - other multiples of 90°

- use the properties of rectangles to deduce related facts and find missing lengths and angles
- distinguish between regular and irregular polygons based on reasoning about equal sides and angles.

Notes and guidance (non-statutory)

Pupils become accurate in drawing lines with a ruler to the nearest millimetre, and measuring with a protractor. They use conventional markings for parallel lines and right angles.

Pupils use the term diagonal and make conjectures about the angles formed between sides, and between diagonals and parallel sides, and other properties of quadrilaterals, for example using dynamic geometry ICT tools.

Pupils use angle sum facts and other properties to make deductions about missing angles and relate these to missing number problems.

Geometry – position and direction

Statutory requirements

Pupils should be taught to:

- identify, describe and represent the position of a shape following a reflection or translation, using the appropriate language, and know that the shape has not changed.

Notes and guidance (non-statutory)

Pupils recognise and use reflection and translation in a variety of diagrams, including continuing to use a 2-D grid and coordinates in the first quadrant. Reflection should be in lines that are parallel to the axes.

Statistics

Statutory requirements

Pupils should be taught to:

- solve comparison, sum and difference problems using information presented in a line graph
- complete, read and interpret information in tables, including timetables.

Notes and guidance (non-statutory)

Pupils connect their work on coordinates and scales to their interpretation of time graphs.
They begin to decide which representations of data are most appropriate and why.

Year 6 programme of study

Number – number and place value

Statutory requirements

Pupils should be taught to:

- read, write, order and compare numbers up to 10 000 000 and determine the value of each digit
- round any whole number to a required degree of accuracy
- use negative numbers in context, and calculate intervals across zero
- solve number and practical problems that involve all of the above.

Notes and guidance (non-statutory)

Pupils use the whole number system, including saying, reading and writing numbers accurately.

Number – addition, subtraction, multiplication and division

Statutory requirements

Pupils should be taught to:

- multiply multi-digit numbers up to 4 digits by a two-digit whole number using the formal written method of long multiplication
- divide numbers up to 4 digits by a two-digit whole number using the formal written method of long division, and interpret remainders as whole number remainders, fractions, or by rounding, as appropriate for the context
- divide numbers up to 4 digits by a two-digit number using the formal written method of short division where appropriate, interpreting remainders according to the context
- perform mental calculations, including with mixed operations and large numbers
- identify common factors, common multiples and prime numbers
- use their knowledge of the order of operations to carry out calculations involving the four operations
- solve addition and subtraction multi-step problems in contexts, deciding which operations and methods to use and why
- solve problems involving addition, subtraction, multiplication and division
- use estimation to check answers to calculations and determine, in the context of a problem, an appropriate degree of accuracy.

Notes and guidance (non-statutory)

Pupils practise addition, subtraction, multiplication and division for larger numbers, using the formal written methods of columnar addition and subtraction, short and long multiplication, and short and long division (see **Mathematics Appendix 1**).

They undertake mental calculations with increasingly large numbers and more complex calculations.

Pupils continue to use all the multiplication tables to calculate mathematical statements in order to maintain their fluency.

Pupils round answers to a specified degree of accuracy, for example, to the nearest 10, 20, 50 etc., but not to a specified number of significant figures.

Pupils explore the order of operations using brackets; for example, $2 + 1 \times 3 = 5$ and $(2 + 1) \times 3 = 9$.

Common factors can be related to finding equivalent fractions.

Number – fractions (including decimals and percentages)

Statutory requirements

Pupils should be taught to:

- use common factors to simplify fractions; use common multiples to express fractions in the same denomination
- compare and order fractions, including fractions > 1

- add and subtract fractions with different denominators and mixed numbers, using the concept of equivalent fractions
- multiply simple pairs of proper fractions, writing the answer in its simplest form [for example, $\frac{1}{4} \times \frac{1}{2} = \frac{1}{8}$]
- divide proper fractions by whole numbers [for example, $\frac{1}{3} \div 2 = \frac{1}{6}$]
- associate a fraction with division and calculate decimal fraction equivalents [for example, 0.375] for a simple fraction [for example, $\frac{3}{8}$]
- identify the value of each digit in numbers given to three decimal places and multiply and divide numbers by 10, 100 and 1000 giving answers up to three decimal places
- multiply one-digit numbers with up to two decimal places by whole numbers
- use written division methods in cases where the answer has up to two decimal places
- solve problems which require answers to be rounded to specified degrees of accuracy
- recall and use equivalences between simple fractions, decimals and percentages, including in different contexts.

Notes and guidance (non-statutory)

Pupils should practise, use and understand the addition and subtraction of fractions with different denominators by identifying equivalent fractions with the same denominator. They should start with fractions where the denominator of one fraction is a multiple of the other (for example, $\frac{1}{2} + \frac{1}{8} = \frac{5}{8}$) and progress to varied and increasingly complex problems.

Pupils should use a variety of images to support their understanding of multiplication with fractions. This follows earlier work about fractions as operators (fractions of), as numbers, and as equal parts of objects, for example as parts of a rectangle.

Pupils use their understanding of the relationship between unit fractions and division to work backwards by multiplying a quantity that represents a unit fraction to find the whole quantity (for example, if $\frac{1}{4}$ of a length is 36cm, then the whole length is $36 \times 4 = 144$cm).

They practise calculations with simple fractions and decimal fraction equivalents to aid fluency, including listing equivalent fractions to identify fractions with common denominators.

Pupils can explore and make conjectures about converting a simple fraction to a decimal fraction (for example, $3 \div 8 = 0.375$). For simple fractions with recurring decimal equivalents, pupils learn about rounding the decimal to three decimal places, or other appropriate approximations depending on the context. Pupils multiply and divide numbers with up to two decimal places by one-digit and two-digit whole numbers. Pupils multiply decimals by whole numbers, starting with the simplest cases, such as $0.4 \times 2 = 0.8$, and in practical contexts, such as measures and money.

Pupils are introduced to the division of decimal numbers by one-digit whole number, initially, in practical contexts involving measures and money. They recognise division calculations as the inverse of multiplication.

Pupils also develop their skills of rounding and estimating as a means of predicting and checking the order of magnitude of their answers to decimal calculations. This includes rounding answers to a specified degree of accuracy and checking the reasonableness of their answers.

Ratio and proportion

Statutory requirements

Pupils should be taught to:

- solve problems involving the relative sizes of two quantities where missing values can be found by using integer multiplication and division facts
- solve problems involving the calculation of percentages [for example, of measures, and such as 15% of 360] and the use of percentages for comparison
- solve problems involving similar shapes where the scale factor is known or can be found
- solve problems involving unequal sharing and grouping using knowledge of fractions and multiples.

Notes and guidance (non-statutory)

Pupils recognise proportionality in contexts when the relations between quantities are in the same ratio (for example, similar shapes and recipes).

Pupils link percentages or 360° to calculating angles of pie charts.

Pupils should consolidate their understanding of ratio when comparing quantities, sizes and scale drawings by solving a variety of problems. They might use the notation $a:b$ to record their work.

Pupils solve problems involving unequal quantities, for example, 'for every egg you need three spoonfuls of flour', '$\frac{3}{5}$ of the class are boys'. These problems are the foundation for later formal approaches to ratio and proportion.

Algebra

Statutory requirements

Pupils should be taught to:

- use simple formulae
- generate and describe linear number sequences
- express missing number problems algebraically
- find pairs of numbers that satisfy an equation with two unknowns
- enumerate possibilities of combinations of two variables.

Notes and guidance (non-statutory)

Pupils should be introduced to the use of symbols and letters to represent variables and unknowns in mathematical situations that they already understand, such as:

- missing numbers, lengths, coordinates and angles
- formulae in mathematics and science

- equivalent expressions (for example, $a + b = b + a$)
- generalisations of number patterns
- number puzzles (for example, what two numbers can add up to).

Measurement

Statutory requirements

Pupils should be taught to:

- solve problems involving the calculation and conversion of units of measure, using decimal notation up to three decimal places where appropriate
- use, read, write and convert between standard units, converting measurements of length, mass, volume and time from a smaller unit of measure to a larger unit, and vice versa, using decimal notation to up to three decimal places
- convert between miles and kilometres
- recognise that shapes with the same areas can have different perimeters and vice versa
- recognise when it is possible to use formulae for area and volume of shapes
- calculate the area of parallelograms and triangles
- calculate, estimate and compare volume of cubes and cuboids using standard units, including cubic centimetres (cm^3) and cubic metres (m^3), and extending to other units [for example, mm^3 and km^3].

Notes and guidance (non-statutory)

Pupils connect conversion (for example, from kilometres to miles) to a graphical representation as preparation for understanding linear/proportional graphs.

They know approximate conversions and are able to tell if an answer is sensible.

Using the number line, pupils use, add and subtract positive and negative integers for measures such as temperature.

They relate the area of rectangles to parallelograms and triangles, for example, by dissection, and calculate their areas, understanding and using the formulae (in words or symbols) to do this.

Pupils could be introduced to compound units for speed, such as miles per hour, and apply their knowledge in science or other subjects as appropriate.

Geometry – properties of shapes

Statutory requirements

Pupils should be taught to:

- draw 2-D shapes using given dimensions and angles
- recognise, describe and build simple 3-D shapes, including making nets

(Continued)

(Continued)

- compare and classify geometric shapes based on their properties and sizes and find unknown angles in any triangles, quadrilaterals, and regular polygons
- illustrate and name parts of circles, including radius, diameter and circumference and know that the diameter is twice the radius
- recognise angles where they meet at a point, are on a straight line, or are vertically opposite, and find missing angles.

Notes and guidance (non-statutory)

Pupils draw shapes and nets accurately, using measuring tools and conventional markings and labels for lines and angles.

Pupils describe the properties of shapes and explain how unknown angles and lengths can be derived from known measurements.

These relationships might be expressed algebraically for example, $d = 2 \times r$; $a = 180 - (b + c)$.

Geometry – position and direction

Statutory requirements

Pupils should be taught to:

- describe positions on the full coordinate grid (all four quadrants)
- draw and translate simple shapes on the coordinate plane, and reflect them in the axes.

Notes and guidance (non-statutory)

Pupils draw and label a pair of axes in all four quadrants with equal scaling. This extends their knowledge of one quadrant to all four quadrants, including the use of negative numbers.

Pupils draw and label rectangles (including squares), parallelograms and rhombuses, specified by coordinates in the four quadrants, predicting missing coordinates using the properties of shapes. These might be expressed algebraically for example, translating vertex (a, b) to $(a - 2, b + 3)$; (a, b) and $(a + d, b + d)$ being opposite vertices of a square of side d.

Statistics

Statutory requirements

Pupils should be taught to:

- interpret and construct pie charts and line graphs and use these to solve problems
- calculate and interpret the mean as an average.

> **Notes and guidance (non-statutory)**
>
> Pupils connect their work on angles, fractions and percentages to the interpretation of pie charts.
>
> Pupils both encounter and draw graphs relating two variables, arising from their own enquiry and in other subjects.
>
> They should connect conversion from kilometres to miles in measurement to its graphical representation.
>
> Pupils know when it is appropriate to find the mean of a data set.

Mathematics Appendix 1: Examples of formal written methods for addition, subtraction, multiplication and division

This appendix sets out some examples of formal written methods for all four operations to illustrate the range of methods that could be taught. It is not intended to be an exhaustive list, nor is it intended to show progression in formal written methods. For example, the exact position of intermediate calculations (superscript and subscript digits) will vary depending on the method and format used.

For multiplication, some pupils may include an addition symbol when adding partial products. For division, some pupils may include a subtraction symbol when subtracting multiples of the divisor.

Addition and subtraction

784 + 642 becomes	874 − 523 becomes	932 − 457 becomes	932 − 457 becomes

$$\begin{array}{r} 7\ 8\ 9 \\ +\ 6\ 4\ 2 \\ \hline 1\ 4\ 3\ 1 \\ {}_1\ {}_1 \end{array}$$

$$\begin{array}{r} 8\ 7\ 4 \\ -\ 5\ 2\ 3 \\ \hline 3\ 5\ 1 \end{array}$$

$$\begin{array}{r} {}^8\cancel{9}\ {}^{12}\cancel{3}\ {}^1 2 \\ -\ 4\ 5\ 7 \\ \hline 4\ 7\ 5 \end{array}$$

$$\begin{array}{r} 9\ {}^1 3\ {}^1 2 \\ -\ \cancel{4}\ \cancel{5}\ 7 \\ {}^5\ {}^6 \\ \hline 4\ 7\ 5 \end{array}$$

Answer: 1431   Answer: 351   Answer: 475   Answer: 475

Short multiplication

24 × 6 becomes	342 × 7 becomes	2741 × 6 becomes

$$\begin{array}{r} 2\ 4 \\ \times\ \ \ 6 \\ \hline 1\ 4\ 4 \\ {}_2 \end{array}$$

$$\begin{array}{r} 3\ 4\ 2 \\ \times\ \ \ \ \ 7 \\ \hline 2\ 3\ 9\ 4 \\ {}_2\ {}_1 \end{array}$$

$$\begin{array}{r} 2\ 7\ 4\ 1 \\ \times\ \ \ \ \ \ \ 6 \\ \hline 1\ 6\ 4\ 4\ 6 \\ {}_4\ {}_2 \end{array}$$

Answer: 144   Answer: 2394   Answer: 16 446

Long multiplication

24 × 16 becomes

```
      2
    2 4
  × 1 6
  2 4 0
  1 4 4
  3 8 4
```

Answer: 384

124 × 26 becomes

```
    1 2
  1 2 4
  ×   2 6
  2 4 8 0
    7 4 4
  3 2 2 4
    1 1
```

Answer: 3224

124 × 26 becomes

```
    1 2
  1 2 4
  ×   2 6
    7 4 4
  2 4 8 0
  3 2 2 4
    1 1
```

Answer: 3224

Short division

98 ÷ 7 becomes

```
    1 4
    2
  7 9 8
```

Answer: 14

432 ÷ 5 becomes

```
      8 6 r2
        3
  5 4 3 2
```

Answer: 86 remainder 2

496 ÷ 11 becomes

```
      4 5 r1
        5
  1 1 4 9 6
```

Answer: $45\frac{1}{11}$

Long division

432 ÷ 15 becomes

```
        2 8 r12
  15 4 3 2
     3 0 0
     1 3 2
     1 2 0
         1 2
```

Answer: 28 remainder 12

432 ÷ 15 becomes

```
        2 8
  15 4 3 2      15 × 20
     3 0 0
     1 3 2      15 × 8
     1 2 0
         1 2
```

$\frac{12}{15} = \frac{4}{5}$

Answer: $28\frac{4}{5}$

432 ÷ 15 becomes

```
        2 8 . 8
  15 4 3 2 . 0
     3 0
     1 3 2
     1 2 0
         1 2 0
         1 2 0
             0
```

Answer: 28.8

FROM THE FRAMEWORK

6 Science

Planning science in the national curriculum

Keira Sewell

Science 1 Principles of planning

This section looks at the key factors which are specific to planning effective science lessons. It builds on the generic factors for planning found in Chapter 1 and should be read in conjunction with these ideas.

Working scientifically

Good science lessons support progress in both procedural (the doing of science) and conceptual (the knowledge and understanding of science) understanding and your planning will need to take account of this. There are a number of ways in which you can do this.

First, you will need to think about your learning objectives for the lesson. While some lessons may be designed to specifically develop children's procedural knowledge (e.g. asking questions, recording data, measurement) and others may focus specifically on the development of concepts (e.g. forces, electricity, habitats), most lessons will need to include objectives which support both procedural and conceptual learning. You will need to consider what progression in procedural and conceptual understanding might look like. For example, in a sequence of lessons you may seek to develop children's understanding of sound so that they move from describing what things make sounds to explaining how things make sounds and how we hear them. This is about developing an understanding of the concept of sound. In the same sequence of lessons you might also develop children's use of the processes which enable them to explore the concept of sound. For example, you may wish to develop their independence in enquiry so that they take more decisions about how and when to record different sounds and what makes those sounds.

Second, you will need to think about how you are asking children to work. Are you asking them to work in a scientific way? This will involve choosing strategies which encourage children to think and work in a scientific way with the ultimate aim of helping them make sense of the scientific ideas you want them to use. (Loxley et al., 2014, Chapter 7 and Peacock et al., 2014, Chapter 2 provide good explanations of these ideas.) Good strategies actively involve children in their learning and

may include dialogue, such as talk partners, using puppets or concept cartoons (see Naylor and Keogh, 2000) and mind maps, and many lessons will incorporate some element of enquiry. The national curriculum for science (DfE, 2013, page 137) suggests enquiry should include observing over time, pattern seeking, identifying, classifying and grouping, comparative and fair testing and researching using secondary sources. It is important to remember that not all scientific enquiry involves practical work and fair testing is not the only type of investigation we want children to be involved in (see Sharp et al., 2014, for further guidance on this).

There are good examples of how you can include enquiry in your teaching in the non-statutory guidance in the national curriculum framework for science so you should read this in conjunction with the statutory programmes of study. Our aim is to move children from directed, illustrative enquiry to more independent enquiry and, therefore, some of the activities you plan will need to teach children how to use the skills and processes of enquiry independently by scaffolding their learning using key questions and more directed enquiry planning formats.

It is also important to remember that children's mastery of scientific processes can often be dependent on their development of key skills and that these may need to be taught specifically. For example, you cannot expect children to know how to make comparisons of the thermal conductivity of different materials if they do not yet know how to use a thermometer. Some of these skills will be learnt in other subject areas, such as drawing graphs or writing a report, and it may be that your science lessons provide a good context for work which is more cross-curricular in nature. (For further discussion of this see Section 3 of this book.)

Third, you will need to think about how you encourage children to work and think scientifically. Often this is dependent on the attitudes you encourage in your classroom. Consider how you can give control of the lesson to the children rather than creating a tightly controlled, teacher-directed format. This approach will enable children to take responsibility for their own learning, to explore new ideas and areas of interest, to discuss and debate alternative approaches and viewpoints and to work collaboratively to solve problems and develop thinking. A good way to do this is to ensure you focus on what the children will be doing rather than simply on what you will be teaching. How do the teaching strategies you have chosen support and promote learning in science? You may also find it useful to allocate roles to each child if they are working as a group. This provides focus and encourages children to develop the interpersonal skills required for effective collaboration. Finally, ask yourself who is working hardest in a lesson; if it is you then you need to reorganise your lesson.

Relevance

OFSTED (2011) identified that one element of good teaching in science was that children *were engaged in science that had relevance to their lives* (page 5). Think carefully about why we teach science in primary schools – what value does it bring? One of the answers to this must be that science is an integral part of all our lives; it influences everything around us and the future of our world. As such, our teaching must reflect this and one way to achieve this is to make our teaching relevant to the children's world. In many cases this may be by focusing on specific local issues, environments, concerns or needs – for example, studying local habitats or thinking about materials used for building in the local area. We should always look for opportunities to link

science to the real world and give relevance to the ideas we are trying to develop. For example, consider how learning about the differences between series and parallel circuits could be developed by incorporating these circuits in a model house to illustrate why parallel circuits are more effective in certain situations.

Because of the real-world relevance of science it is often difficult to separate science from learning in other curriculum areas. As a result science lends itself well to cross-curricular work and it is common for science lessons to provide opportunities for children to develop or demonstrate learning both across the science curriculum and in other subject areas. For example, within the science curriculum there are obvious links between properties and changes of materials and forces and magnets, and links across the curriculum can be made using approaches such as: reporting scientific enquiry through writing a report (English); learning about how sounds can be changed in musical instruments (music); or healthy eating (design and technology). Wherever possible these opportunities should be exploited.

Assessment

Assessing learning in science can be more problematic given the active, and sometimes practical, nature of science. It may not always be easy to use an outcome (such as a piece of writing or a presentation) to assess understanding, particularly of scientific processes, and there is some debate about whether a written outcome can capture the thinking behind the understanding of a scientific concept. As such, we need to use a range of assessment strategies to ensure we capture children's learning. Such strategies may include observations, discussion and questioning, drawings, photographs and video, written tests, data records (e.g. graphs and tables) and concept maps, and often we need to be with children at specific moments to assess effectively. (See Naylor et al., 2004, for a good range of assessment strategies.)

Your choice of strategy will also impact on the organisation in your classroom. For example, if you need to listen to a group discussing their predictions you need to plan that you are working with this group at the appropriate time in the lesson structure.

You may also find that you cannot do the same activity with all children at the same time if you need to be with them to assess learning. One way to address this is to have a circus of activities, where other activities are more self-sustaining or have more permanent outcomes, while you work closely alongside the activity where outcomes are more ephemeral. Other approaches include a more staggered lesson structure to ensure you are with groups at opportune moments.

Vocabulary

Teaching scientific vocabulary is an important aspect of effective science education and, as such, should be an integral part of planning. This does not mean you should write down all the words you will use but, rather, that you should identify key words which are important in understanding the science you want children to learn. It is useful to think of scientific words as follows:

- names: e.g. hydrogen, granite, artery;
- processes: e.g. evaporation, respiration, digestion, prediction, recording, measuring;
- concepts: e.g. energy, force, atom, habitat.

 Identifying scientific vocabulary is important as it ensures you fully understand the meaning of the words before you start teaching so that you can explain the concepts behind the vocabulary clearly. For example, when teaching electricity you may use the word 'circuit' but what does this actually mean? What constitutes a circuit? What principles of electricity and electrical current do children need to understand in order to make a circuit?

Some scientific words have common roots which are useful for children to learn. For example, 'photo-' (meaning light) is common to 'photosynthesis', 'photograph' and 'photosensitive'. What other word roots would be useful for children to know?

It is also important to remember that some words have different meanings in our everyday life which may influence our understanding of scientific concepts. Consider the words 'force' and 'hard' – what do they mean in everyday life and does this reflect their scientific meanings? Asking children what they know about a word such as 'force' can be a good starting point for a sequence of lessons around this concept and can support children in building up concept or mind maps around an area of understanding.

Misconceptions

Scientific concepts are complex and, because of the way in which we construct knowledge, misconceptions are common when learning science. Identifying the common misconceptions before you start planning can often mean you avoid these and adapt your teaching accordingly. For example, a common misconception is that when a solid dissolves it 'disappears' and teachers can sometimes reinforce this idea by using the word 'disappear' in their descriptions. Being aware of this ensures we are careful with the vocabulary we use and that we adopt teaching approaches which enable children to understand that just because we cannot see something does not mean it is not there. Some teaching approaches can also, unwittingly, reinforce misconceptions. Analogies and models can be very effective but if used without understanding they can over-simplify complex scientific ideas and lead to misconceptions. (Allen, 2010, provides a good starting point for identifying misconceptions in science.)

Health and safety

Because of the practical and active nature of science it is important to identify any hazards associated with planned activities. A hazard is something which could cause harm, and a risk assessment will enable you to identify the potential for this to occur and the ways in which you could minimise or remove the risk. Even seemingly harmless activities such as planting seeds have risks associated with them – for example, many seeds are coated in fungicides which could be harmful if ingested. There are many texts designed to support risk assessments in science both within and outside the classroom but a good starting point is *Be Safe!* (ASE, 2011).

The learning environment

Science lends itself particularly well to learning in environments other than the classroom. The use of outdoor learning spaces is obvious when we look at environmental work and many teachers will take children into the outdoors to look at

habitats or to study living things in context. Many other areas of science benefit from being taught in larger spaces than the classroom – the school playground, the hall or the local park can often provide a more appropriate environment. For example, learning about how sounds get quieter the further away you are from the source can be difficult to manage in the classroom but fantastic to do on the school playground. Dunne and Peacock (2012) and Loxley et al. (2014) both have chapters which provide a good starting point for learning outside the classroom.

Resources

Resourcing science does not have to be expensive. Many things we use in our daily lives make science relevant to everyday life and ensure children understand the role of science around them. However, good resourcing needs careful thought and a well-planned lesson needs to consider the following.

- Which resources would best support the learning intended? If you want children to identify living/non-living things will you get the best outcome if you just use photographs of objects (after all, none of these are living)?
- Which resources need to be ordered/booked/organised with other agencies? Health education centres, wildlife organisations, libraries, etc. can all be good sources but you will probably need to book items or services well in advance.
- How will resources be organised to encourage children to work independently? Will children have a choice of resources or be able to collect their own according to need?
- Do resources enable children to continue to develop their understanding of the processes of science? Using a measuring cylinder is a much more accurate way of measuring liquids than a dropping pipette but requires an understanding of number and the ways in which liquid behaves when put into a container.
- Do the resources available mean that children can only conduct an enquiry in one way? What if they want to do something different – are they encouraged to seek alternative approaches?
- Do selected resources suggest or reinforce a particular perspective of science (e.g. many posters and books give a perception that science is the domain of white, male scientists)?
- Are selected resources safe to use (e.g. do any children have food allergies which need to be accommodated)?

Using information and communications technology (ICT) in science

The relationship between science and ICT is extremely important. We can use ICT in a wide variety of ways, however, the important factor is to remember that ICT should be used to support learning and not simply make your teaching easier or used as a wow factor. For example, using a digital microscope can be extremely effective in enabling children to examine objects in close detail but there may be times when using hand lenses can be even more effective. Consider what you want ICT to do in terms of the learning outcomes for your lesson or sequence of lessons.

Good uses of ICT include writing reports (e.g. word-processing programmes, digital images), presenting data (e.g. presentation programmes, video or audio reports, posters), communicating data (e.g. emails, blogs, social media), capturing

 data (e.g. data logging, sensors, images from video, cameras, digital microscopes), introducing ideas or problems (e.g. using the interactive whiteboard, video links), using simulation software to model ideas or predict outcomes, researching ideas from electronic sources (e.g. websites, CD-ROMS), and storing and manipulating data (e.g. spreadsheets and databases). Sharp et al. (2014), Chapter 10, explores these ideas in more detail.

Activity length

Not all science activities fit neatly into a normal lesson time. Some are more long-term projects and may require a slightly different approach to planning than in other subjects. Good examples include such things as monitoring the apparent movement of the sun across the sky or the germination of seeds and the growth of plants. Although you could plan these as separate lessons, there is scope to plan longer-term activities which span a longer period of time. In such plans you would identify what activities would take place on each date but include them all on the same plan as they share the learning and other organisational characteristics.

Further reading

Allen, M. (2010) *Misconceptions in Primary Science*. Maidenhead: Open University Press.

ASE (2011) *Be Safe! Health and Safety in School Science and Technology for Teachers of 3- to 12-year-olds* (4th edition). Hatfield: ASE.

ASE *Primary Science*. (The primary journal of the Association for Science Education – see **ase.org.uk** for details.)

Dunne, M. and Peacock, A. (2012) *Primary Science: A Guide to Teaching Practice*. London: Sage.

Goldsworthy, A. and Feasey, R. (1997) *Making Sense of Primary Science Investigations*. Hatfield: ASE.

Harlen, W. (2000) *The Teaching of Science in Primary Schools*. London: David Fulton.

Harlen, W. (ed.) (2006) *ASE Guide to Primary Science*. Hatfield: ASE.

Loxley, P., Dawes, L., Nicholls, L. and Dore, B. (2014) *Teaching Primary Science: Promoting Enjoyment and Developing Understanding* (2nd edition). London: Routledge.

Naylor, S. and Keogh, B. (2000) *Concept Cartoons in Science Education*. Sandbach: Millgate House Publishers. (Also available on CD-ROM)

Naylor, S., Keogh, B. and Goldsworthy, A. (2004) *Active Assessment*. London: David Fulton.

OFSTED (2011) Successful science. [online] Available at: **http://dera.ioe.ac.uk/2148**

OFSTED (2013) Maintaining curiosity: Science education in schools. [online] Available at: **http://www.gov.uk/government/publications/maintaining-curiosity-a-survey-into-science-education-in-schools**

Peacock, G. A. (2002) *Teaching Science in Primary Schools*. London: Letts.

Peacock, G., Sharp, J., Johnsey, R. and Wright, D. (2014) *Primary Science: Knowledge and Understanding* (7th edition). London: Sage/Learning Matters.

Sharp, J. (ed.) (2004) *Developing Primary Science*. Exeter: Learning Matters.

Sharp, J., Peacock, G., Johnsey, R., Simon, S., Smith, R., Cross, A. and Harris, D. (2014) *Primary Science: Teaching Theory and Practice* (7th edition). London: Sage/Learning Matters.

Science 2 Examples of planning

The following three lesson plans are provided as examples of planning in science. They do not contain the detail you will probably wish to have on your plans but do illustrate some of the points discussed previously.

Lesson One

Subject/topic:	Date: 23/10/2016	Teaching group/set: Y3
Rocks – grouping and classifying	Time: 1.15 p.m.	No. of pupils: 28

Intended learning:	NC reference/context:
Children will learn to: • make systematic and careful observations of rocks and group them on the basis of physical appearance • communicate their findings using digital records.	Rocks, Y3 PoS Lower KS2 – Working scientifically

Success criteria:	Assessment strategy:
All children will be able to: • group eight samples of rocks using one aspect of their physical appearance • compose an email which includes a written record of their classification and digital photograph(s) of their grouping(s). Some children will be able to: • list three or more aspects of the physical appearance of rocks in their presentation and group them accordingly.	• Observation of groupings and discussion which informs these. • Email correspondence with incorporated photographs of groupings.

Key vocabulary:	Resources:	Risk assessment:
grains, crystals, words associated with texture and colour	Letter from Sarah the builder on IWB. Eight labelled rock samples from a local quarry. Hand lenses Digital microscopes Digital cameras Sorting rings	Potential hazard of dust and rock particles in eyes or ingested – wash hands thoroughly after handling rock samples. Warn children not to look at the sun or light sources through lenses.

Time	Teacher focus	Pupil focus
10 mins	Introduce the challenge of finding a rock which could be used to replace the building materials in the school. Sarah the builder has sent in an email to ask for your help in choosing which of the eight rock samples she has would be best in replacing the parts of the school damaged by a recent storm.	Sitting at group tables (six per table), read letter and identify challenge set. As a group, highlight key phrases and words. Group to work as building team from now.

There are obvious links with geography, English and computing in these lessons which could be developed.

Outcomes are specific and differentiated.

Labelling the samples means children can focus on finding out how the rocks behave rather than what they are called.

Hook provides context for learning and relevance to a real-life context.

Collaborative working, encouraging pupil–pupil dialogue.

| 30 mins | Identify as many differences as you can between the eight samples Sarah is thinking of using. Group the rocks according to their physical features.

Assess discussions to identify children's understanding of physical differences. | Each building team to identify physical differences between rock samples.

Group rocks according to physical features and take photographs of groupings.

Develop initial hypothesis of which three of the eight samples may be best to use to repair building with reasons for their choice. |
| 20 mins | Chair 5-minute discussion to elicit key ideas emerging.

Focus children on what information should be contained in the email. | Write email to Sarah's building firm which identifies initial findings and thoughts. Include photographs of groupings. |

Focus on processes of science enables children to develop conceptual understanding of rocks.

Mid-lesson assessments provide the opportunity for teachers to provide further input or develop children's thinking to a higher level.

Lesson Two

Subject/topic:	Date: 27/10/2016	Teaching group/set: Y3
Rocks – physical properties	Time: 10.30 a.m.	No. of pupils: 28

Intended learning:	NC reference/context:
Children will learn how to: • use a variety of sources to research scientific facts and use this information to develop a reasoned argument • plan a fair test.	Rocks, Y3 PoS Everyday materials, Y2 PoS

Success criteria:	Assessment strategy:
All children will be able to: • use one source to identify what kind of rock (igneous, sedimentary, metamorphic) their samples are • plan a simple fair test involving one dependent variable with support. Some children will be able to: • use a range of sources to identify rock samples and use research to inform their ideas about its potential use as a building material • plan a fair test independently involving one dependent variable.	• Marking of 'What do we know?' sheet • Marking of investigation plan

Key vocabulary:	Resources:	Risk assessment:
igneous, sedimentary, metamorphic, erosion.	Email from Sarah the builder on IWB. Access to websites and texts on types of rock. Hand lenses, digital microscopes.	Potential hazard of dust and rock particles in eyes or ingested – wash hands thoroughly after handling rock samples. Warn children not to look at the sun or light sources through lenses.

Use of ICT to communicate findings and ideas.

LOs provide opportunity for children to repeat assessments not achieved in previous year group or to demonstrate understanding in alternative contexts.

Enquiry-based research using a range of sources. Encourages children to become more critical of those available and to check out information using other sources.

Time	Teacher focus	Pupil focus
10 mins	Sarah has asked each team of builders to choose their top three rock samples and investigate them further. She has sent instructions via email as to what should be investigated – strength and durability in poor weather.	Read email and consider the key points from Sarah's letter. Each team to collect their three samples for further investigation.
20 mins	Direct teams to research their chosen samples. Work with teams to identify relevant sources and information.	Teams to identify name and source of samples chosen. Using websites and selected books teams to identify source of their samples. Should be able to identify how their rock may have been formed and how this may affect the strength/durability of it. Record their information on a 'What do we know?' sheet.
40 mins	Direct teams to plan an investigation to find out how their chosen samples will react to erosion. Support given to **blue group** (LA) by teacher to construct an investigation – scaffolded planning sheet and teacher support for planning phase. TA to work with **red group** (HA) to consider other aspects they could investigate in order to identify the best rock to repair the school. Mini-plenary after 20 mins to discuss foci of investigation and methods of enquiry.	Work in building teams to identify the focus of further enquiry – erosion by rubbing or by water. Some teams may choose to investigate both factors. Teams to plan an investigation to compare how their chosen samples will react to being rubbed together or immersed in water. Use scaffolding sheet which has key questions for structuring investigations – e.g. What do you want to find out? What do you predict will happen? What will you keep the same, change, measure or record? Teams to complete planning sheet with equipment order and submit to teacher for the following lesson.

Encourages children to identify key aspects of an investigation rather than it being teacher-directed.

Opportunity for children to extend their thinking through differentiated outcomes.

Children given opportunity to plan independently; allows for alternative approaches and encourages discussion. Teacher and TA scaffold learning of different attainment groups.

Mini-plenaries enable the teacher to reinforce ideas, expectations and outcomes and encourage children to share ideas and listen to alternative approaches and perspectives.

Lesson Three

Subject/topic:	Date: 31/10/2016	Teaching group/set: Y3
Rocks – effects of erosion	Time: 1.15 p.m.	No. of pupils: 28

Intended learning:	NC reference/ context:
Children will learn to: • make systematic and careful observations of changes to their samples during an investigation • record their observations in an appropriate and relevant way • interpret their findings and communicate these using email.	Rocks, Y3 PoS Everyday materials, Y2 PoS

Success criteria:	Assessment strategy:
All children will be able to: • record their observations in a way which is appropriate to the changes occurring. Some children will be able to: • take accurate measurements of the changes affecting their rocks during the investigation.	• Observation of investigative approaches • Assessment of presentations

Key vocabulary:	Resources:	Risk assessment:
interpret, conclusion, record, erode, absorb, porous	As on team equipment orders but may include: plastic trays, 10 ml syringes, small watering cans, 50 ml measuring cylinders, dropping pipettes, plastic cups, digital microscopes, hand lenses, fine sieves, digital scales 'Sarah the builder' to receive presentations (could be dressed up member of staff or a local parent or builder) Laptops with PowerPoint and video/digital photo software	Potential hazard of dust and rock particles in eyes or ingested – wear goggles when rubbing rock samples and wash hands thoroughly after investigation. Risk of slipping on wet floors – have paper towels ready to mop up spillages. Warn children not to look at the sun or light sources through lenses. Other hazards to be identified following receipt of equipment lists.

Time	Teacher focus	Pupil focus
40 mins	Provide equipment trays as ordered. Support given to each group to develop their enquiry. TA to work with **blue group** (LA) as scribe and facilitator	Teams to carry out planned investigation and record results. Recording will vary depending on the variables selected. Scaffolded sheets given to teams who find recording challenging (e.g. pre-prepared tables for writing results or drawing appearance of rocks following testing).
10 mins	Teacher and TA support development of presentations.	Teams to organise presentation of their findings and conclusions. Use PowerPoint to present.
30 mins	Distribute peer evaluation forms focusing on key questions relating to the learning objectives over the sequence of lessons. Teacher welcomes 'Sarah' to the classroom and chairs presentations. Probing questions asked by Sarah and by peers where appropriate.	Teams to present their final ideas to Sarah the builder. Peers to record their evaluations of the ideas presented using the sheet prepared and submit their thoughts to the teacher.

Peer assessment focused on learning objectives – enables children to see how they could develop their ideas and continue to make progress and engages them with the presentations.

Teams experience real-life context of reporting results to a client – working scientifically.

Lesson time extended to allow for more in-depth project work. Potential to include assessment of other subject areas thus maximising use of time. (See Section 3 for further guidance.)

Support given to groups who understand the nature of enquiry but find reporting their ideas difficult.

Focus on findings and conclusions means children do not have to report on the whole of their investigation.

Presence of Sarah retains context and enables children to report as scientists.

Questions enable knowledge and understanding to be probed and encourages children to be critical of their own and others' work and develop skills in giving feedback.

FROM THE FRAMEWORK

Science 3 The framework for science

Purpose of study

A high-quality science education provides the foundations for understanding the world through the specific disciplines of biology, chemistry and physics. Science has changed our lives and is vital to the world's future prosperity, and all pupils should be taught essential aspects of the knowledge, methods, processes and uses of science. Through building up a body of key foundational knowledge and concepts, pupils should be encouraged to recognise the power of rational explanation and develop a sense of excitement and curiosity about natural phenomena. They should be encouraged to understand how science can be used to explain what is occurring, predict how things will behave, and analyse causes.

Aims

The national curriculum for science aims to ensure that all pupils:

- develop **scientific knowledge and conceptual understanding** through the specific disciplines of biology, chemistry and physics
- develop understanding of the **nature, processes and methods of science** through different types of science enquiries that help them to answer scientific questions about the world around them
- are equipped with the scientific knowledge required to understand the **uses and implications** of science, today and for the future.

Scientific knowledge and conceptual understanding

The programmes of study describe a sequence of knowledge and concepts. While it is important that pupils make progress, it is also vitally important that they develop secure understanding of each key block of knowledge and concepts in order to progress to the next stage. Insecure, superficial understanding will not allow genuine progression: pupils may struggle at key points of transition (such as between primary and secondary school), build up serious misconceptions, and/or have significant difficulties in understanding higher-order content.

Pupils should be able to describe associated processes and key characteristics in common language, but they should also be familiar with, and use, technical terminology accurately and precisely. They should build up an extended specialist vocabulary. They should also apply their mathematical knowledge to their understanding of science, including collecting, presenting and analysing data. The social and economic implications of science are important but, generally, they are taught most appropriately within the wider school curriculum: teachers will wish to use different contexts to maximise their pupils' engagement with and motivation to study science.

The nature, processes and methods of science

'Working scientifically' specifies the understanding of the nature, processes and methods of science for each year group. It should not be taught as a separate strand.

The notes and guidance give examples of how 'working scientifically' might be embedded within the content of biology, chemistry and physics, focusing on the key features of scientific enquiry, so that pupils learn to use a variety of approaches to answer relevant scientific questions. These types of scientific enquiry should include: observing over time; pattern seeking; identifying, classifying and grouping; comparative and fair testing (controlled investigations); and researching using secondary sources. Pupils should seek answers to questions through collecting, analysing and presenting data. 'Working scientifically' will be developed further at key stages 3 and 4, once pupils have built up sufficient understanding of science to engage meaningfully in more sophisticated discussion of experimental design and control.

Spoken language

The national curriculum for science reflects the importance of spoken language in pupils' development across the whole curriculum – cognitively, socially and linguistically. The quality and variety of language that pupils hear and speak are key factors in developing their scientific vocabulary and articulating scientific concepts clearly and precisely. They must be assisted in making their thinking clear, both to themselves and others, and teachers should ensure that pupils build secure foundations by using discussion to probe and remedy their misconceptions.

School curriculum

The programmes of study for science are set out year-by-year for key stages 1 and 2. Schools are, however, only required to teach the relevant programme of study by the end of the key stage. Within each key stage, schools therefore have the flexibility to introduce content earlier or later than set out in the programme of study. In addition, schools can introduce key stage content during an earlier key stage if appropriate. All schools are also required to set out their school curriculum for science on a year-by-year basis and make this information available online.

Attainment targets

By the end of each key stage, pupils are expected to know, apply and understand the matters, skills and processes specified in the relevant programme of study.

Schools are not required by law to teach the content indicated as being 'non-statutory'.

Key stage 1

The principal focus of science teaching in key stage 1 is to enable pupils to experience and observe phenomena, looking more closely at the natural and humanly-constructed world around them. They should be encouraged to be curious and ask questions about what they notice. They should be helped to develop their understanding of scientific ideas by using different types of scientific enquiry to answer their own questions, including observing

changes over a period of time, noticing patterns, grouping and classifying things, carrying out simple comparative tests, and finding things out using secondary sources of information. They should begin to use simple scientific language to talk about what they have found out and communicate their ideas to a range of audiences in a variety of ways. Most of the learning about science should be done through the use of first-hand practical experiences, but there should also be some use of appropriate secondary sources, such as books, photographs and videos.

'Working scientifically' is described separately in the programme of study, but must **always** be taught through and clearly related to the teaching of substantive science content in the programme of study. Throughout the notes and guidance, examples show how scientific methods and skills might be linked to specific elements of the content.

Pupils should read and spell scientific vocabulary at a level consistent with their increasing word reading and spelling knowledge at key stage 1.

Key stage 1 programme of study – years 1 and 2

Working scientifically

Statutory requirements

During years 1 and 2, pupils should be taught to use the following practical scientific methods, processes and skills through the teaching of the programme of study content:

- asking simple questions and recognising that they can be answered in different ways
- observing closely, using simple equipment
- performing simple tests
- identifying and classifying
- using their observations and ideas to suggest answers to questions
- gathering and recording data to help in answering questions.

Notes and guidance (non-statutory)

Pupils in years 1 and 2 should explore the world around them and raise their own questions. They should experience different types of scientific enquiries, including practical activities, and begin to recognise ways in which they might answer scientific questions. They should use simple features to compare objects, materials and living things and, with help, decide how to sort and group them, observe changes over time, and, with guidance, they should begin to notice patterns and relationships. They should ask people questions and use simple secondary sources to find answers. They should use simple measurements and equipment (for example, hand lenses, egg timers) to gather data, carry out simple tests, record simple data, and talk about what they have found out and how they found it out. With help, they should record and communicate their findings in a range of ways and begin to use simple scientific language.

These opportunities for working scientifically should be provided across years 1 and 2 so that the expectations in the programme of study can be met by the end of year 2. Pupils are not expected to cover each aspect for every area of study.

Year 1 programme of study

Plants

Statutory requirements

Pupils should be taught to:

- identify and name a variety of common wild and garden plants, including deciduous and evergreen trees
- identify and describe the basic structure of a variety of common flowering plants, including trees.

Notes and guidance (non-statutory)

Pupils should use the local environment throughout the year to explore and answer questions about plants growing in their habitat. Where possible, they should observe the growth of flowers and vegetables that they have planted.

They should become familiar with common names of flowers, examples of deciduous and evergreen trees, and plant structures (including leaves, flowers (blossom), petals, fruit, roots, bulb, seed, trunk, branches, stem).

Pupils might work scientifically by: observing closely, perhaps using magnifying glasses, and comparing and contrasting familiar plants; describing how they were able to identify and group them, and drawing diagrams showing the parts of different plants including trees. Pupils might keep records of how plants have changed over time, for example the leaves falling off trees and buds opening; and compare and contrast what they have found out about different plants.

Animals, including humans

Statutory requirements

Pupils should be taught to:

- identify and name a variety of common animals including fish, amphibians, reptiles, birds and mammals
- identify and name a variety of common animals that are carnivores, herbivores and omnivores
- describe and compare the structure of a variety of common animals (fish, amphibians, reptiles, birds and mammals, including pets)
- identify, name, draw and label the basic parts of the human body and say which part of the body is associated with each sense.

Notes and guidance (non-statutory)

Pupils should use the local environment throughout the year to explore and answer questions about animals in their habitat. They should understand how to take care of

animals taken from their local environment and the need to return them safely after study. Pupils should become familiar with the common names of some fish, amphibians, reptiles, birds and mammals, including those that are kept as pets.

Pupils should have plenty of opportunities to learn the names of the main body parts (including head, neck, arms, elbows, legs, knees, face, ears, eyes, hair, mouth, teeth) through games, actions, songs and rhymes.

Pupils might work scientifically by: using their observations to compare and contrast animals at first hand or through videos and photographs, describing how they identify and group them; grouping animals according to what they eat; and using their senses to compare different textures, sounds and smells.

Everyday materials

Statutory requirements

Pupils should be taught to:

- distinguish between an object and the material from which it is made
- identify and name a variety of everyday materials, including wood, plastic, glass, metal, water, and rock
- describe the simple physical properties of a variety of everyday materials
- compare and group together a variety of everyday materials on the basis of their simple physical properties.

Notes and guidance (non-statutory)

Pupils should explore, name, discuss and raise and answer questions about everyday materials so that they become familiar with the names of materials and properties such as: hard/soft; stretchy/stiff; shiny/dull; rough/smooth; bendy/not bendy; waterproof/not waterproof; absorbent/not absorbent; opaque/transparent. Pupils should explore and experiment with a wide variety of materials, not only those listed in the programme of study, but including for example: brick, paper, fabrics, elastic, foil.

Pupils might work scientifically by: performing simple tests to explore questions, for example: 'What is the best material for an umbrella? . . . for lining a dog basket? . . . for curtains? . . . for a bookshelf? . . . for a gymnast's leotard?'

Seasonal changes

Statutory requirements

Pupils should be taught to:

- observe changes across the four seasons
- observe and describe weather associated with the seasons and how day length varies.

Notes and guidance (non-statutory)

Pupils should observe and talk about changes in the weather and the seasons.
   Note: Pupils should be warned that it is not safe to look directly at the Sun, even when wearing dark glasses.
   Pupils might work scientifically by: making tables and charts about the weather; and making displays of what happens in the world around them, including day length, as the seasons change.

Year 2 programme of study

Living things and their habitats

Statutory requirements

Pupils should be taught to:

- explore and compare the differences between things that are living, dead, and things that have never been alive
- identify that most living things live in habitats to which they are suited and describe how different habitats provide for the basic needs of different kinds of animals and plants, and how they depend on each other
- identify and name a variety of plants and animals in their habitats, including micro-habitats
- describe how animals obtain their food from plants and other animals, using the idea of a simple food chain, and identify and name different sources of food.

Notes and guidance (non-statutory)

Pupils should be introduced to the idea that all living things have certain characteristics that are essential for keeping them alive and healthy. They should raise and answer questions that help them to become familiar with the life processes that are common to all living things. Pupils should be introduced to the terms 'habitat' (a natural environment or home of a variety of plants and animals) and 'micro-habitat' (a very small habitat, for example for woodlice under stones, logs or leaf litter). They should raise and answer questions about the local environment that help them to identify and study a variety of plants and animals within their habitat and observe how living things depend on each other, for example, plants serving as a source of food and shelter for animals. Pupils should compare animals in familiar habitats with animals found in less familiar habitats, for example, on the seashore, in woodland, in the ocean, in the rainforest.
   Pupils might work scientifically by: sorting and classifying things according to whether they are living, dead or were never alive, and recording their findings using charts. They should describe how they decided where to place things, exploring questions for example: 'Is a flame alive? Is a deciduous tree dead in winter?' and talk about ways of answering their questions. They could construct a simple food chain that includes humans (e.g. grass, cow, human). They could describe the conditions in different habitats and micro-habitats (under log, on stony path, under bushes) and find out how the conditions affect the number and type(s) of plants and animals that live there.

Plants

Statutory requirements

Pupils should be taught to:

- observe and describe how seeds and bulbs grow into mature plants
- find out and describe how plants need water, light and a suitable temperature to grow and stay healthy.

Notes and guidance (non-statutory)

Pupils should use the local environment throughout the year to observe how different plants grow. Pupils should be introduced to the requirements of plants for germination, growth and survival, as well as to the processes of reproduction and growth in plants.

Note: Seeds and bulbs need water to grow but most do not need light; seeds and bulbs have a store of food inside them.

Pupils might work scientifically by: observing and recording, with some accuracy, the growth of a variety of plants as they change over time from a seed or bulb, or observing similar plants at different stages of growth; setting up a comparative test to show that plants need light and water to stay healthy.

Animals, including humans

Statutory requirements

Pupils should be taught to:

- notice that animals, including humans, have offspring which grow into adults
- find out about and describe the basic needs of animals, including humans, for survival (water, food and air)
- describe the importance for humans of exercise, eating the right amounts of different types of food, and hygiene.

Notes and guidance (non-statutory)

Pupils should be introduced to the basic needs of animals for survival, as well as the importance of exercise and nutrition for humans. They should also be introduced to the processes of reproduction and growth in animals. The focus at this stage should be on questions that help pupils to recognise growth; they should not be expected to understand how reproduction occurs.

The following examples might be used: egg, chick, chicken; egg, caterpillar, pupa, butterfly; spawn, tadpole, frog; lamb, sheep. Growing into adults can include reference to baby, toddler, child, teenager, adult.

Pupils might work scientifically by: observing, through video or first-hand observation and measurement, how different animals, including humans, grow; asking questions about what things animals need for survival and what humans need to stay healthy; and suggesting ways to find answers to their questions.

Uses of everyday materials

Statutory requirements

Pupils should be taught to:

- identify and compare the suitability of a variety of everyday materials, including wood, metal, plastic, glass, brick, rock, paper and cardboard for particular uses
- find out how the shapes of solid objects made from some materials can be changed by squashing, bending, twisting and stretching.

Notes and guidance (non-statutory)

Pupils should identify and discuss the uses of different everyday materials so that they become familiar with how some materials are used for more than one thing (metal can be used for coins, cans, cars and table legs; wood can be used for matches, floors, and telegraph poles) or different materials are used for the same thing (spoons can be made from plastic, wood, metal, but not normally from glass). They should think about the properties of materials that make them suitable or unsuitable for particular purposes and they should be encouraged to think about unusual and creative uses for everyday materials. Pupils might find out about people who have developed useful new materials, for example John Dunlop, Charles Macintosh or John McAdam.

Pupils might work scientifically by: comparing the uses of everyday materials in and around the school with materials found in other places (at home, the journey to school, on visits, and in stories, rhymes and songs); observing closely, identifying and classifying the uses of different materials, and recording their observations.

Lower key stage 2 – years 3 and 4

The principal focus of science teaching in lower key stage 2 is to enable pupils to broaden their scientific view of the world around them. They should do this through exploring, talking about, testing and developing ideas about everyday phenomena and the relationships between living things and familiar environments, and by beginning to develop their ideas about functions, relationships and interactions. They should ask their own questions about what they observe and make some decisions about which types of scientific enquiry are likely to be the best ways of answering them, including observing changes over time, noticing patterns, grouping and classifying things, carrying out simple comparative and fair tests and finding things out using secondary sources of information. They should draw simple conclusions and use some scientific language, first, to talk about and, later, to write about what they have found out.

'Working scientifically' is described separately at the beginning of the programme of study, but must **always** be taught through and clearly related to substantive science content in the programme of study. Throughout the notes and guidance, examples show how scientific methods and skills might be linked to specific elements of the content.

Pupils should read and spell scientific vocabulary correctly and with confidence, using their growing word reading and spelling knowledge.

Lower key stage 2 programme of study

Working scientifically

Statutory requirements

During years 3 and 4, pupils should be taught to use the following practical scientific methods, processes and skills through the teaching of the programme of study content:

- asking relevant questions and using different types of scientific enquiries to answer them
- setting up simple practical enquiries, comparative and fair tests
- making systematic and careful observations and, where appropriate, taking accurate measurements using standard units, using a range of equipment, including thermometers and data loggers
- gathering, recording, classifying and presenting data in a variety of ways to help in answering questions
- recording findings using simple scientific language, drawings, labelled diagrams, keys, bar charts, and tables
- reporting on findings from enquiries, including oral and written explanations, displays or presentations of results and conclusions
- using results to draw simple conclusions, make predictions for new values, suggest improvements and raise further questions
- identifying differences, similarities or changes related to simple scientific ideas and processes
- using straightforward scientific evidence to answer questions or to support their findings.

Notes and guidance (non-statutory)

Pupils in years 3 and 4 should be given a range of scientific experiences to enable them to raise their own questions about the world around them. They should start to make their own decisions about the most appropriate type of scientific enquiry they might use to answer questions; recognise when a simple fair test is necessary and help to decide how to set it up; talk about criteria for grouping, sorting and classifying; and use simple keys. They should begin to look for naturally occurring patterns and relationships and decide what data to collect to identify them. They should help to make decisions about what observations to make, how long to make them for and the type of simple equipment that might be used.

They should learn how to use new equipment, such as data loggers, appropriately. They should collect data from their own observations and measurements, using notes, simple tables and standard units, and help to make decisions about how to record and analyse this data. With help, pupils should look for changes, patterns, similarities and differences in their data in order to draw simple conclusions and answer questions. With support, they should identify new questions arising from the data, making predictions for new values within or beyond the data they have collected and finding ways of improving what they have already done. They should also recognise when and how secondary sources might help them to answer questions that cannot be answered through practical investigations. Pupils should use relevant scientific language to discuss their ideas and communicate their findings in ways that are appropriate for different audiences.

These opportunities for working scientifically should be provided across years 3 and 4 so that the expectations in the programme of study can be met by the end of year 4. Pupils are not expected to cover each aspect for every area of study.

Year 3 programme of study

Plants

Statutory requirements

Pupils should be taught to:

- identify and describe the functions of different parts of flowering plants: roots, stem/trunk, leaves and flowers
- explore the requirements of plants for life and growth (air, light, water, nutrients from soil, and room to grow) and how they vary from plant to plant
- investigate the way in which water is transported within plants
- explore the part that flowers play in the life cycle of flowering plants, including pollination, seed formation and seed dispersal.

Notes and guidance (non-statutory)

Pupils should be introduced to the relationship between structure and function: the idea that every part has a job to do. They should explore questions that focus on the role of the roots and stem in nutrition and support, leaves for nutrition and flowers for reproduction.

Note: Pupils can be introduced to the idea that plants can make their own food, but at this stage they do not need to understand how this happens.

Pupils might work scientifically by: comparing the effect of different factors on plant growth, for example, the amount of light, the amount of fertiliser; discovering how seeds are formed by observing the different stages of plant life cycles over a period of time; looking for patterns in the structure of fruits that relate to how the seeds are dispersed. They might observe how water is transported in plants, for example, by putting cut, white carnations into coloured water and observing how water travels up the stem to the flowers.

Animals, including humans

Statutory requirements

Pupils should be taught to:

- identify that animals, including humans, need the right types and amount of nutrition, and that they cannot make their own food; they get nutrition from what they eat
- identify that humans and some other animals have skeletons and muscles for support, protection and movement.

Notes and guidance (non-statutory)

Pupils should continue to learn about the importance of nutrition and should be introduced to the main body parts associated with the skeleton and muscles, finding out how different parts of the body have special functions.

Pupils might work scientifically by: identifying and grouping animals with and without skeletons and observing and comparing their movement; exploring ideas about what would happen if humans did not have skeletons. They might compare and contrast the diets of different animals (including their pets) and decide ways of grouping them according to what they eat. They might research different food groups and how they keep us healthy and design meals based on what they find out.

Rocks

Statutory requirements

Pupils should be taught to:

- compare and group together different kinds of rocks on the basis of their appearance and simple physical properties
- describe in simple terms how fossils are formed when things that have lived are trapped within rock
- recognise that soils are made from rocks and organic matter.

Notes and guidance (non-statutory)

Linked with work in geography, pupils should explore different kinds of rocks and soils, including those in the local environment.

Pupils might work scientifically by: observing rocks, including those used in buildings and gravestones, and exploring how and why they might have changed over time; using a hand lens or microscope to help them to identify and classify rocks according to whether they have grains or crystals, and whether they have fossils in them. Pupils might research and discuss the different kinds of living things whose fossils are found in sedimentary rock and explore how fossils are formed. Pupils could explore different soils and identify similarities and differences between them and investigate what happens when rocks are rubbed together or what changes occur when they are in water. They can raise and answer questions about the way soils are formed.

Light

Statutory requirements

Pupils should be taught to:

- recognise that they need light in order to see things and that dark is the absence of light
- notice that light is reflected from surfaces
- recognise that light from the sun can be dangerous and that there are ways to protect their eyes
- recognise that shadows are formed when the light from a light source is blocked by a solid object
- find patterns in the way that the size of shadows change.

Notes and guidance (non-statutory)

Pupils should explore what happens when light reflects off a mirror or other reflective surfaces, including playing mirror games to help them to answer questions about how light behaves. They should think about why it is important to protect their eyes from bright lights. They should look for, and measure, shadows, and find out how they are formed and what might cause the shadows to change.

Note: Pupils should be warned that it is not safe to look directly at the Sun, even when wearing dark glasses.

Pupils might work scientifically by: looking for patterns in what happens to shadows when the light source moves or the distance between the light source and the object changes.

Forces and magnets

Statutory requirements

Pupils should be taught to:

- compare how things move on different surfaces
- notice that some forces need contact between two objects, but magnetic forces can act at a distance
- observe how magnets attract or repel each other and attract some materials and not others
- compare and group together a variety of everyday materials on the basis of whether they are attracted to a magnet, and identify some magnetic materials
- describe magnets as having two poles
- predict whether two magnets will attract or repel each other, depending on which poles are facing.

Notes and guidance (non-statutory)

Pupils should observe that magnetic forces can act without direct contact, unlike most forces, where direct contact is necessary (for example, opening a door, pushing a swing). They should explore the behaviour and everyday uses of different magnets (for example, bar, ring, button and horseshoe).

Pupils might work scientifically by: comparing how different things move and grouping them; raising questions and carrying out tests to find out how far things move on different surfaces and gathering and recording data to find answers to their questions; exploring the strengths of different magnets and finding a fair way to compare them; sorting materials into those that are magnetic and those that are not; looking for patterns in the way that magnets behave in relation to each other and what might affect this, for example, the strength of the magnet or which pole faces another; identifying how these properties make magnets useful in everyday items and suggesting creative uses for different magnets.

Year 4 programme of study

Living things and their habitats

Statutory requirements

Pupils should be taught to:

- recognise that living things can be grouped in a variety of ways
- explore and use classification keys to help group, identify and name a variety of living things in their local and wider environment
- recognise that environments can change and that this can sometimes pose dangers to living things.

Notes and guidance (non-statutory)

Pupils should use the local environment throughout the year to raise and answer questions that help them to identify and study plants and animals in their habitat. They should identify how the habitat changes throughout the year. Pupils should explore possible ways of grouping a wide selection of living things that include animals and flowering plants and non-flowering plants. Pupils could begin to put vertebrate animals into groups such as fish, amphibians, reptiles, birds, and mammals; and invertebrates into snails and slugs, worms, spiders, and insects.

Note: Plants can be grouped into categories such as flowering plants (including grasses) and non-flowering plants, such as ferns and mosses.

Pupils should explore examples of human impact (both positive and negative) on environments, for example, the positive effects of nature reserves, ecologically planned parks, or garden ponds, and the negative effects of population and development, litter or deforestation.

Pupils might work scientifically by: using and making simple guides or keys to explore and identify local plants and animals; making a guide to local living things; raising and answering questions based on their observations of animals and what they have found out about other animals that they have researched.

Animals, including humans

Statutory requirements

Pupils should be taught to:

- describe the simple functions of the basic parts of the digestive system in humans
- identify the different types of teeth in humans and their simple functions
- construct and interpret a variety of food chains, identifying producers, predators and prey.

Notes and guidance (non-statutory)

Pupils should be introduced to the main body parts associated with the digestive system, for example, mouth, tongue, teeth, oesophagus, stomach and small and large intestine and explore questions that help them to understand their special functions.

Pupils might work scientifically by: comparing the teeth of carnivores and herbivores, and suggesting reasons for differences; finding out what damages teeth and how to look after them. They might draw and discuss their ideas about the digestive system and compare them with models or images.

States of matter

Statutory requirements

Pupils should be taught to:

- compare and group materials together, according to whether they are solids, liquids or gases
- observe that some materials change state when they are heated or cooled, and measure or research the temperature at which this happens in degrees Celsius (°C)
- identify the part played by evaporation and condensation in the water cycle and associate the rate of evaporation with temperature.

Notes and guidance (non-statutory)

Pupils should explore a variety of everyday materials and develop simple descriptions of the states of matter (solids hold their shape; liquids form a pool not a pile; gases escape from an unsealed container). Pupils should observe water as a solid, a liquid and a gas and should note the changes to water when it is heated or cooled.

Note: Teachers should avoid using materials where heating is associated with chemical change, for example, through baking or burning.

Pupils might work scientifically by: grouping and classifying a variety of different materials; exploring the effect of temperature on substances such as chocolate, butter, cream (for example, to make food such as chocolate crispy cakes and ice-cream for a party). They could research the temperature at which materials change state, for example, when iron melts or when oxygen condenses into a liquid. They might observe and record evaporation over a period of time, for example, a puddle in the playground or washing on a line, and investigate the effect of temperature on washing drying or snowmen melting.

Sound

Statutory requirements

Pupils should be taught to:

- identify how sounds are made, associating some of them with something vibrating
- recognise that vibrations from sounds travel through a medium to the ear

- find patterns between the pitch of a sound and features of the object that produced it
- find patterns between the volume of a sound and the strength of the vibrations that produced it
- recognise that sounds get fainter as the distance from the sound source increases.

Notes and guidance (non-statutory)

Pupils should explore and identify the way sound is made through vibration in a range of different musical instruments from around the world; and find out how the pitch and volume of sounds can be changed in a variety of ways.

Pupils might work scientifically by: finding patterns in the sounds that are made by different objects such as saucepan lids of different sizes or elastic bands of different thicknesses. They might make earmuffs from a variety of different materials to investigate which provides the best insulation against sound. They could make and play their own instruments by using what they have found out about pitch and volume.

Electricity

Statutory requirements

Pupils should be taught to:

- identify common appliances that run on electricity
- construct a simple series electrical circuit, identifying and naming its basic parts, including cells, wires, bulbs, switches and buzzers
- identify whether or not a lamp will light in a simple series circuit, based on whether or not the lamp is part of a complete loop with a battery
- recognise that a switch opens and closes a circuit and associate this with whether or not a lamp lights in a simple series circuit
- recognise some common conductors and insulators, and associate metals with being good conductors.

Notes and guidance (non-statutory)

Pupils should construct simple series circuits, trying different components, for example, bulbs, buzzers and motors, and including switches, and use their circuits to create simple devices. Pupils should draw the circuit as a pictorial representation, not necessarily using conventional circuit symbols at this stage; these will be introduced in year 6.

Note: Pupils might use the terms current and voltage, but these should not be introduced or defined formally at this stage. Pupils should be taught about precautions for working safely with electricity.

Pupils might work scientifically by: observing patterns, for example, that bulbs get brighter if more cells are added, that metals tend to be conductors of electricity, and that some materials can and some cannot be used to connect across a gap in a circuit.

Upper key stage 2 – years 5 and 6

The principal focus of science teaching in upper key stage 2 is to enable pupils to develop a deeper understanding of a wide range of scientific ideas. They should do this through exploring and talking about their ideas; asking their own questions about scientific phenomena; and analysing functions, relationships and interactions more systematically. At upper key stage 2, they should encounter more abstract ideas and begin to recognise how these ideas help them to understand and predict how the world operates. They should also begin to recognise that scientific ideas change and develop over time. They should select the most appropriate ways to answer science questions using different types of scientific enquiry, including observing changes over different periods of time, noticing patterns, grouping and classifying things, carrying out comparative and fair tests and finding things out using a wide range of secondary sources of information. Pupils should draw conclusions based on their data and observations, use evidence to justify their ideas, and use their scientific knowledge and understanding to explain their findings.

'Working and thinking scientifically' is described separately at the beginning of the programme of study, but must **always** be taught through and clearly related to substantive science content in the programme of study. Throughout the notes and guidance, examples show how scientific methods and skills might be linked to specific elements of the content.

Pupils should read, spell and pronounce scientific vocabulary correctly.

Upper key stage 2 programme of study

Working scientifically

Statutory requirements

During years 5 and 6, pupils should be taught to use the following practical scientific methods, processes and skills through the teaching of the programme of study content:

- planning different types of scientific enquiries to answer questions, including recognising and controlling variables where necessary
- taking measurements, using a range of scientific equipment, with increasing accuracy and precision, taking repeat readings when appropriate
- recording data and results of increasing complexity using scientific diagrams and labels, classification keys, tables, scatter graphs, bar and line graphs
- using test results to make predictions to set up further comparative and fair tests
- reporting and presenting findings from enquiries, including conclusions, causal relationships and explanations of and degree of trust in results, in oral and written forms such as displays and other presentations
- identifying scientific evidence that has been used to support or refute ideas or arguments.

Notes and guidance (non-statutory)

Pupils in years 5 and 6 should use their science experiences to: explore ideas and raise different kinds of questions; select and plan the most appropriate type of scientific enquiry to use to answer scientific questions; recognise when and how to set up

comparative and fair tests and explain which variables need to be controlled and why. They should use and develop keys and other information records to identify, classify and describe living things and materials, and identify patterns that might be found in the natural environment. They should make their own decisions about what observations to make, what measurements to use and how long to make them for, and whether to repeat them; choose the most appropriate equipment to make measurements and explain how to use it accurately. They should decide how to record data from a choice of familiar approaches; look for different causal relationships in their data and identify evidence that refutes or supports their ideas. They should use their results to identify when further tests and observations might be needed; recognise which secondary sources will be most useful to research their ideas and begin to separate opinion from fact. They should use relevant scientific language and illustrations to discuss, communicate and justify their scientific ideas and should talk about how scientific ideas have developed over time.

These opportunities for working scientifically should be provided across years 5 and 6 so that the expectations in the programme of study can be met by the end of year 6. Pupils are not expected to cover each aspect for every area of study.

Year 5 programme of study

Living things and their habitats

Statutory requirements

Pupils should be taught to:

- describe the differences in the life cycles of a mammal, an amphibian, an insect and a bird
- describe the life process of reproduction in some plants and animals.

Notes and guidance (non-statutory)

Pupils should study and raise questions about their local environment throughout the year. They should observe life-cycle changes in a variety of living things, for example, plants in the vegetable garden or flower border, and animals in the local environment. They should find out about the work of naturalists and animal behaviourists, for example, David Attenborough and Jane Goodall.

Pupils should find out about different types of reproduction, including sexual and asexual reproduction in plants, and sexual reproduction in animals.

Pupils might work scientifically by: observing and comparing the life cycles of plants and animals in their local environment with other plants and animals around the world (in the rainforest, in the oceans, in desert areas and in prehistoric times), asking pertinent questions and suggesting reasons for similarities and differences. They might try to grow new plants from different parts of the parent plant, for example, seeds, stem and root cuttings, tubers, bulbs. They might observe changes in an animal over a period of time (for example, by hatching and rearing chicks), comparing how different animals reproduce and grow.

Animals, including humans

Statutory requirements

Pupils should be taught to:

- describe the changes as humans develop to old age.

Notes and guidance (non-statutory)

Pupils should draw a timeline to indicate stages in the growth and development of humans. They should learn about the changes experienced in puberty.

Pupils could work scientifically by researching the gestation periods of other animals and comparing them with humans; by finding out and recording the length and mass of a baby as it grows.

Properties and changes of materials

Statutory requirements

Pupils should be taught to:

- compare and group together everyday materials on the basis of their properties, including their hardness, solubility, transparency, conductivity (electrical and thermal), and response to magnets
- know that some materials will dissolve in liquid to form a solution, and describe how to recover a substance from a solution
- use knowledge of solids, liquids and gases to decide how mixtures might be separated, including through filtering, sieving and evaporating
- give reasons, based on evidence from comparative and fair tests, for the particular uses of everyday materials, including metals, wood and plastic
- demonstrate that dissolving, mixing and changes of state are reversible changes
- explain that some changes result in the formation of new materials, and that this kind of change is not usually reversible, including changes associated with burning and the action of acid on bicarbonate of soda.

Notes and guidance (non-statutory)

Pupils should build a more systematic understanding of materials by exploring and comparing the properties of a broad range of materials, including relating these to what they learnt about magnetism in year 3 and about electricity in year 4. They should explore reversible changes, including, evaporating, filtering, sieving, melting and dissolving, recognising that melting and dissolving are different processes. Pupils should explore changes that are difficult to reverse, for example, burning, rusting and other reactions, for example, vinegar with bicarbonate of soda. They should find out about

how chemists create new materials, for example, Spencer Silver, who invented the glue for sticky notes or Ruth Benerito, who invented wrinkle-free cotton.

Note: Pupils are not required to make quantitative measurements about conductivity and insulation at this stage. It is sufficient for them to observe that some conductors will produce a brighter bulb in a circuit than others and that some materials will feel hotter than others when a heat source is placed against them. Safety guidelines should be followed when burning materials.

Pupils might work scientifically by: carrying out tests to answer questions, for example, 'Which materials would be the most effective for making a warm jacket, for wrapping ice cream to stop it melting, or for making blackout curtains?' They might compare materials in order to make a switch in a circuit. They could observe and compare the changes that take place, for example, when burning different materials or baking bread or cakes. They might research and discuss how chemical changes have an impact on our lives, for example, cooking, and discuss the creative use of new materials such as polymers, super-sticky and super-thin materials.

Earth and space

Statutory requirements

Pupils should be taught to:

- describe the movement of the Earth, and other planets, relative to the Sun in the solar system
- describe the movement of the Moon relative to the Earth
- describe the Sun, Earth and Moon as approximately spherical bodies
- use the idea of the Earth's rotation to explain day and night and the apparent movement of the sun across the sky.

Notes and guidance (non-statutory)

Pupils should be introduced to a model of the Sun and Earth that enables them to explain day and night. Pupils should learn that the Sun is a star at the centre of our solar system and that it has eight planets: Mercury, Venus, Earth, Mars, Jupiter, Saturn, Uranus and Neptune (Pluto was reclassified as a 'dwarf planet' in 2006). They should understand that a moon is a celestial body that orbits a planet (Earth has one moon; Jupiter has four large moons and numerous smaller ones).

Note: Pupils should be warned that it is not safe to look directly at the Sun, even when wearing dark glasses.

Pupils should find out about the way that ideas about the solar system have developed, understanding how the geocentric model of the solar system gave way to the heliocentric model by considering the work of scientists such as Ptolemy, Alhazen and Copernicus.

Pupils might work scientifically by: comparing the time of day at different places on the Earth through internet links and direct communication; creating simple models of the solar system; constructing simple shadow clocks and sundials, calibrated to show midday and the start and end of the school day; finding out why some people think that structures such as Stonehenge might have been used as astronomical clocks.

Forces

Statutory requirements

Pupils should be taught to:

- explain that unsupported objects fall towards the Earth because of the force of gravity acting between the Earth and the falling object
- identify the effects of air resistance, water resistance and friction, that act between moving surfaces
- recognise that some mechanisms, including levers, pulleys and gears, allow a smaller force to have a greater effect.

Notes and guidance (non-statutory)

Pupils should explore falling objects and raise questions about the effects of air resistance. They should explore the effects of air resistance by observing how different objects such as parachutes and sycamore seeds fall. They should experience forces that make things begin to move, get faster or slow down. Pupils should explore the effects of friction on movement and find out how it slows or stops moving objects, for example, by observing the effects of a brake on a bicycle wheel. Pupils should explore the effects of levers, pulleys and simple machines on movement. Pupils might find out how scientists, for example, Galileo Galilei and Isaac Newton helped to develop the theory of gravitation.

Pupils might work scientifically by: exploring falling paper cones or cup-cake cases, and designing and making a variety of parachutes and carrying out fair tests to determine which designs are the most effective. They might explore resistance in water by making and testing boats of different shapes. They might design and make products that use levers, pulleys, gears and/or springs and explore their effects.

Year 6 programme of study

Living things and their habitats

Statutory requirements

Pupils should be taught to:

- describe how living things are classified into broad groups according to common observable characteristics and based on similarities and differences, including micro-organisms, plants and animals
- give reasons for classifying plants and animals based on specific characteristics.

Notes and guidance (non-statutory)

Pupils should build on their learning about grouping living things in year 4 by looking at the classification system in more detail. They should be introduced to the idea that broad groupings, such as micro-organisms, plants and animals can be subdivided.

Through direct observations where possible, they should classify animals into commonly found invertebrates (such as insects, spiders, snails, worms) and vertebrates (fish, amphibians, reptiles, birds and mammals). They should discuss reasons why living things are placed in one group and not another.

Pupils might find out about the significance of the work of scientists such as Carl Linnaeus, a pioneer of classification.

Pupils might work scientifically by: using classification systems and keys to identify some animals and plants in the immediate environment. They could research unfamiliar animals and plants from a broad range of other habitats and decide where they belong in the classification system.

Animals including humans

Statutory requirements

Pupils should be taught to:

- identify and name the main parts of the human circulatory system, and describe the functions of the heart, blood vessels and blood
- recognise the impact of diet, exercise, drugs and lifestyle on the way their bodies function
- describe the ways in which nutrients and water are transported within animals, including humans.

Notes and guidance (non-statutory)

Pupils should build on their learning from years 3 and 4 about the main body parts and internal organs (skeletal, muscular and digestive system) to explore and answer questions that help them to understand how the circulatory system enables the body to function.

Pupils should learn how to keep their bodies healthy and how their bodies might be damaged – including how some drugs and other substances can be harmful to the human body.

Pupils might work scientifically by: exploring the work of scientists and scientific research about the relationship between diet, exercise, drugs, lifestyle and health.

Evolution and inheritance

Statutory requirements

Pupils should be taught to:

- recognise that living things have changed over time and that fossils provide information about living things that inhabited the Earth millions of years ago
- recognise that living things produce offspring of the same kind, but normally offspring vary and are not identical to their parents
- identify how animals and plants are adapted to suit their environment in different ways and that adaptation may lead to evolution.

Notes and guidance (non-statutory)

Building on what they learnt about fossils in the topic on rocks in year 3, pupils should find out more about how living things on earth have changed over time. They should be introduced to the idea that characteristics are passed from parents to their offspring, for instance by considering different breeds of dogs, and what happens when, for example, labradors are crossed with poodles. They should also appreciate that variation in offspring over time can make animals more or less able to survive in particular environments, for example, by exploring how giraffes' necks got longer, or the development of insulating fur on the arctic fox. Pupils might find out about the work of palaeontologists such as Mary Anning and about how Charles Darwin and Alfred Wallace developed their ideas on evolution.

Note: At this stage, pupils are not expected to understand how genes and chromosomes work.

Pupils might work scientifically by: observing and raising questions about local animals and how they are adapted to their environment; comparing how some living things are adapted to survive in extreme conditions, for example, cactuses, penguins and camels. They might analyse the advantages and disadvantages of specific adaptations, such as being on two feet rather than four, having a long or a short beak, having gills or lungs, tendrils on climbing plants, brightly coloured and scented flowers.

Light

Statutory requirements

Pupils should be taught to:

- recognise that light appears to travel in straight lines
- use the idea that light travels in straight lines to explain that objects are seen because they give out or reflect light into the eye
- explain that we see things because light travels from light sources to our eyes or from light sources to objects and then to our eyes
- use the idea that light travels in straight lines to explain why shadows have the same shape as the objects that cast them.

Notes and guidance (non-statutory)

Pupils should build on the work on light in year 3, exploring the way that light behaves, including light sources, reflection and shadows. They should talk about what happens and make predictions.

Pupils might work scientifically by: deciding where to place rear-view mirrors on cars; designing and making a periscope and using the idea that light appears to travel in straight lines to explain how it works. They might investigate the relationship between light sources, objects and shadows by using shadow puppets. They could extend their experience of light by looking a range of phenomena including rainbows, colours on soap bubbles, objects looking bent in water and coloured filters (they do not need to explain why these phenomena occur).

Electricity

Statutory requirements

Pupils should be taught to:

- associate the brightness of a lamp or the volume of a buzzer with the number and voltage of cells used in the circuit
- compare and give reasons for variations in how components function, including the brightness of bulbs, the loudness of buzzers and the on/off position of switches
- use recognised symbols when representing a simple circuit in a diagram.

Notes and guidance (non-statutory)

Building on their work in year 4, pupils should construct simple series circuits, to help them to answer questions about what happens when they try different components, for example, switches, bulbs, buzzers and motors. They should learn how to represent a simple circuit in a diagram using recognised symbols.

Note: Pupils are expected to learn only about series circuits, not parallel circuits. Pupils should be taught to take the necessary precautions for working safely with electricity.

Pupils might work scientifically by: systematically identifying the effect of changing one component at a time in a circuit; designing and making a set of traffic lights, a burglar alarm or some other useful circuit.

7 Art and design

Planning art and design in the national curriculum

Karen Hosack Janes

Art and design 1 Principles of planning

This section looks at the key factors that are specific to planning effective art and design lessons. It builds on the generic factors for planning found in Chapter 1 and should be read in conjunction with these ideas.

Art making and art appreciation

High-quality art and design lessons support pupils in both their art making *and* in their art appreciation. First, your planning will need to give pupils opportunities to be taught a range of artistic skills, including drawing, painting and sculptural modelling, showing them how to follow through the design process of generating ideas, researching, presenting and evaluating their work. Second, as an integral part to their art and design education, you will need to introduce pupils to a variety of work by artists, crafts people and designers from our own time and the past, and from their own and different cultures. It is only when art making and art appreciation are taught as one and the same that pupils will draw links between their own work and that of others, and see clearly how, by creating art, we can all partake in a practice that connects people across time, place and cultures.

Relevance

Art and design education focuses on the visual arts. The term 'visual art forms' is used to define the different types of visual art. This includes: drawing, painting, sculpture, printmaking, photography and craft (also known as the decorative arts – ceramics, textiles, jewellery-making, glassmaking, papermaking, stonemasonry, woodwork and metalwork), and design (including architecture, interior design, graphic design and fashion design). Jobs involving these visual art forms, together with those in TV, radio and software designing, are known as the creative industries. This sector makes up over five per cent of the UK economy, and is rapidly growing.

Children first start to explore the world around them using their eyes. Therefore, the visual arts are particularly accessible for children to learn from. Their visual development begins shortly after birth, when they initially simply see contrasting tones, and then, as they mature, they begin to recognise similarities and differences between the things they observe. Later, children start to communicate these visual experiences in their mark and model making, for example with crayons and dough. It is through this play-based learning that children build their knowledge and express what they have learnt. Their art and design education at school should be an extension of this early learning, with experiences – and opportunities to respond to these experiences – becoming increasingly challenging.

Creativity

Art and design is synonymous with creativity because the design process of generating ideas, researching, presenting and evaluating requires teaching approaches that promote experimentation, sensitivity and inquisitiveness – qualities that the pre-eminent educational theorist Dewey (1997) described as essential for effective learning to take place. When pupils are given opportunities to work in this way they are more likely to make connections with further experiences they have, therefore ensuring progression in learning. It is a principle that Dewey called the experiential continuum, more widely known today as experiential learning.

Creativity, of course, is not exclusively the domain of art and design. The skills that pupils develop in art and design lessons can be used across the curriculum, which makes art and design particularly appropriate to use alongside teaching other subject areas. For example, observational drawing can be taught by studying plant specimens in a science project (also perhaps introducing pupils to the scientific studies of plants made during the Renaissance by Leonardo da Vinci), or a design technology and literacy project could have a painting of a local building of interest as a central stimulus (the Your Paintings online database is an invaluable resource for finding such works of art), or historical investigations can be prompted from first looking at objects like the Bayeux Tapestry or a commemorative piece of jewellery.

The learning environment and resources

Most art and design lessons will take place in your classroom. You will need to arrange it in such a way as to allow pupils to create their work and to dry, store and display it. Also, fundamental to high-quality art and design lessons is the use of good quality materials. Pupils will need to be shown how to take care of these.

Where possible, aim to expose pupils to original works of art. This might mean, for example, a trip to a local park to see a war memorial or to a museum or gallery. As Deasy (2005), director of the US Art Education Partnership, eloquently explains: *If we want to understand the values, morals, philosophies, aesthetics, and qualities of life in an historical period or geographical region (including our own), we study the arts of that time and place* (page vi). This is why museums and galleries exist. The impact on pupils of being in a space that is specifically designated to celebrate 'the highest forms of human creativity' (the phrase used in the national curriculum purpose of study) should not be underestimated.

Large museums and galleries have websites and education officers that can guide you in using their collections to deliver the national curriculum. Online digital images of collections can be sourced through such websites. In addition, it is worth investing in large physical reproductions to use as central visual stimuli in the classroom. These can be returned to during a project to ensure that learning is focused.

Vocabulary

There are some key words that your pupils need to be taught to enable them to engage with their own and others' art, craft and design. The national curriculum only stipulates what constitutes very basic subject knowledge for the visual arts; therefore, you will need to extend this.

Pupils should build an understanding of each visual art form through being introduced to a range of examples from different times and cultures. No examples of artists, craft people and designers are given in the national curriculum, although the word 'great' is used. This allows for lots of flexibility when it comes to your planning. Note that the word 'great' is very subjective: what one person thinks of as 'great', another might not. This debate, in itself, is educationally valuable to have with pupils.

The phase 'thinking critically' is used in the purpose of study, but not specified in these terms until key stage 3. However, at key stage 1 pupils are required to be taught to describe 'the differences and similarities between the different practices and disciplines'. Recognising and discussing these differences and similarities are the first steps in thinking critically, as is comparing their own practice in making artwork to that of others.

Pupils need to know that drawing is central to art and design. First-hand observational drawing is when artists draw what is in front of them. This is a discipline that is practised by all artists, whether it is in front of, for example, a landscape, or cityscape, an object (such as a vase of flowers) or a figure (known as a life model). You will need to be confident in your own first-hand observational drawing ability before teaching your class. The OFSTED report *Making a Mark: Art, Craft and Design 2008–11* (OFSTED, 2012) highlights teachers' lack of confidence in drawing as a barrier to pupils making progress in art and design. Techniques such as 'bug drawing' (tracking an imaginary bug crawling around an object and recording its path with pencil on paper) will help you if this is not your area of expertise. The knack is not to take your eyes off the subject that you are drawing. (The Campaign for Drawing has useful web resources.)

The terms 'form', 'tone' and 'texture' are called 'formal elements'.

- Form relates to how three-dimensional a drawing looks.
- Tone is making light and dark marks to give the impression that a light source is shining on the subject.
- Texture is how these marks can describe the surface of a subject (for example, rough or smooth).

You will also need to teach your pupils about colour theory using a colour wheel – showing them how to mix secondary colours from primary colours, and how tertiary colours are made. To enable them to mix an array of colours they will need two shades of each primary colour paint and black and white to learn how tones of colours are achieved (ready mix is ideal paint to use in the classroom as it is economical and washable).

Assessment

When assessing pupils' art and design work it is important to look at the levels of control being used in mastering techniques and pupils' willingness to engage with the design process. Sketchbooks are the perfect place for pupils to practise their artistic skills and for teachers to assess their pupils' improvement with techniques and engagement in the activities. By dating each page the pupils, and you, will be able to gauge their progress. At key stage 2 pupils are required to keep a sketchbook but it is never too early to start. As well as a central place for their drawings, pupils can also use sketchbooks for:

- mind maps;
- observations throughout a project in words and sketches;
- experimentations with media (i.e. art materials);
- collections of photographs, cuttings from magazines, newspapers, internet printouts, leaflets, etc;
- photographs of experiences during a project and reflective comments (i.e. step-by-step images of a piece of artwork being made, showing evaluation and modification) and visits to museums and galleries, etc;
- evidence of directed and self-directed tasks completed at home.

Further reading

Deasy, R.J. (2005) *Third Space: When Learning Matters*. Washington, DC: Arts Education Partnership.

Dewey, J. (1997) *Experience and Education*. New York: Touchstone.

Downing, D., Johnson, F. and Kaur, S. (2003) *Saving a Place for the Arts? A Survey of the Arts in Primary Schools in England*. Berkshire: The National Foundation for Educational Research (NfER).

Giudici, C., Rinaldi, C. and Krechevsky, M. (eds) (2001) *Making Learning Visible: Children as Individuals and Group Learners*. Reggio Emilia: Reggio Children Publications.

Hosack Janes, K. (2014) *Using the Visual Arts for Cross-Curricular Teaching and Learning: Imaginative Ideas for the Primary School*. London: Routledge.

Kolb, D.A. (1984) *Experiential Learning: Experience as the Source of Learning and Development*. New Jersey: Prentice Hall.

National Advisory Committee on Creative and Cultural Education (1999) *All Our Futures: Creativity, Culture and Education*. London: HMSO. [online] Available at: **www.sirkenrobinson.com/skr/pdf/allourfutures.pdf**

OFSTED (2010) *Learning: Creative Approaches that Raise Standards*. London: HMSO. [online] Available at: **www.creativitycultureeducation.org/wp-content/uploads/learning-creative-approaches-that-raise-standards-250.pdf**

OFSTED (2012) *Making a Mark: Art, Craft and Design 2008–11*. London: HMSO. [online] Available at: **http://webarchive.nationalarchives.gov.uk/20141124154759/http://www.ofsted.gov.uk/resources/making-mark-art-craft-and-design-education-2008-11**

Seidel, S., Tishman, S., Winner, E., Hetland, L. and Palmer, P. (2009) *The Qualities of Quality: Understanding Excellence in Arts Education*. Cambridge, MA: Project Zero, Harvard Graduate School of Education.

Useful websites

The Campaign for Drawing: **www.thebigdraw.org.uk/home/index.aspx**
The Cultural Learning Alliance: **www.culturallearningalliance.org.uk**
Your Paintings: **www.bbc.co.uk/arts/yourpaintings**

Art and design 2 Examples of planning

The following three lesson plans are provided as examples of planning in art and design. They do not contain the detail you will probably wish to have on your plans but do illustrate some of the points discussed previously.

Lesson One

Subject/topic: Rainforests	Date: 15/1/2016 Time: 9.15 a.m.		Teaching group/set: Y1 No. of pupils: 29
Intended learning: Children will learn to: • look carefully at a work of art, developing visual literacy • develop observational drawing skills.			**NC reference/context:** Pupils should be taught drawing skills Pupils should be introduced to works of art and taught about the practices and disciplines of making art
Success criteria: All children will be able to: • comment on what they can see in the painting and contribute to group discussion • make sketching lines with some control that resemble the leaves that they have collected. Some children will be able to: • use key vocabulary during discussions about the painting • make convincing accurate first-hand observational drawings of the leaves that they have collected.			**Assessment strategy:** • Observation of group discussions when generating comments for 'What can we see?' sheets • Assessment of accuracy of observational drawing
Key vocabulary: First-hand observational drawing, original and reproduction, image, painting, sketching	**Resources:** 1 x A1 and 10 x A4 printed reproductions of Henri Rousseau's 'Tiger in a Tropical Storm (Surprised!)' (1891), and access to zoomable image on the National Gallery website and BBC Class Clip; leaf ID sheets; pupil sketchbooks. 2B pencils and sharpeners	**Risk assessment:**	
Time	**Teacher focus**		**Pupil focus**
30 mins	Introduce the challenge of discussing as a group and writing down 'What can we see?' in the stimulus image. Checking pupils' understanding of the challenge and assessing the level of pupils' prior knowledge. Introduce zoomable digital image on the whiteboard and watch the BBC Class Clip about the painting (stepping into the painting).		Sitting at group tables (six per table) look at the reproductions (1 x A4 per three pupils). Generate responses to 'What can we see?' question on large sheets of paper. Watch Class Clip and discussing as whole class how it might feel to be in a rainforest – thinking about all the senses. Learn about how Rousseau never went to a real rainforest or saw a real tiger, instead doing his studies for his painting at the zoo and botanical gardens in Paris.

Collaborative working encouraging pupil–pupil dialogue.

Link to science/animals including humans.

Use of ICT for research.

Hook provides a context for learning and relevance to a real-life context.

	Discuss as a group the pupil comments sheets and think about how it would feel to be in a rainforest. This will inform further enquiry. Outline that the next three art lessons will focus on (1) observational drawing of plants, (2) colour mixing and painting of plants, (3) making models of animals that could be found in a tropical forest.	
30 mins	Discuss the difference between the plants in a rainforest and those in the school playground. Challenge the pupils to collect leaves in the playground and identify them from a leaf ID sheet.	Discuss as a whole group the difference between trees found in the school playground and the plants in a rainforest. Collect leaves in the playground and match to a leaf ID sheet.
30 mins	Demonstrate first-hand observational drawing technique with 2B sketching pencil using collected leaves as a subject. **Home Learning** – bring in a house/ tropical plant for next lesson.	Listen carefully to demonstration. Individuals practise sketching techniques in their sketchbooks.

Link to science – plants.

Lesson Two

Subject/topic: Rainforests	Date: 22/1/2016 Time: 9.15 a.m.	Teaching group/set: Y1 No. of pupils: 29

Intended learning:	NC reference/context:
Children will learn: • to develop their first-hand observational drawing techniques • about colour theory (primary and secondary colours) • painting techniques.	Pupils should be taught drawing and painting skills, including developing techniques in using colour, line and form Pupils should be introduced to works of art and taught about the practices and disciplines of making art
Success criteria: All children will be able to : • identify the primary and secondary colours and talk about how green is mixed • make drawings with some control that resemble the house/ tropical plants • mix a few shades of green and use these to paint their drawings. Some children will be able to: • explain how all secondary colours are mixed from primary colours • make convincing accurate first-hand observational drawings of house/tropical plants • mix a more extensive range of shades of green and use these to paint their drawings, demonstrating a considered painting technique.	**Assessment strategy:** • Marking colour wheel sheets • Assessment of first-hand observational drawings • Observation of group colour-mixing work

Key vocabulary:	Resources	Risk assessment:
First-hand observational drawing, painting, colour wheel, primary and secondary colours	Henri Rousseau's 'Tiger in a Tropical Storm (Surprised!)' reproductions Ready mix paint in two shades of each primary colour Palettes, paint brushes, water pots, paper towels 2B pencils, A4 cartridge paper	Risk of slipping on wet floors – paper towels needed

Time	Teacher focus	Pupil focus
10 mins	Record using time-lapse app the house/tropical plants arriving. Write first challenge on whiteboard – Think about the differences between the plants in the school playground and the house/tropical plants. Write individual observations in sketchbooks.	Place house/tropical plants on a centre table. Think about the differences between the plants in the school playground and the house/tropical plants. Write individual observations in sketchbooks.
50 mins	Demonstrate colour wheel and discuss how mixing primary colours makes secondary colours. Support pupils in drawing colour wheel and mixing colours. TA to support blue group (LA).	Draw a colour wheel. Paint primary colours. Mix secondary colours. Paint secondary colours.
30 mins	Encourage pupils to mix as many shades of green as possible and show them how to colour match with the green shades in the painting. Demonstrate painting technique.	Sitting at group tables (six per table) and working in twos, count the number of green shades in the 'Tiger in a Tropical Storm (Surprised!)' painting. Experiment with mixing as many shades as possible. Working individually on single sheets of cartridge paper, use sketching technique to make a first-hand observational drawing of a house/tropical plant. Use shades of green to carefully paint the drawings.

Side annotations:

This can be used in a final sharing presentation of the pupils' work.

Opportunity for children to demonstrate what they remember from the previous lesson.

Link to science – plants.

Only use one shade of each primary colour.

Use two shades of each primary colour to enable a wider range of green shades.

Lesson Three

Subject/topic:	Date: 29/1/2016	Teaching group/set: Y1
Rainforests	Time: 9.15 a.m.	No. of pupils: 29

Intended learning:	NC reference/context:
Children will learn to: • choose appropriate materials to make a sculptural model • develop painting techniques which describe texture.	Pupils should be taught to use a range of materials creatively (including sculptural materials) Pupils should be introduced to works of art and taught about the practices and disciplines of making art

Success criteria:	Assessment strategy:
All children will be able to: • work collaboratively to produce a model of an animal that lives in a rain forest • use a 2D image to inform the making of their 3D model • experiment with painting techniques to describe texture (e.g. fur). Some children will be able to: • contribute significantly to the collaborative work • understand clearly that a 2D image shows a single angle and that more research is needed to inform making a 3D model • convincingly describe texture using painting techniques.	• Observation of group work • Assessment of willingness to experiment with painting techniques • Assessment of final model during group presentations

Key vocabulary:	Resources:	Risk assessment:
Sculpture/model Texture Experiment 2D/3D	Henri Rousseau's 'Tiger in a Tropical Storm (Surprised!)' reproductions	Risk of slipping on wet floors – paper towels needed
	Images of animals that live in a rainforest	
	Modelling materials (newspaper/ masking tape/elastic bands/ modelling clay, etc.)	

Opportunity for children to collect/research.

Time	Teacher focus	Pupil focus
20 mins	Introduce the challenge of making a model of an animal that lives in a rain forest. Demonstrate how a 2D image of the body of an animal can be visualised in 3D geometric shapes	Working in groups of three (mixed-ability) sitting at group tables (six per table), look at, discuss and choose an image of an animal to make a model of. Watch demonstration. Sketch geometrical shapes to make a drawing of the model.
40 mins	Demonstrate model-making techniques. Support groups in their discussions and their choice of materials. TA to support groups in need. Demonstration of painting techniques to describe texture.	Choose and experiment with making techniques. Complete a collaborative model. Experimentation of painting techniques and final painting of model.
20 mins	Group presentations of their models. Ask probing questions to assist pupils in evaluating work.	Pupils present model to the class and describe their making techniques.

Collaborative working, encouraging pupil–pupil dialogue.

Link to science – animals.

Obvious links to mathematics, geometry – properties of shapes.

Real-life computer modelling could be shown – hook provides relevance.

Opportunities for self and peer–peer evaluation.

Art and design 3 The framework for art and design

Purpose of study

Art, craft and design embody some of the highest forms of human creativity. A high-quality art and design education should engage, inspire and challenge pupils, equipping them with the knowledge and skills to experiment, invent and create their own works of art, craft and design. As pupils progress, they should be able to think critically and develop a more rigorous understanding of art and design. They should also know how art and design both reflect and shape our history, and contribute to the culture, creativity and wealth of our nation.

Aims

The national curriculum for art and design aims to ensure that all pupils:

- produce creative work, exploring their ideas and recording their experiences
- become proficient in drawing, painting, sculpture and other art, craft and design techniques
- evaluate and analyse creative works using the language of art, craft and design
- know about great artists, craft makers and designers, and understand the historical and cultural development of their art forms.

Attainment targets

By the end of each key stage, pupils are expected to know, apply and understand the matters, skills and processes specified in the relevant programme of study.

Schools are not required by law to teach the content in [square brackets].

Subject content

Key stage 1

Pupils should be taught:

- to use a range of materials creatively to design and make products
- to use drawing, painting and sculpture to develop and share their ideas, experiences and imagination
- to develop a wide range of art and design techniques in using colour, pattern, texture, line, shape, form and space
- about the work of a range of artists, craft makers and designers, describing the differences and similarities between different practices and disciplines, and making links to their own work

Key stage 2

Pupils should be taught to develop their techniques, including their control and their use of materials, with creativity, experimentation and an increasing awareness of different kinds of art, craft and design.

Pupils should be taught:

- to create sketch books to record their observations and use them to review and revisit ideas
- to improve their mastery of art and design techniques, including drawing, painting and sculpture with a range of materials [for example, pencil, charcoal, paint, clay]
- about great artists, architects and designers in history.

@ 8 Computing

Planning computing in the national curriculum

Helen Caldwell and Sway Grantham

Computing 1 Principles of planning

This section looks at the key factors which are specific to planning effective computing lessons. It builds on the generic factors for planning found in Chapter 1 and should be read in conjunction with these ideas.

National curriculum (NC) guidance

The national curriculum purpose of study begins by stating that *a high-quality computing education equips pupils to use computational thinking and creativity to understand and change the world*. That is quite a claim. It suggests that we should be ambitious in our plans and encourage children to feel empowered by their computing skills to make a difference. Code.org echo this idea when they say, *the programmers of tomorrow are the wizards of the future!* This approach shifts the emphasis from children as users to children as makers and from consumers to creators. It puts them in a more central role, making decisions about what to make and share using their digital skills, and gives teachers the job of filtering information rather than just imparting it. Our goal is for children to be active and discerning, synthesising and evaluating information as they create a range of digital products such as blogs, podcasts, websites, eBooks or slideshows, as well as computer programs.

In planning for this type of scenario, it is worth keeping in mind the broader ideas associated with computational thinking, which are often represented as a set of *concepts* and *approaches*. Concepts can include logic, algorithms, decomposition, patterns, abstraction and evaluation. Approaches are often described as tinkering, creating, debugging, persevering and collaborating. For more about this, look at the 'computational thinker' diagram in the Barefoot Computing resources. An obvious starting point is to begin to assimilate the relevant vocabulary into our classrooms so that children develop an ability to discuss computing concepts and talk about their learning. Simple examples of the use of words such as 'algorithm', 'decomposition', 'abstraction', 'conditionals' and 'debugging' can be introduced in contexts away from computers. For example, we might refer to how we can write an algorithm (a set of instructions) to make a Lego® model, or to how we use the process of decomposition in maths to break down a problem into manageable chunks. We could point out the similarities between debugging computer programs and editing writing, or find everyday examples of loops (days of the week) and conditionals (if it is raining I pick up an umbrella). To take this idea a stage further, we can build in physical activities exploring computing concepts away from the technology such as writing algorithms for how to moonwalk or how to play tag. Such activities are generally known as *unplugged computing*.

In considering approaches to computational thinking, you may notice that the terms imply an environment in which children are exploring, identifying challenges and solving problems together. One key aspect is allowing time for playful exploring or 'tinkering', a phase that is full of questions and trying things out. Another is the collaborative process of remixing and reusing each other's ideas in order to 'generalise' solutions. A third is the process of testing and refining ideas bit-by-bit and debugging errors in order to build an efficient solution to a programming problem. There is also the concept of 'persevering' or, as the computing pioneer Seymour Papert puts it, *hard fun* (Papert, 1980). Papert suggests that it is important to encourage children to be independent learners who find ways to solve problems for themselves, and that teachers should model effective strategies in order to show that we too are learning through exploring, developing and testing ideas.

Together, these computational thinking concepts and approaches represent how problems are typically tackled in real-world computing projects. In planning for a classroom that nurtures this type of learning, your role is to provide the conditions for all children to be productive makers using technology, giving them opportunities to take on personally relevant challenges and a chance to talk, reflect and share.

Cross-curricular computing

To refer back to the national curriculum guidance, alongside the concept of computational thinking is the notion that children can use technology *creatively* as a learning tool and an expressive medium across the primary curriculum. If you are to make this approach work well you will need to plan your learning objectives to balance computing with other subject areas. As an example, your computing focus may be to learn to write programs using repetition by drawing shapes with the repeat block in Scratch. Your more able children may go on to use nested loops to draw more complex patterns. You have identified clear links with maths and also with art and design, and have taken time to review knowledge of angles, coordinates and degrees. In a follow-up lesson, you then plan to look at the properties of geometric shapes from an art and design perspective and to compare Islamic and Celtic patterns. Similar cross-curricular opportunities using Scratch might include creating animations to illustrate animal life cycles, preparing a quiz on animal habitats, making a science game on the properties of materials, or writing a program to work out the area of a rectangle.

When the focus is on two curriculum areas, it is important to identify opportunities for reinforcing computational thinking within the activity at the curriculum planning stage. For example, if you were creating a water cycle animation you might plan your algorithm in advance by sequencing the steps of the process. At this point you could introduce the idea of abstraction, the process of leaving out unnecessary detail and focusing on the main relevant factors. Making connections across the curriculum in this way will help to make computing activities more meaningful for children and they will be better able to understand the relevance of their work. There is a similar advantage in reinforcing computational thinking concepts via a different platform such as through the apps Hopscotch, Cargo-Bot, A.L.E.X, Kodable, Tynker or Scratch Junior. Bear in mind that the need to develop a broad understanding of computing concepts and approaches is more important than learning one programming language.

Planning for talk

Talk is central to building understanding about learning within the computing curriculum. By articulating and building upon their reasoning, children learn more than just the facts and skills – they learn to think about themselves as learners. Building explicit knowledge about strategies for learning and problem-solving means that children are more likely to use them. You should therefore aim to include discussion points in your computing planning, allowing time for children to share solutions, explain their choices of code, make comparisons and say why they are useful. They could also add written comments to blocks of code in Scratch.

Resources

Computing is a subject that requires you to give careful thought to the physical environment and resources. Learning can be a very different experience depending on whether you are teaching in an ICT suite once a week, using a set of laptops on a daily basis, or sharing a set of iPads with the class next door. You will need to consider how you can make the most of what you have already in terms of access to equipment and prioritise which additional resources you think you need well in advance. For example, a robust set of iPad cases will give you the chance to explore learning beyond the classroom and think about how children's use of technology can enhance their engagement with the outdoor learning. Planning a circus of activities or planning for paired work can free up equipment and enable all to have a turn. Indeed, paired programming is an established software development technique in which two programmers work together at one workstation and switch roles frequently, with the 'driver' writing the code while the 'navigator' reviews each line of code as it is typed in.

Differentiation

Your curriculum planning needs to address ways to provide additional support or extra challenges for those who need it. Computing offers a different way of learning and can be a good subject for reaching out to learners who may not achieve in other areas. It can be constructive to work with laminated Scratch blocks to predict what the code will do before moving to the computer. Children can take on the roles of sprites acting out the commands as a friend 'runs' the code, and they can begin to debug their programs before they go near the computer. Teachers or pupils modelling the process of constructing algorithms can be helpful. You might provide template files, partly completed problems to finish for those who need it or pre-prepared help sheets, hints and prompts. Another option is to use mixed ability pairs to provide support for less confident pupils. You will need to give particular thought as to how the computing curriculum can be adapted for students with special educational needs and disabilities.

It is inevitable that some children will take to computing like ducks to water and you will need to ensure that your high attainers are sufficiently challenged. Encourage them to generalise their programming solutions to other situations or to enhance their programs by adding blocks for sound or more user control. Suggest that they look for ways to make their programs more efficient and to explain how they fixed their bugs. Ask them to explain their reasoning using the comments option in Scratch, taking care to use the correct terminology.

Assessment

Assessment is an essential aspect of any curriculum, completing the cycle of planning, teaching and evaluating. A set of 'I can' statements or progression statements to complement your scheme of work will be an invaluable starting point for assessment. One option is to use or adapt the Progression Pathways Assessment Framework developed by the Computing at Schools organisation (CAS). This framework organises the curriculum across the three strands of computer science, information technology and digital literacy, and specifies learning outcomes linked to computational thinking concepts. It can be used alongside a digital badge scheme to provide a motivating context for learning.

In addition to this, your planning will need to identify opportunities for teacher assessment for learning (AfL) during the main task and discussions, using pupils' explanations and demonstrations as evidence of understanding. Talk is vital for checking whether children have developed real understanding. Adding questions to your planning will help focus the talk opportunities during your lessons and highlight the assessment opportunities. You could use voice recorders or screencasts to capture children's explanations.

It is likely that you will end up with children pursuing tasks at different rates and setting their own challenges. You will need to build in time for them to try out each other's projects and provide some positive feedback and suggestions for improvement. This makes your plenary an important time for recapping the steps their projects have in common, such as choosing commands and writing the algorithm, testing and debugging the program, and getting feedback from users. A well-planned plenary will use peer-assessment techniques such as 'think-pair-share' to help pupils share their work with an audience and reflect on the learning process. It will give you a chance to reinforce relevant computational thinking strategies. Children's finished projects might be used for summative assessment and you can allow children a chance to make the refinements you suggest as a result of this feedback.

Classroom environment

We have focused on how to plan computing lessons that enable children to become creative makers and thinkers using the medium of technology, and apply their powers of invention to become innovative problem-solvers across many spheres. The classroom environment we have described has the following elements.

- A workshop atmosphere in which children are encouraged to help each other solve open problems.
- Time for children to tinker and explore, and therefore to develop ownership over computing challenges.

- Unplugged exploration of computational thinking concepts away from the computer and reference to real-world examples.
- The use of computing as a creative tool for making digital artefacts across other primary curriculum areas.
- A mix of open-ended inquiry-based challenges and the teaching of specific subject knowledge and skills.

Progression

It is likely that key stage 1 will include a good deal of 'unplugged' activities and work with floor robots such as Beebots. Children might begin by looking at technology around us and by understanding that input and output devices control computers. This could be followed up with sequencing and sorting tasks, perhaps related to dance and music. They could create and debug algorithms to program remote-controlled toys and cars, or progress from controlling human 'Beebots' to real Beebots, reinforcing the idea that technology is controlled by people. All of these experiences can be related to their understanding of the uses of technology in the real world.

Towards the end of key stage 1 you might move into directional programming with screen robots. In key stage 2 you would continue to develop children's experiences of physical computing alongside their use of visual programming tools on the computer, using resources such as Lego®, WeDo, MakeyMakeys, robots, Raspberry Pis and Scratch. Children's understanding of networks, email and the internet will be developed to include an understanding of how webpages are constructed. eSafety and digital citizenship will be themes that run throughout, and will need to be revisited regularly as you aim to teach children to take responsibility for their use of technology, and to respect copyright and confidentiality. Again, the emphasis is on children taking an active role in order to become not just digitally literate and safe, but critical and responsible, so that they develop a real understanding of computers and society that goes beyond the practical skills.

Much of your curriculum may be covered in an entirely cross-curricular way, in particular the strand which focuses on *using technology purposefully to create, organise, store, manipulate and retrieve digital content*. This is likely to encompass skills such as researching and communicating ideas, using spreadsheets, databases and tools to present data, working with media to produce video and audio, and making a range of digital artefacts and presentations, including eBooks.

While you are likely to draw upon some ready-made sets of lesson ideas to help build knowledge of programming techniques, when planning your programming lessons you should bear in mind the advantages we discussed earlier of adopting an inquiry-led approach, and you should aim to build in open-ended challenges and choices so that children can learn to define problems, experiment and find out how to solve problems for themselves, rather than restrict them to pre-defined steps and goals. Be guided by your pupils' growing enthusiasm for the subject and have the courage to make time for developing an exciting set of thinking strategies that they will be able to draw upon throughout their careers, regardless of whether or not they become future computer programmers. Above all, we would agree with Seymour Papert when he says that, *The role of the teacher is to create the conditions for invention rather than provide ready-made knowledge* (Papert, 1996).

Further reading

Active Teaching and Learning Strategies for Key Stages 1 & 2 from Northern Ireland Curriculum. Available at: **www.nicurriculum.org.uk/docs/key_stages_1_and_2/altm-ks12.pdf**

Barefoot Computing. Available at: **www.barefootcas.org.uk**

Bird, J., Caldwell, H. and Mayne, P. (2014) *Lessons in Teaching Primary Computing*. London: Sage.

Code.org. The programmers of tomorrow are the wizards of the future. Available at: **http://contest.catalysts.cc/en/ccc/the-wizards-of-the-future**

Computer Science Unplugged. Available at: **www.csunplugged.org**

Computing At School CAS resources. Available at: **www.computingatschool.org.uk/index.php?id=primary-national-curriculum-guidance**

Creative Computing: An introductory computing curriculum using Scratch. Available at: **www.scratched.gse.harvard.edu/guide**

Digital Leader Network. Available at: **www.digitalleadernetwork.co.uk**

Digital SchoolHouse resources. Available at: **www.resources.digitalschoolhouse.org.uk**

Hunt, S. (2014) Computational thinking: A special way to look at problems. Available at: **www.computingatschool.org.uk/data/uploads/newsletter-spring-2014.pdf**

Junior Computer Science. Available at: **www.code-it.co.uk/index.html**

NAACE Guidance for Primary Teachers. Available at: **www.naace.co.uk/curriculum/primaryguide**

Papert, S. (1980) *Mindstorms: Children, Computers, and Powerful Ideas*. New York: Basic Books, Inc.

Papert, S. (1996) *The Connected Family: Bridging the Digital Generation Gap*. Atlanta, GA: Longstreet Press.

Wing, J. (2012) What is computational thinking? Available at: **www.cs.cmu.edu/~CompThink**

Computing 2 Examples of planning

The following three lesson plans are provided as examples of planning in computing. They do not contain the detail you will probably wish to have on your plans but do illustrate some of the points discussed previously.

Lesson One

Subject/topic: Programming	Date: 23/10/2016 Time: 1.15 p.m.	Teaching group/set: Y1 No. of pupils: 32

Intended learning:	NC reference/context:
Children will learn to: • create a program to suit a specific purpose • debug errors in a program.	Create and debug simple programs, KS1 PoS Use logical reasoning to predict the behaviour of simple programs, KS1 PoS

Success criteria:	Assessment strategy:
All children will be able to: • predict what will happen when the program is run • write a program • find the error (debug) the program. Some children will be able to: • correct the error in the program.	• Voice recordings of predictions • Observation of groupings and discussion, which informs these • Photos of rearranged program

Key vocabulary:	Resources:	Risk assessment:
program, debug, errors, predict	*The Jolly Postman* or *Other People's Letters* ideally on IWB Beebots (at least six) Giant arrow cards and 'Go' button x six Beebot mats Easi-Speak mp3 microphone iPad with Beebot app	Make sure children have clear work areas to avoid tripping over or treading on the Beebots.

Time	Teacher focus	Pupil focus
10 mins	Before lesson stack tables Lead discussion and retelling of *The Jolly Postman* or *Other People's Letters* Introduce task of delivering the letters using a Beebot.	Sitting on the floor space looking at the IWB and discussing what happened in the story. Look at the Beebot 'map' of the places the Jolly Postman visited in the story as they are discussing.
40 mins	Introduce activity circus and put children in groups of four. Teacher supports debugging group. TA to support predicting programming group.	Four activities with two groups of four children working on each activity at the same time. Ten minutes on each activity.

(margin notes)

Assessment appropriate to the age and ability of the children.

Does not have to be written tasks.

Be specific. When you're in a rush before a lesson begins you want to know you have everything you need, including the amount!

	Assess discussions to identify children's understanding of debugging. TA's group can record their predictions using the Easi-Speak mp3 microphone to share at the end.	Activity 1 (T supported): Beebot gets lost taking the post from the post box to the three bears' house, so the children need to find the problem in the program. Activity 2 (TA supported): Guess where Beebot is going next by looking at the program. Then test it out by running the Beebot program. Activity 3: Beebot needs to get to the giant's house. Can you write the program? Use the cards to help you and then take a photo of your program. Activity 4: Get iPad Beebot where he needs to go.
10 mins	Encourage the children to speak to the group about their learning, including any debugging groups highlighted.	Sit back on the carpet and share what they have learnt. Each group explains their photo and talks about their prediction.

Make it clear who is doing what. It is clear where each adult needs to be and doing what.

Amend what you want to share as you go. Some things you can't plan for so leave them open!

Lesson Two

Subject/topic:	Date: 27/10/2016	Teaching group/set: Y4
Programming	Time: 10.30 a.m.	No. of pupils: 32

Intended learning:	NC reference/context:
Children will learn to: • write programs • use repetition in my programs.	design, write and debug programs, KS2 PoS use sequence, selection and repetition in programs, KS2 PoS

Success criteria:	Assessment strategy:
All children will be able to: • recognise that a computer will only do what it's told • explain that their program runs from start to finish • use repetition in their programs. Some children will be able to: • discuss the different types of loops • embed loops within loops.	• Children comment their code to explain what their loop is doing • HA: screencast and talk through their code to explain more complicated concepts such as embedded loops

Key vocabulary:	Resources:	Risk assessment:
programming, repetition, loops, Scratch, sprites, embed, sequence	Computers with internet access Dance video Loops sheets Self-assessment checklist	Children must carry laptops with two hands and only carry one at a time. Internet filters are in place and children know the school's ICT code of conduct to ensure they know what to do if they find anything they're not happy with.

eSafety is really important and should be taught whenever computers are used.

Time	Teacher focus	Pupil focus
10 mins	Give out laptops from trolley. Play dance video	Collect laptops and log them in. While they're loading: Volunteers leave the room. Then are given instructions to repeat dance.

It is particularly important to plan the logistics of getting the computers to the children or the children to the computers. Think ahead!

		Lead discussion about what you'd need to include to program a dance routine in Scratch	Begin to create a flowchart thinking through how they will create their own dance routine.
	10 mins	Outline task – to create a dancing animation in Scratch including a loop Observe how different children approach the task ready to address in a minute	Look through example code on the Scratch project. Begin creating their own dance routine. LA can 'remix' existing code if necessary.
Plan opportunities for talk and discussion.	10 mins	Introduce LO and the specific focus on repetition Hand out example code loop sheets Focus the children on the use of repetition to reduce the amount of programming they have to write	Discuss what they notice and talk through the code with learning partners. Look at 'self-assessment checklist' and refer to it throughout the lesson.
Planning questions can focus you when you are working around the room with your pupils.	40 mins	Monitor the children as they write their programs. Encourage them to debug their own code and question their use of loops – why there? Why have you used this block? Explain what your program does. Can you think of a reason why you would need to use two loops together? Explain it.	Create their dance routines including loops.
Don't feel you have to stick to a '3 part lesson'. Suit the needs of your learners and plan for it.	10 mins	Bring the lesson to a close by reminding the children they should have been commenting their code	Complete a 'self-assessment checklist' and rate their own learning before saving it (including comments).

Lesson Three

Subject/topic: Programming	**Date:** 31/10/2016 **Time:** 1.15 p.m.	**Teaching group/set:** Y6 **No. of pupils:** 32	

<table>
<tr><td colspan="2">Intended learning:
Children will learn to:

• write programs for a specific purpose
• use repetition in my programs.</td><td>NC reference/context:

design, write and debug programs, KS2 PoS use sequence, selection and repetition in programs, KS2 PoS</td></tr>
<tr><td colspan="2">Success criteria:
All children will be able to:

• write a program to meet a specific purpose
• use repetition in their programs
• explain the different types of loops.

Some children will be able to:

• embed loops within loops
• include variables which change as a loop progresses.</td><td>Assessment strategy:

• Peer assessment during 'gallery' gives pupils an opportunity to reflect on other pupils' and their own work
• Observe pupils' use of loops
• Note pupils' understanding of loops during final discussion</td></tr>
</table>

Same NC context as the previous year 4 lesson so evidence of progress must come from within the lesson. Careful planning ensures you're building on prior learning.

When pupils see how others have written their program they can consider if theirs was the best approach

Key vocabulary:	Resources:	Risk assessment:
programming, repetition, loops, embed, variables, purpose, Python, LEDs	Raspberry Pi incl. monitors, SD cards, keyboards and mouse x 16	Trailing extension leads – cover with anti-trip mats and draw children's attention to them
	Pibrella x 16 Extension leads 'Cheat sheets'	Do not use electrical equipment if any signs of wear are causing problems

Time	Teacher focus	Pupil focus
10 mins	Hand out the equipment for the Raspberry Pis in sets including Pibrella Show children a video of traffic lights	Connect the Raspberry Pis and check with a teacher before plugging it into the electricity. Note the sequence of the lights and rough timings.
40 mins	Encourage pupils to first break down their program into smaller parts – what do they need to achieve first? Model independence by suggesting the children use cheat sheet cards to give them prompts.	In pairs pupils write a computer program to control traffic lights on their Pibrella in Python. LA, or dyslexic, learners can use Scratch to program without the problem of syntax. Use cheat sheet card for specific examples of code.
10 mins	Host a gallery where the children present their code to the class. Lead a discussion on what the most efficient way to write that code was. How many children used loops effectively?	One in the pair stays with the Pi presenting their program, the other looks at their peers' work around the room. Then swop. Reflect on what they've seen of their peers' program.

Even though key vocabulary is often the same, it needs to be continually revisited to ensure language is not a barrier to learning.

Careful planning means that the same 'Intended Learning' can occur through different mediums to meet the needs of individual learners.

Computing 3 The framework for computing

Purpose of study

A high-quality computing education equips pupils to use computational thinking and creativity to understand and change the world. Computing has deep links with mathematics, science and design and technology, and provides insights into both natural and artificial systems. The core of computing is computer science, in which pupils are taught the principles of information and computation, how digital systems work and how to put this knowledge to use through programming. Building on this knowledge and understanding, pupils are equipped to use information technology to create programs, systems and a range of content. Computing also ensures that pupils become digitally literate – able to use, and express themselves and develop their ideas through, information and communication technology – at a level suitable for the future workplace and as active participants in a digital world.

Aims

The national curriculum for computing aims to ensure that all pupils:

- can understand and apply the fundamental principles and concepts of computer science, including abstraction, logic, algorithms and data representation
- can analyse problems in computational terms, and have repeated practical experience of writing computer programs in order to solve such problems
- can evaluate and apply information technology, including new or unfamiliar technologies, analytically to solve problems
- are responsible, competent, confident and creative users of information and communication technology.

Attainment targets

By the end of each key stage, pupils are expected to know, apply and understand the matters, skills and processes specified in the relevant programme of study.

Schools are not required by law to teach the example content in [square brackets].

Subject content

Key stage 1

Pupils should be taught to:

- understand what algorithms are, how they are implemented as programs on digital devices, and that programs execute by following precise and unambiguous instructions
- create and debug simple programs
- use logical reasoning to predict the behaviour of simple programs
- use technology purposefully to create, organise, store, manipulate and retrieve digital content

- recognise common uses of information technology beyond school
- use technology safely and respectfully, keeping personal information private; identify where to go for help and support when they have concerns about content or contact on the internet or other online technologies.

Key stage 2

Pupils should be taught to:

- design, write and debug programs that accomplish specific goals, including controlling or simulating physical systems; solve problems by decomposing them into smaller parts
- use sequence, selection, and repetition in programs; work with variables and various forms of input and output
- use logical reasoning to explain how some simple algorithms work and to detect and correct errors in algorithms and programs
- understand computer networks, including the internet; how they can provide multiple services, such as the World Wide Web, and the opportunities they offer for communication and collaboration
- use search technologies effectively, appreciate how results are selected and ranked, and be discerning in evaluating digital content
- select, use and combine a variety of software (including internet services) on a range of digital devices to design and create a range of programs, systems and content that accomplish given goals, including collecting, analysing, evaluating and presenting data and information
- use technology safely, respectfully and responsibly; recognise acceptable/unacceptable behaviour; identify a range of ways to report concerns about content and contact.

9 Design and technology

Planning design and technology in the national curriculum

Sue Dutson

Design and technology 1 Principles of planning

This section looks at the key factors which are specific to planning effective design and technology lessons. It builds on the generic factors for planning found in Chapter 1 and should be read in conjunction with these ideas.

Design and technology is a bridge between the arts and the sciences. It is a rigorous, practical subject requiring children to use literacy and numeracy to design, make and evaluate products that solve real and relevant problems in a variety of contexts.

The national curriculum for design and technology has a very clear focus; it seeks to ensure that Foundation subjects are used to inform and enhance numeracy and mathematics, language, literacy and vocabulary development while also enabling teachers to effectively address inclusion issues.

While underpinning and enhancing the core subjects, design and technology brings the curriculum to life and is enjoyed and valued by all children and, to this end, it becomes an excellent tool for behaviour management because children are engaged, enthused and enjoy the practical, interactive challenges that are set up.

A further dimension to design and technology through the 2014 curriculum is the requirement that all children in key stage 1 and key stage 2 engage in work with food, learning how to cook and to apply the principles of cooking, nutrition and healthy eating. There are obvious links with science here.

Thus, planning for design and technology now has two strands: the design, make, evaluate process, whereby children design and make products for an identified purpose, and the cooking and nutrition strand. It is important that both these requirements are covered and that one is not planned to the exclusion of the other. It follows, therefore, that due to the extra requirement in design and technology use of curriculum time is maximised through the exploration of cross-curricular links and opportunities.

Effective implementation of design and technology ensures that children have regular, planned opportunities to engage with designing, making and evaluating processes, set in real-life contexts that have relevance to the children. Regular planning ensures that children get used to routines and systems and have opportunities to get used to working with and managing equipment. It also means that classrooms are more likely to have a design and make or 'busy' table that is permanently set up so that children can dip in and out of activities as their day permits. One-off, whole-day or even whole-week design and technology planning usually leads to the children becoming unmanageably excitable and activities tend to lose context while staff become frustrated and find it difficult to keep children on task.

The curriculum asserts that design and technology is an iterative process and thus it is essential that planning happens at both class and whole-school level in order to ensure that activities facilitate cumulative progression.

Design and technology is great for promoting and developing cross-curricular ideas and yet it is essential that it retains its own integrity, allowing children to identify the purpose of the task and the needs of the user. It is essential that children have the opportunity to make choices, and therefore the range of availability of resources requires careful consideration.

Relevance

Good practice requires that all children engage in design and technology activities that allow them to evaluate past and present design ideas. They are allowed to take risks with their ideas and know that design and technology education recognises the essential contribution that designers make to the creativity, culture, wealth and wellbeing of the nation. It is essential that children develop a range of skills and their ability to perform tasks confidently – particularly significant in the preparation of food.

OFSTED subject surveys (2012) cite a range of well-contextualised and appropriate activities that have relevance to children in primary schools.

Assessment

Assessing children's design and technology is frequently an observational and intuitive process. Children who find reading and writing difficult are often the best designers and makers. Empowering children to evaluate their own work and that of others against their project design criteria is usually the best place to start. Your own professional expertise will also stand you in good stead for making a start with assessing children's work. For example, ask yourself 'What would my expectations be if I conducted this project (e.g. designing and making a rain jacket for teddy) with year 1 or year 6?' With food work the progression in skills and management of ingredients requires consideration, and the British Nutrition Association website is particularly helpful here.

Vocabulary

Design and technology has its own range of subject-specific terminology. However, it is an excellent vehicle for contextualising children's speaking and listening in a secure and non-threatening way and can also be used to incorporate a range of

other subjects while addressing design ideas. For example, children working on a playground design might also use scientific forces vocabulary but might equally incorporate geographical location vocabulary.

Resourcing design and technology

- Resourcing design and technology requires careful planning; in order to provide the children with choices a range of resources are required. Textiles can frequently be taught using reclaimed or recycled fabrics while resistant materials in the form of soft wood and balsa are best bought from the relevant suppliers because the junior hacksaws used in primary schools are not sufficiently heavy duty to cope with harder wood.
- Using batteries and bulbs in conjunction with science activities ensures that battery use is maximised.
- Most design and technology can happen on a shoestring budget and asking children to discuss ideas and projects at home is a great way of both involving parents and raising their awareness of the need for resources.
- Planning across the whole school ensures that ordering of resources can be streamlined and budgeted for in the most cost-effective way.
- Do the resources enable children to experience a range of tools and media with which to work (textiles, resistant materials, mouldable materials, etc.)?
- Are the resources appropriate to the needs of the children (e.g. children in Reception and year 1 still need scissors that have sharp blades with which to practise and refine their cutting skills but the scissors should have rounded ends)?
- Who will manage the resources and how will they be distributed to ensure that the children can work independently?
- With the food requirement schools should have a range of child-appropriate cooking equipment – ideally containers made from transparent material so that children can see what is happening to the ingredients. Are heating devices placed at child height for maximum involvement/engagement, rather than improvising with the staff room facilities?
- Health and safety issues relating to the washing of hands and safe storage of food must be addressed and implemented; encouraging at least one member of staff to achieve a Food Hygiene Level 2 certificate is desirable and can have a significant impact on the confidence of all staff.
- Schools should have a system to enable teachers and support staff to claim for incidental expenses from a designated petty cash budget.
- Given the food requirement for design and technology it makes sense that schools keep a database of children's allergies. This enables teachers to ensure that children's claims of allergies do not become synonymous to 'do not like' or 'never tried'.

Safety issues

Design and technology is a practical subject and it is important that children have the opportunity to use as wide a range of resources as possible. Some resources and tools can be deemed hazardous, but a simple risk assessment citing a sharp pencil as a potential risk can hopefully put your concerns into perspective. Most accidents in design and technology happen because children are excitable and unused to using

certain equipment – notably hacksaws and glue guns. The more opportunities children have to use them the more responsible and sensible they become because they recognise the potential advantages of their use. For example, children are frequently disappointed or get into mischief while waiting for PVA glue to bond whereas a low-melt glue gun provides immediate results and provides greater versatility with the range of materials that can be joined. Table 9.1 illustrates a simple risk assessment on a sharp pencil versus a low-melt glue gun.

Table 9.1 A simple risk assessment on a sharp pencil versus low-melt glue gun

Resource	Likely number available in class of 30 children	Potential risk posed by resource, 1–5 scale (1 = min, 5 = max)	Potential risk posed (= number x risk)
Sharp pencil	30	5	150
Low-melt glue gun	3	3	9

Clearly the low-melt glue gun poses fewer potential risks but initially requires the children to become familiar with its use.

The learning environment

Design and technology potentially lends itself to a very fluid way of working. Children become involved in the interactive and practical nature of the tasks and the classroom can become a busy, sometimes noisy but just as often quiet, work space. While design and technology can frequently make use of local resources – playgrounds, shops, care homes, museums – it is vital that ALL children remain in planned design and technology sessions and are not withdrawn for 'extra reading' or similar as this immediately devalues the status of the subject.

Activity length

The length of design and technology activities can vary more than in almost any other subject. Often children become engrossed and involved in tasks that then take much longer than was initially planned. Finding extra time for activities that overrun can be managed in various ways.

- Children take their project home with them (great for promoting home–school links).
- Children can refer to their design and technology when they have completed other tasks.
- The setting up of a work table in the classroom where children can work semi-independently provides extra time for completing tasks.

Using information and communication technology (ICT)

Incorporation of tasks whereby products can be operated using a computer (e.g. fairground ride or traffic light system) allows links to be made between design technology and computing. Equally the use of digital recording devices

enables children to record progress within the design process and to retain a record of the finished product.

Further reading

Adams, K. (2007) *Behaviour for Learning in the Primary School*. Exeter: Learning Matters.

Barlex, D. (ed.) (2007) *Design and Technology for the Next Generation: A Collection of Provocative Pieces, Written by Experts in Their Field to Stimulate Reflection and Curriculum Innovation*. Shropshire: Cliffeco.

Bold, C. (1999) *Progression in Primary Design and Technology*. London: Fulton.

Desailly, J. (2012) *Creativity in the Primary Classroom*. London: Sage.

Fisher, R. and Williams, W. (2004) *Unlocking Creativity: A Teacher's Guide to Creativity Across the Curriculum*. London: Fulton.

Hayes, D. (2006) *Inspiring Primary Teaching: Insights into Excellent Primary Practice*. Exeter: Learning Matters.

Hope, G. (2006) *Teaching Design and Technology at Key Stages 1 and 2*. Exeter: Learning Matters.

Jackson, G. (2013) *Debates in Design and Technology*. London: Taylor and Francis.

Jarman, E. (2009) *A Place to Talk Outside*. London: Featherstone Publishing.

Jarman, E. (2011) *A Place to Talk for Boys*. London: Featherstone Publishing.

Kerry, T. (2011) *Cross-Curricular Teaching in the Primary School*. London: Routledge.

Sigman, A. (2008) *Practically Minded*. Stroud: RMET.

Watkins, C. (2009) Collaborative learning. *School Leadership Today*, 1(1): 22–5.

Watkins, C. (2009) Learner-driven learning. *School Leadership Today*, 1(2): 28–31.

Wilson, A. (2009) *Creativity in Primary Education*. Exeter: Learning Matters.

Useful websites

The Design and Technology Association: **www.data.org.uk**

British Nutrition Foundation: **www.foodafactoflife.org.uk**

Multicultural packed lunch: **www.loveyourlunch.org.uk**

Ofsted Primary Subject Surveys: **www.ofsted.gov.uk/inspection-reports**

The School Food Plan: **www.schoolfoodplan.com**

Design and technology 2 Examples of planning

The following three lesson plans are provided as examples of planning in design and technology. They do not contain the detail you will probably wish to have on your plans but do illustrate some key points for consideration.

Lesson One

Subject/topic:	Date: 23/10/2016	Teaching group/set: Y3
Using construction kits	Time: 1.15 p.m.	No. of pupils: 28

Intended learning:	NC reference/context:
Children will learn to: • develop technical and practical expertise • design a functional product based on design criteria • select from a range of equipment • generate, develop and model their ideas through discussion, annotated sketches and diagrams • evaluate their products against their own design criteria.	Lower KS2 Children generate, develop, model and communicate their ideas through discussion and annotated sketches

Success criteria:	Assessment strategy:
All children will be able to: • listen to the story, select one component or aspect of the story to build using either purpose-made construction kits or modelling clay, lollipop sticks, pipe cleaners. Some children will be able to: • consider resources they might like to use to improve/enhance/stabilise their model • make suggestions about what they would like to do next/utilise ideas that they see around the classroom in order to improve their own design.	• Observation of groups and individual children and the outcomes of their designs • Observation of the social skills of children • Ability of children to verbally articulate their ideas and to make suggestions about how they might improve/enhance their work

Key vocabulary:	Resources:	Risk assessment:
Build, construct, design, stability, assemble, components	*The Trouble with Dad* by Babette Cole Construction kits Modelling clay, pipe cleaners, lollipop sticks, pieces of correx	Responsible use of all resources

Time	Teacher focus	Pupil focus
10 mins	Read the story *The Trouble with Dad* by Babette Cole	Children sitting on carpet to hear the story. Allow them to discuss briefly.
30 mins	Ask the children to make something using the resources provided that will help them to tell the story	Children to work in twos or threes – may ask the children to sketch their intended structure/model but most children prefer to explore the resources, designing and reviewing/evaluating as they go along.

Whatever is available.

You can decide whether to show the pictures to the children or leave them to visualise the images.

Group work enables children to share and discuss ideas.

Distribute kits/resources appropriately on tables or floor depending on size.

20 mins		Ask the children to identify what they have made and then reread/retell the story using the children's models as appropriate Photograph the children's work to record evidence. Put models to one side so that they can be used as a basis for children's drawing/recording	Ask children to evaluate their models: What do they like best/like least? If they had more time what else would they like to have incorporated? Are there other resources that they would like to have had available?

Can do this as a whole class or can discuss with each group of children before sequencing.

Lesson Two

Subject/topic:	Date: 27/10/2016	Teaching group/set: Y3
Construction kits/modelling materials part 2	Time: 10.30 a.m.	No. of pupils: 28

Intended learning:	NC reference/context:
Children will learn to: • record their work considering the appearance of their models from different perspectives • discuss why the model, unless symmetrical, appears different when viewed from different angles • consider how construction kits can be assembled for mass production.	Communicate their ideas through discussion, annotated sketches, cross-sectional drawings and through the use of pattern (component) pieces

Success criteria:	Assessment strategy:
All children will be able to: • record their model from at least one perspective • discuss the type/number of components used and sort components used into 'types' • offer ideas and suggestions to develop their model, e.g. mention symmetry, even, uneven, did not have enough components to make the model 'match'. Some children will be able to: • extend the activity: Can you disassemble your model and record the stages so that your friend could use your recordings to make the model? • suggest a range of resources that have not already been used that would enable them to make a construction kit of their own (clothes pegs, drinking straws, card triangles, lolly sticks with/without holes, masking tape, electrical wire, paper fasteners, paper clips)	• Ability of children to record their models and relate their drawing to the different observational positions • Questioning of children to elicit ideas and component choice • Marking of written record of stages in construction • Observation of construction kit assembly

Key vocabulary:	Resources:	Risk assessment:
components, design, models, perspective, plan view	large sheets sugar paper, chalk, potential ideas that children may have for building their own construction kit	Wash hands after using chalk

Time	Teacher focus	Pupil focus
10 mins	Set out models from last time and arrange children so that models can be viewed from different perspectives	Children discuss and review the models
20 mins	Ask children to discuss their recordings and then to work with another group to decide how drawings correspond to models	Children draw the model from their own seating position
10 mins	Evaluate and discuss – including plan view – links to maps and geography	Children set up 'working wall' type display with their drawings

Peer evaluation supports critical review.

Working walls demonstrate progression and support children in reviewing the development of their design.

Lesson Three

Subject/topic:	Date: 31/10/2016	Teaching group/set: Y3
Modelling using found materials	Time: 1.15 p.m.	No. of pupils: 28

Intended learning:	NC reference/context:
Children will learn to: • explore a range of available materials • use the materials selected to their best advantage • evaluate a range of joining techniques • use temporary fixings.	Make – Select from a wider range of materials and components, including construction materials according to their functional and aesthetic properties

Success criteria:	Assessment strategy:
All children will be able to: • collect a variety of available/reclaimed materials appropriate to modelling • draw and talk about the materials and resources they wish to use. Some children will be able to: • review their work and make improvements and suggestions as they work.	• Observation of children's collection and use of materials • Observation and questioning of ideas • Questioning relating to review

Key vocabulary:	Resources:	Risk assessment:
texture, material, mouldable, strengthen, reinforce, stiffen, investigate, explore, evaluate	*Henry's Exercises* by Rodney Peppe Clothes pegs, drinking straws, card triangles, lolly sticks with/without holes, masking tape, electrical wire, paper fasteners, paper clips, sticky labels, pieces of correx chalk, A3 paper	Hacksaws, low-melt glue guns Children have been taught to use the tools safely and are aware of risks and risk 'benefits'

Book is very old but available at very low cost. It is great because it is written with humour and yet is very immediate.

May have other resources available – plasticised garden wire is great and can be bought as cheaply as £1 in budget shops.

Time	Teacher focus	Pupil focus
10 mins	Read the book *Henry's Exercises*, by Rodney Peppe. Reread and ask children to discuss. Set the design brief – children are going to design and make a model to help Henry to exercise. Henry is an elephant!	Children sit on the carpet – the story is short and teachers may wish to consider whether the children are shown the illustrations in the book or whether the children are left to visualise. Teacher shows children range of resources/ materials that are available for use
30 mins	Teacher circulates – discusses children's ideas and helps the children consider the use of temporary fixings to allow a 'mock up'/prototype of the model	Children can work in twos to develop their design, consider the materials they will use (and why), make large labelled drawing of their construction – they may wish to fold their paper to draw different perspectives
40 mins	Teacher circulates and discusses progress with the children and supports/ suggests as is required Teacher records/photographs children's models for display	Children collect resources and work on their models. Children engage with design, make, evaluate cycle and make adaptations to their model ideas Children share/evaluate/ explain their ideas during the next literacy lesson to facilitate speaking and listening opportunity

Children paired or grouped at teacher's discretion to maximise involvement and engagement.

Will carry over to another lesson to provide speaking and listening context.

Design and technology 3 The framework for design and technology

Purpose of study

Design and technology is an inspiring, rigorous and practical subject. Using creativity and imagination, pupils design and make products that solve real and relevant problems within a variety of contexts, considering their own and others' needs, wants and values. They acquire a broad range of subject knowledge and draw on disciplines such as mathematics, science, engineering, computing and art. Pupils learn how to take risks, becoming resourceful, innovative, enterprising and capable citizens. Through the evaluation of past and present design and technology, they develop a critical understanding of its impact on daily life and the wider world. High-quality design and technology education makes an essential contribution to the creativity, culture, wealth and well-being of the nation.

Aims

The national curriculum for design and technology aims to ensure that all pupils:

- develop the creative, technical and practical expertise needed to perform everyday tasks confidently and to participate successfully in an increasingly technological world
- build and apply a repertoire of knowledge, understanding and skills in order to design and make high-quality prototypes and products for a wide range of users
- critique, evaluate and test their ideas and products and the work of others
- understand and apply the principles of nutrition and learn how to cook.

Attainment targets

By the end of each key stage, pupils are expected to know, apply and understand the matters, skills and processes specified in the relevant programme of study.

Schools are not required by law to teach the example content in [square brackets].

Subject content

Key stage 1

Through a variety of creative and practical activities, pupils should be taught the knowledge, understanding and skills needed to engage in an iterative process of designing and making. They should work in a range of relevant contexts [for example, the home and school, gardens and playgrounds, the local community, industry and the wider environment].

When designing and making, pupils should be taught to:

Design

- design purposeful, functional, appealing products for themselves and other users based on design criteria
- generate, develop, model and communicate their ideas through talking, drawing, templates, mock-ups and, where appropriate, information and communication technology

Make

- select from and use a range of tools and equipment to perform practical tasks [for example, cutting, shaping, joining and finishing]
- select from and use a wide range of materials and components, including construction materials, textiles and ingredients, according to their characteristics

Evaluate

- explore and evaluate a range of existing products
- evaluate their ideas and products against design criteria

Technical knowledge

- build structures, exploring how they can be made stronger, stiffer and more stable
- explore and use mechanisms [for example, levers, sliders, wheels and axles], in their products.

Key stage 2

Through a variety of creative and practical activities, pupils should be taught the knowledge, understanding and skills needed to engage in an iterative process of designing and making. They should work in a range of relevant contexts [for example, the home, school, leisure, culture, enterprise, industry and the wider environment].

When designing and making, pupils should be taught to:

Design

- use research and develop design criteria to inform the design of innovative, functional, appealing products that are fit for purpose, aimed at particular individuals or groups
- generate, develop, model and communicate their ideas through discussion, annotated sketches, cross-sectional and exploded diagrams, prototypes, pattern pieces and computer-aided design

Make

- select from and use a wider range of tools and equipment to perform practical tasks [for example, cutting, shaping, joining and finishing], accurately
- select from and use a wider range of materials and components, including construction materials, textiles and ingredients, according to their functional properties and aesthetic qualities

Evaluate

- investigate and analyse a range of existing products
- evaluate their ideas and products against their own design criteria and consider the views of others to improve their work
- understand how key events and individuals in design and technology have helped shape the world

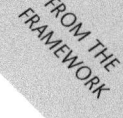

Technical knowledge

- apply their understanding of how to strengthen, stiffen and reinforce more complex structures
- understand and use mechanical systems in their products [for example, gears, pulleys, cams, levers and linkages]
- understand and use electrical systems in their products [for example, series circuits incorporating switches, bulbs, buzzers and motors]
- apply their understanding of computing to program, monitor and control their products.

Cooking and nutrition

As part of their work with food, pupils should be taught how to cook and apply the principles of nutrition and healthy eating. Instilling a love of cooking in pupils will also open a door to one of the great expressions of human creativity. Learning how to cook is a crucial life skill that enables pupils to feed themselves and others affordably and well, now and in later life.

Pupils should be taught to:

Key stage 1

- use the basic principles of a healthy and varied diet to prepare dishes
- understand where food comes from.

Key stage 2

- understand and apply the principles of a healthy and varied diet
- prepare and cook a variety of predominantly savoury dishes using a range of cooking techniques
- understand seasonality, and know where and how a variety of ingredients are grown, reared, caught and processed.

🌧 10 Geography

Planning geography in the national curriculum

Deborah Wilkinson

Geography 1 Principles of planning

This section looks at the key factors which are specific to planning effective geography lessons. It builds on the generic factors for planning found in Chapter 1 and should be read in conjunction with these ideas.

Good geography lessons should be creative, imaginative and relevant to children (Geographical Association, 2005). Planned lessons should teach children about places, people and issues (both local and global). The national curriculum purpose of study statement is based on a framework of core subject knowledge, understanding and skills, and geographical topics are defined as either human or physical geography. Geographical skills such as mapping should be used to help children to interpret data and should be woven into planning wherever possible, as should fieldwork, which is a statutory part of the curriculum.

Fieldwork and enquiry

Fieldwork helps children to develop core competencies (such as mapping skills) that enable them to engage with the world in a more meaningful way. The local area provides children with a context for learning and understanding local issues – a key skill if they are to connect with the wider world. As a teacher it is, therefore, imperative that you have a good awareness of the area surrounding the school (local streets, parks and amenities) as these locations will provide you with a key resource when planning fieldwork opportunities. Children who have engaged in fieldwork relating to their local area are better positioned to identify similarities and differences between their region and that of another. OFSTED (2011, page 9) identified that pupils whose learning was outstanding were *very familiar with their own location and were able to make connections between their lives and those of others in a contrasting location.* There is, however, a need to avoid the issue of presenting an inaccurate and biased or over-simplified view of a country. Oxfam's *Education for Global Citizenship: A Guide for Schools* (2006) and Chapter 16 of the Geographical Association's *Primary Geography Handbook* (2005) provide guidance relating to how comparisons can be taught so that racist, discriminatory and stereotypical views can be challenged.

Although there is no requirement for enquiry, it could be argued that this is an essential feature of effective geography planning and is implicit in supporting children to understand their world. Good enquiry-based lessons provide a powerful vehicle for developing geographical knowledge and understanding and lie at the heart of good geography in school (Kinder, 2013). Your planning should provide children with a purpose and a context and allow children to question and investigate an issue. Enquiry should not be viewed as a 'bolt on' but should be informing the planning. The idea is to develop understanding rather than to simply 'deliver content' via a transmission style of teaching. During an enquiry lesson a teacher should view themselves as a facilitator rather than someone who delivers or transmits facts to children. During the process of enquiry-based learning children are partners in determining the process of learning and should be actively engaged in discovering things for themselves. This way of working can be outlined in an 'input/output' chart, as shown in Figure 10.1.

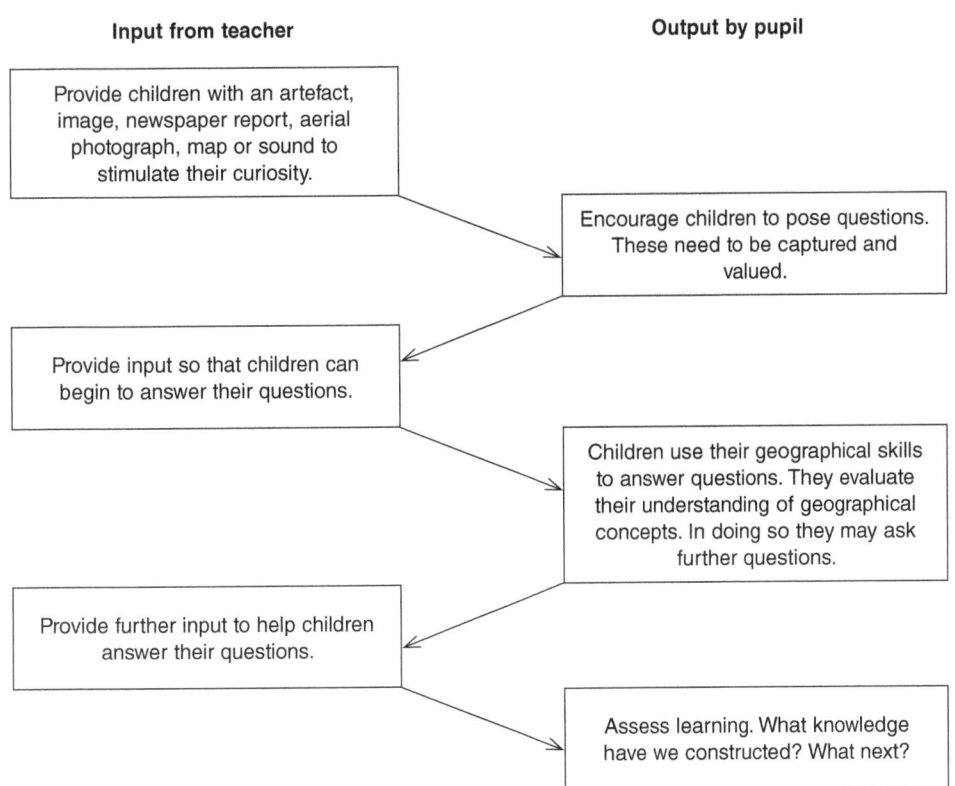

Figure 10.1   Input/output planning chart

The challenge faced with the input/output planning model is to consider motivating ways in which the content of the curriculum can be stimulated. Encouraging children to raise questions can be hard but is worth the effort as it provides children with ownership over their learning. *A Different View* (Geographical Association, 2000) provides a useful source of questions that can be used to model effective questioning skills to children. OFSTED also publishes good practice examples of geography planning in their examples of good practice.

Further reading

Geographical Association (2005) *Primary Geography Handbook.* Sheffield: Geographical Association.

Geographical Association (2009) *A Different View: A Manifesto from the Geographical Association.* Sheffield: Geographical Association.

Kinder, A. (2013) Questioning Geography. *Teaching Geography*, Spring: 6–7.

OFSTED (2011) Learning to make a world of difference. [Online] Available at: **http://dera. ioe.ac.uk/2154/1/Geography%20declining%20in%20schools.pdf**

OFSTED. Good practice examples can be found at: **https://www.gov.uk/government/ collections/ofsted-examples-of-good-practice-in-geography-teaching**

Oxfam (2006) *Education for Global Citizenship: A Guide for Schools.* Available at: **www.oxfam. org.uk/education/global-citizenship**

Geography 2 Examples of planning

The following three lesson plans are provided as examples of planning in geography. They do not contain the detail you will probably wish to have on your plans but do illustrate some of the points discussed previously.

Lesson One

Subject/topic: Mapping skills	Date: 23/10/2016 Time: 12:45 p.m.	Teaching group/set: Y2 No. of pupils: 28
Intended learning: Children will learn to: • identify key physical and human features in a landscape, e.g. hill, mountain, farm, house • use simple directions and locational language.	**NC reference/context:** Human and physical geography Mapping skills	
Success criteria: All children will be able to: • use geographical language to identify physical and human features in a landscape • use a Beebot to develop their directional understanding (using words such as forward).	**Assessment strategy:** • Observation of groupings and discussion which informs these • Working with a group	

Key vocabulary: mountain, hill, house, woods, bungalow, palace, next to, opposite, near, far, left, right	Resources: *The Jolly Postman or Other People's Letters* by J. and A. Ahlberg Scanned image of the final double page of the book for IWB Crayons and wall paper Beebots	Risk assessment: Working in groups – ensure children are aware of sharing and turn-taking.

A story is a good 'hook' to engage children in the learning.

Time	Teacher focus	Pupil focus
10 mins	Read *The Jolly Postman or Other People's Letters* to the children. Highlight the address of each of the recipient's letters in relation to key physical features (e.g. mountain, hill, woods) and human features (town, house and cottage).	Children to be seated on the carpet as the story is shared with them. As the story is being read to the children ask TA to stick the envelopes onto the whiteboard so that children have a visual prompt of the Jolly Postman's journey. Write key words (e.g. hills, woods) that are presented in the story.
30 mins	In groups, children to draw a story map showing the Jolly Postman's route on rolls of wall paper. They will then label the physical and human features. Children to say where houses are in relation to each other using directional language – opposite, next to, etc.	Scan the final page of the book onto the IWB so that children have a visual overview of all of the places visited by the Jolly Postman. In groups of six, children to map the story.

| 30 mins | Children to use Beebots to map the quickest journey between the places that the Jolly Postman visits on his route. | **Challenge:** The Jolly Postman has been taking too long to deliver his letters. Can you find the quickest route between the different locations? Children will decide how to plan their routes and will use the Beebot, using directional language, e.g. opposite, next to, forward, right and left. |
| 10 mins | Children to report which is the best route for the Jolly Postman to take. | Children will orally explain why a particular route is best for the Jolly Postman. Encourage children to use geographical language. |

Children will have ownership as they can decide upon the 'best' route. This will also stimulate the children to use geographical language.

Lesson Two

Subject/topic:	Date: 27/10/2016	Teaching group/set: Y2
Mapping skills	Time: 10.30 a.m.	No. of pupils: 28

Intended learning:	NC reference/context:
Children will learn to: • use aerial views to recognise local landmarks • use maps to plan a simple route.	Geographical skills

Success criteria:	Assessment strategy:
All children will be able to: • identify the school and their home on an aerial map • begin to plan a simple route (with support). Some children will be able to: • recognise some key local landmarks • begin to plan a route.	• Presentation of maps, listening to geographical language used

Key vocabulary:	Resources:	Risk assessment:
aerial map, maps, build on language introduced last week relating to physical and human geography	iPads Maps of the local area	None

Time	Teacher focus	Pupil focus
10 mins	Start the lesson using Google Maps and zoom into the school grounds and surrounding area. Does anyone recognise this place? (Focus on local landmarks)	What is this place like? Gather children's questions so they can answer the questions next week.
20 mins	Children to explore their local area using learning pads or iPads. Can they find their route to school from home? Can they find their house on the map? Children will work in pairs to plan a route from school to a local amenity for next week when they find out what the place is like. They will start with the aerial view and will then use printed maps (simple maps of the local area).	Children to use iPads/learning pads to identify different locations locally. Children will also begin to plan the route between the school and the local area.

Collecting children's questions is important so that children are able to answer them in the next session.

You have provided the stimulus in the form of maps; now children will have the opportunity to explore ideas.

10 mins	Children to share the route that they will walk next week with the rest of the class. Children will vote on the best route.	Provide children with maps and using a red pencil draw in the route children will walk next week.

Lesson Three

Subject/topic:	Date: 31/10/2016	Teaching group/set: Y2
Mapping skills	Time: 11 a.m.	No. of pupils: 28

Intended learning:	NC reference/context:
Children will learn to: • identify key features in the environment that they like and dislike and record these using cameras/iPads • use their maps from last week to locate the local area.	Fieldwork and geographical skills

The fieldwork provides children with the opportunity to answer their questions.

Success criteria:	Assessment strategy:
All children will be able to: • record their observations using pictures and words • follow a map with support. Some children will be able to: • record using pictures and charts • follow a map.	• Observation • Assessment of presentations

Key vocabulary:	Resources:	Risk assessment:
Language relating to human geography developed in the previous 2 lessons	Maps from previous week ICT equipment for recording	You will need to follow the school guidelines in relation to planning a fieldwork opportunity for children.

Time	Teacher focus	Pupil focus
90 mins	Children to go on a 'welly walk' to a local area to make an environmental quality analysis (how good or bad a place is). Children will use their maps from the previous lesson to find their way to the local area.	Children will complete an environmental analysis of the local area. Children will take digital camera pictures (or will use iPads or learning pads to record their feelings and thoughts). They will focus on recording things they like and things they dislike about the area. Children will work in pairs. Children's work will be unpacked in the following lesson when they consider how the location could be made better – this may include inviting a person from the local council into school so that children can feed back to someone who has the power to make change happen.

Use of technology will serve as a reminder of the fieldwork when back in class.

Children may pose further questions that will need answering. A visitor to the school can help with this.

Geography 3 The framework for geography

Purpose of study

A high-quality geography education should inspire in pupils a curiosity and fascination about the world and its people that will remain with them for the rest of their lives. Teaching should equip pupils with knowledge about diverse places, people, resources and natural and human environments, together with a deep understanding of the Earth's key physical and human processes. As pupils progress, their growing knowledge about the world should help them to deepen their understanding of the interaction between physical and human processes, and of the formation and use of landscapes and environments. Geographical knowledge, understanding and skills provide the framework and approaches that explain how the Earth's features at different scales are shaped, interconnected and change over time.

Aims

The national curriculum for geography aims to ensure that all pupils:

- develop contextual knowledge of the location of globally significant places – both terrestrial and marine – including their defining physical and human characteristics and how these provide a geographical context for understanding the actions of processes
- understand the processes that give rise to key physical and human geographical features of the world, how these are interdependent and how they bring about spatial variation and change over time
- are competent in the geographical skills needed to:

  o collect, analyse and communicate with a range of data gathered through experiences of fieldwork that deepen their understanding of geographical processes
  o interpret a range of sources of geographical information, including maps, diagrams, globes, aerial photographs and Geographical Information Systems (GIS)
  o communicate geographical information in a variety of ways, including through maps, numerical and quantitative skills and writing at length.

Schools are not required by law to teach the example content in [square brackets].

Attainment targets

By the end of each key stage, pupils are expected to know, apply and understand the matters, skills and processes specified in the relevant programme of study.

Subject content

Key stage 1

Pupils should develop knowledge about the world, the United Kingdom and their locality. They should understand basic subject-specific vocabulary relating to human and physical geography and begin to use geographical skills, including first-hand observation, to enhance their locational awareness.

Pupils should be taught to:

Locational knowledge

- name and locate the world's 7 continents and 5 oceans
- name, locate and identify characteristics of the 4 countries and capital cities of the United Kingdom and its surrounding seas

Place knowledge

- understand geographical similarities and differences through studying the human and physical geography of a small area of the United Kingdom, and of a small area in a contrasting non-European country

Human and physical geography

- identify seasonal and daily weather patterns in the United Kingdom and the location of hot and cold areas of the world in relation to the Equator and the North and South Poles
- use basic geographical vocabulary to refer to:
  - o key physical features, including: beach, cliff, coast, forest, hill, mountain, sea, ocean, river, soil, valley, vegetation, season and weather
  - o key human features, including: city, town, village, factory, farm, house, office, port, harbour and shop

Geographical skills and fieldwork

- use world maps, atlases and globes to identify the United Kingdom and its countries, as well as the countries, continents and oceans studied at this key stage
- use simple compass directions (north, south, east and west) and locational and directional language [for example, near and far, left and right], to describe the location of features and routes on a map
- use aerial photographs and plan perspectives to recognise landmarks and basic human and physical features; devise a simple map; and use and construct basic symbols in a key
- use simple fieldwork and observational skills to study the geography of their school and its grounds and the key human and physical features of its surrounding environment.

Key stage 2

Pupils should extend their knowledge and understanding beyond the local area to include the United Kingdom and Europe, North and South America. This will include the location and characteristics of a range of the world's most significant human and physical features. They should develop their use of geographical knowledge, understanding and skills to enhance their locational and place knowledge.

Pupils should be taught to:

Locational knowledge

- locate the world's countries, using maps to focus on Europe (including the location of Russia) and North and South America, concentrating on their environmental regions, key physical and human characteristics, countries, and major cities

- name and locate counties and cities of the United Kingdom, geographical regions and their identifying human and physical characteristics, key topographical features (including hills, mountains, coasts and rivers), and land-use patterns; and understand how some of these aspects have changed over time
- identify the position and significance of latitude, longitude, Equator, Northern Hemisphere, Southern Hemisphere, the Tropics of Cancer and Capricorn, Arctic and Antarctic Circle, the Prime/Greenwich Meridian and time zones (including day and night)

Place knowledge

- understand geographical similarities and differences through the study of human and physical geography of a region of the United Kingdom, a region in a European country, and a region in North or South America

Human and physical geography

- describe and understand key aspects of:
  - o physical geography, including: climate zones, biomes and vegetation belts, rivers, mountains, volcanoes and earthquakes, and the water cycle
  - o human geography, including: types of settlement and land use, economic activity including trade links, and the distribution of natural resources including energy, food, minerals and water

Geographical skills and fieldwork

- use maps, atlases, globes and digital/computer mapping to locate countries and describe features studied
- use the 8 points of a compass, 4- and 6-figure grid references, symbols and keys (including the use of Ordnance Survey maps) to build their knowledge of the United Kingdom and the wider world
- use fieldwork to observe, measure, record and present the human and physical features in the local area using a range of methods, including sketch maps, plans and graphs, and digital technologies.

11 History

Planning history in the national curriculum

Linda Cooper

History 1 Principles of planning

This section looks at the key factors which are specific to planning effective history lessons. It builds on the generic factors for planning found in Chapter 1 and should be read in conjunction with these ideas.

History is an essential part of the learning journey of the primary school pupil. Lessons with our young historians should be both engaging and memorable. We need to be planning for learning that helps children understand their personal, cultural and national heritage in order to help them develop their identity and sense of belonging to their family, their school, their community, their locality and their nation. In doing so, children discover and explore their own place in the wider world and the presence of history in the curriculum makes learning a more compelling experience as a result. As outlined in Chapter 2, good planning does not necessarily guarantee good learning. However, the themes that are outlined in this chapter should help you to focus your planning in ways calculated to ensure that lessons follow the principles of effective pedagogy in this subject.

Using the curriculum framework effectively

In common with the other curriculum subjects the programme of study (PoS) for history starts by defining the 'purpose of study' and provides a list of historical aims. This is then followed by a section on subject content, where the nature of historical learning and the areas covered are defined at each key stage. It is tempting to turn straight to the part of the PoS that details 'what' you should be teaching. It is a natural impulse to examine the 'content' of the curriculum as it is this that makes this subject so immensely intriguing. However, when planning lessons, you need to pause and carefully examine the purpose of study and the aims for this subject. By doing so you will come to understand the skills and concepts that make for an effective young historian and will ensure that your planned history lessons have depth and realise opportunities for good history teaching. It is this area of the PoS that we will now explore in more detail.

Planning for the development of historical concepts and skills

Good planning is based on an appreciation of the importance of developing historical concepts and skills in lessons. The initial preamble and the aims of the PoS outline these essential key concepts and skills, and important examples include:

- continuity and change – pupils need to understand changes over time and analyse their impact;
- cause and consequence – pupils need to investigate why people acted in a certain way and explain reasons for this;
- similarity and difference – pupils need to analyse similarities and differences between people, beliefs and cultures;
- significance of people – pupils need to consider the nature of significance and how notable individuals have impacted in local, national and global terms;
- the use of evidence – questions, deductions and hypotheses about the past need to be formed via the use of primary sources;
- interpretations of history – pupils need to think about the different ways the past is portrayed and the reasons for this.

Every lesson plan should identify which of these concepts are targeted and how they will be developed. However, there are other generalised skills that require careful consideration when planning history. You need to ensure that your planning supports the development of questioning, observation skills, classifying and analysing, hypothesising, deducting and making connections through a developing awareness of how different aspects of history interrelate – these are all skills that are required of a historian.

A note about chronology . . .

Chronology, the understanding of the passing of time, is another key concept that needs to be considered as part of the planning process. This has been given particular consideration in this chapter, reflecting the new emphasis placed on chronology in the PoS where it is prominent in the section on the aims of the curriculum and is emphasised in statements about content at each key stage.

This emphasis on chronology is not surprising. OFSTED (2011) found that many primary school children had a poorly developed understanding of the passing of time and could not link periods and events together. In addition, OFSTED (2011) argued that the way schools planned history emphasised an episodic understanding of time periods that resulted in children being unable to grasp an overview of the passing of time. While children might have in-depth knowledge of one period, they could not place it in a bigger time-frame or make connections between the period studied and what came before and after.

Planning for chronology, therefore, needs to be carefully considered so that children are able to place events in a long-term narrative. To help achieve this some topics might be planned as in-depth topics and some might be planned to be delivered as overviews in order that children are helped to build up a full and coherent knowledge of chronology such that they come to appreciate the 'long arc' of history. For more information as to how to plan chronology Cooper (2013) includes a very useful chapter on this theme.

Planning for substantive knowledge

While planning for historical skills and concepts is vital, historical knowledge should also be a major element of the planning process. Good history plans should use a combination of approaches that support the development of historical thinking alongside the acquisition of historical knowledge. Maddison (2014) notes the importance of historical knowledge when he asserts that *pupils' knowledge and understanding of topics studied is not as good as it was at the time of OFSTED's (2011) last subject report* (page 5). Byrom (2013) also discusses the importance of the development of historical knowledge and suggests that it would be a *travesty to suggest that the subject was simply about skills* (page 8). It is the 'knowledge' part of the curriculum that makes history so very fascinating and provides the foundation on which historical skills can be developed securely.

Byrom (2013) suggests that substantive knowledge is engendered in children by teachers equipped with good subject knowledge of their own. He suggests that planning should be 'grounded' in strong subject knowledge that is made up from a combination of familiarity with historical events, an understanding of the issues and dilemmas that dominated the period to be studied and 'nuggets' of information, based on a smaller scale, which serve to illustrate and evoke the character of human lives from the past (Byrom, 2013).

Developing subject knowledge in some areas defined in the new history curriculum may be challenging for some practitioners. Some areas, such as British history before 1066 or early civilisations like the Ancient Sumer or the Shang Dynasty of Ancient China, may require teachers to undertake research in order to improve their own understanding before embarking on planning a new topic. However, the investment of time is worthwhile as good subject knowledge enables teachers to create windows into the past that are more interesting and more likely to promote historical knowledge and skills in their pupils. A really good place to start is The Historical Association website (**www.history.org.uk**) where you will find sections dedicated to updating subject knowledge.

Planning via enquiry

Good historical learning is that which is based around enquiry. An enquiry-led approach is one that encourages *pupils to ask relevant questions, to pose and define problems, to plan what to and how to research, to predict outcomes and anticipate consequences, and to test conclusions and improve ideas* (DfEE/QCA, 1999: 22). Enquiry-based learning encourages independent learning and OFSTED (2011) notes that *the most effective schools use a well focused enquiry-based approach to achieve this* (pages 6–7). Adopting an enquiry-based approach helps teachers move away from teacher-centred approaches and promotes a socio-constructivist environment where children are active participants in the learning journey.

Utilising an enquiry-based approach to learning has direct implications for the planning process. Good learning will be encouraged by the creation of initial, enquiry-based questions that will lead the learning for the class. These should help to imbue themes with a sense of mystery and inspire interest and curiosity in the subject being taught. Questions that start with 'how does', 'what is', 'who were', 'how much' and 'which' help to initiate enquiry and encourage children to actively engage in the application of historical concepts or in making comparisons between

 time periods. For instance, the question 'In which house would you prefer to live?' could be a useful starter to help children spot similarity and difference as well as encouraging comparative reasoning. *Primary Humanities* by Pickford et al. (2013) provides a useful chapter on enquiry-based learning and gives numerous examples of enquiry-based questions.

Resources

Your plans need to show how you will use resources to bring your lesson to life as effective use of good resources is integral to helping children imagine 'what it was really like'. You need to plan to make use of a wide variety of resources using a combination of primary (evidence that was created at the time of the period being studied) and secondary (information written after the event) sources. These might include, among other things, pictures, portraits, objects, museums, archives, local and national monuments, people, buildings, digital resources and documentary papers. Planning to resource units of work that are based in the more distant past (e.g. pre-1066) can be challenging as there is much less available primary evidence to use. You will need to think carefully about how you overcome this challenge. Look at your locality and see if any buildings or monuments date back to pre-1066 – you may be surprised at what you find. Make the most of local museums as they can provide a wealth of resources. Many of the national museums provide a bank of high-quality digital images of objects found before 1066 and the websites of the British Museum (**www.britishmuseum.org**) and English Heritage (**www.english-heritage.org.uk**) provide good images of settlement, hill forts and Stone Age objects.

Planning for assessment of progression

Ensuring you have a good understanding of historical conceptual development is essential in helping you to plan for effective assessment. Teachers need to be aware that their plans should cater for the assessment of historical knowledge and children's acquisition of skills and concepts. For instance, children should progress in their conceptual understanding of chronology and the way they express their attainment in this subject should be very different between year 1 and year 6. Furthermore, assessment of historical understanding should not just be about the written product, but should offer children the opportunity to demonstrate their understanding in a whole range of outputs.

Further reading

Byrom, J. (2013) Alive and kicking? Some personal reflections on the revised National Curriculum (2014) and what we might do with it. *Teaching History. Curriculum Evolution. The Historical Association Curriculum Supplement*, 6–12.

Cooper, H. (2013) *Teaching History Creativity*. Abingdon: Routledge.

Maddison, M. (2014) The National Curriculum for History from Sept 2014: The view from OFSTED. *Primary History*, 66 (Spring): 5–7.

OFSTED (2011) *History for All: History in English Schools 2007/10*. Manchester: Crown Copyright.

Pickford, T., Garner, W. and Jackson, E. (2013) *Primary Humanities*. London: Sage.

Turner-Bisset, R. (2005) *Creative Teaching: History in the Primary Classroom*. London: David Fulton.

History 2 Examples of planning

The following three lesson plans are provided as examples of planning in history. They do not contain the detail you will probably wish to have on your plans but do illustrate some of the points discussed previously.

Lesson One

Subject/topic:	Date: 23/10/2016	Teaching group/set: Y5
Houses through time	Time: 1.00 p.m.	No. of pupils: 28

Intended learning:	NC reference/context:
KEY QUESTION: How have houses changed over time? Children will learn to: • make observations about the interior of homes through time • observe continuity and change across different periods of time.	A study of an aspect or theme in British history that extends pupils' chronological knowledge beyond 1066 Key concept: continuity and change

Note the overarching enquiry question.

Note that the learning objective is related to the development of a historical concept.

Success criteria:	Assessment strategy:
All children will be able to: • make observations about what has changed and what has remained the same when studying living rooms from different time periods • make simple deductions about society in the time period being observed. Some children will be able to: • make comparisons between time periods • explain the impact of change over time.	• Observation of groupings and discussion which informs these • Marking of table that lists changes over time • Assessment of whether children have been able to make comparative statements • Evidence of deductive reasoning

Key vocabulary:	Resources:	Risk assessment:
continuity, change, same, difference, deduction, hypothesis	Pictures of living rooms from 1930s, 2000 and 2014 (one set for each table) wireless, radio, digital radio/iPad Pictures of one of the dwellings from Skara Brae (a Stone Age/Neolithic home)	

Time	Teacher focus	Pupil focus
15 mins	Introduce the lesson by showing the children a wireless and asking them what it might have been used for. Once they have deduced what it is used for, ask the children how the radios they use today have changed and how they have stayed the same. Show the children the analogue and digital radio/iPad and think about how these gadgets have changed.	

The lesson starts with an artefact (primary evidence) in order to create interest and intrigue.

		Continue by showing the children pictures of three living rooms from the past and compare them to the one from the present. Ask them to spot the differences, but also get them to think about what has stayed the same. Ask the children to work as history detectives and use the photographs to note how the rooms have changed.	Sitting at group tables (six per table) ask children to look at pictures provided and ask them to talk about what is different and what has stayed the same.
	25 mins	Teacher to explain to the children a table on which they record changes between the living rooms and things that have stayed the same. Also explain a third column in which deductions about life in the past and present are made.	Encourage the children to try to make simple deductions about the past. For instance, is there any evidence of how families used their leisure time? Note changes in things like technology but also note developments that include changes in attitudes – for instance, is the most modern room more environmentally friendly? What is the **evidence** for this?
Note the use of pictures of primary evidence.	20 mins	Get children to specify some of the changes they have noted. Now extend the task and show the children a picture of the inside of one of the dwellings of Skara Brae – a Stone Age/Neolithic dwelling.	When showing the picture of Skara Brae the children will probably initially think it is very different and will easily point out these differences. Encourage children to use this **evidence** to consider whether there are actually any similarities, e.g. the presence of a 'stone dresser' in the room at Skara Brae where objects of value may have been stored. Also, the hearth providing warmth and a natural meeting place would be similar to sitting rooms through the ages.

Note the use of pictures of primary evidence.

Note the emphasis on making comparisons across time periods – children need to grasp the long arc of history.

Lesson Two

Subject/topic:	Date: 27/10/2016	Teaching group/set: Y5
Houses through time	Time: 10.00 a.m.	No. of pupils: 28
KEY QUESTION: How have houses changed over time? **Intended learning:** Children will: • learn about changes and continuity in houses across time periods • learn to associate features of houses with a particular period • undertake research in order to answer questions about the past • communicate their findings using a digital resource.	**NC reference/context:** A study of an aspect or theme in British history that extends pupils' chronological knowledge beyond 1066 Key concept: continuity and change Key concept: chronology	

Remember to be aware of the importance of developing chronological understanding.

Success criteria: All children will be able to: • make at least three comparative statements about differences in the external features of two houses from different time periods • associate features of a house with a historical period • carry out research with some support • present their work on a PowerPoint slide with support. Some children will be able to: • carry out research independently • make value judgements about which house they would prefer to live in and give reasons for this • present their work on a PowerPoint slide independently.	**Assessment strategy:** • Observation of the ability of the children to undertake independent research • Assessment of quality of comparative statements on the PowerPoint slide

Key vocabulary:	**Resources:**	**Risk assessment:**
Iron Age wattle, Roman daub, Anglo Saxon, Viking, Tudor, Georgian, Victorian, oldest, newest	Pictures of houses from different time periods from the Iron Age to houses built in more modern times, placed in six envelopes Laptops (ensure they are fully charged) with internet connection Secondary sources on homes through time	Give children a selected list of websites through which they can investigate houses and homes – check websites for validity of content.

Time	Teacher focus	Pupil focus
15 mins	Recall the learning from the previous lesson and reintroduce the overarching enquiry focus of how houses have changed over time. Ask children to open the envelopes on their desks and look at the pictures of the houses. Have pictures of these houses up on the IWB. Ask the following questions about the houses: • Which of the houses are similar to your house? • What materials have been used to build the houses in the pictures? • Which houses have windows, which do not? Do they open and close? • Which houses have just one room, which have more than one? • Do the houses have chimneys? • Do you notice anything about the front doors? • What time periods do you think the houses belong to? Why do you think this?	Emphasis will be on children working in pairs and talking about the pictures. Encourage the children to study the pictures carefully and to raise questions about them.

Remember to build on prior knowledge.

Note the emphasis on trying to make the past visual in order to capture the curiosity of the children.

Consider how your questioning encourages historical thinking and comparative reasoning.

Give an opportunity for children to extend their thinking.

35 mins	Ask pairs to pick two houses they wish to investigate further via research.	Using websites and selected books, pairs to research their two chosen houses.
	Teacher to support blue group (LA) when carrying out research.	Children to create a PowerPoint slide that compares and contrasts their two houses – particular categories of room numbers, building materials, doors and windows should be focused on. Using the information some children might make a judgement about which house they would prefer to live in and give reasons for this.
	Teacher to remind children to allocate a time period to their chosen houses (e.g. I think one house is Roman, one house is from the Iron Age).	
	Encourage the children to try to hypothesise about the past using the pictures and secondary sources (e.g. some Tudor houses had windows containing glass. In Tudor houses the windows were small as glass was very expensive).	
20 mins	Teacher to ask children to share their PowerPoint slide.	Children to assess the contributions of their peers using the phrases:
	Teacher to make one resource out of all the slides to be used in the next session	I liked . . .
	Teacher to set homework: children to take a picture of a house in their locality, to print out and bring in.	It would be even better if . . .

Lesson Three

Subject/topic:	Date: 3/10/2016	Teaching group/set: Y5
Houses through time	Time: 9.00 a.m.	No. of pupils: 28

KEY QUESTION: How have houses changed over time?	NC reference/context:
Intended learning:	A study of an aspect or theme in British history that extends pupils' chronological knowledge beyond 1066
Children will learn to:	
• classify features of houses and relate them to distinct time periods • sequence houses according to their age from oldest to newest • note when and why architecture changes and to comment on the impact of this.	Key concept: chronology

Success criteria:	Assessment strategy:
All children will be able to: • sequence their houses in the correct order • associate at least five of their houses with correct time periods • make judgement statements about change over time. Some children will be able to: • place all their houses in time order • associate the house with a period of time	• Assessment of timelines • Assessment of the level of chronological vocabulary used on the timeline • Assessment of statements made about change and the impact of change • Interrogation of the database for accuracy of information

- allocate dates to their timeline
- make a very simple database based on houses through time.

Key vocabulary:	Resources:	Risk assessment:
Iron Age century, Roman millennium, Anglo Saxon, BCE/CE, Viking, Tudor, Georgian, Victorian, oldest, newest	Photographs brought in by children PowerPoint made by the children in the previous lesson Six envelopes containing colour pictures of houses Black and white pictures of the houses in the envelope – enough for one for each child Glue Information books on houses through time Pictures of the houses being discussed should also be accessible on laptops (for one group of children who make a database)	

Note the importance of developing a vocabulary associated with chronology.

Time	Teacher focus	Pupil focus
10 mins	Revisit the pictures from the last lesson – these pictures will have been supplemented by the pictures the children have brought in of houses in their locality. Teacher to have these pictures on the IWB. Teacher to also share the PowerPoint from the last lesson.	
40 mins	Teacher to support blue group (LA) when carrying out the research. TA to support the red group (HA) to use laptops in order for the children to create data-files on houses through time. TA to compile a data cards into a simple database.	Children to use the black and white pictures of houses and place them in order from oldest to newest to create a simple visual timeline. Using their knowledge gained from the prior lesson and the PowerPoint resource, the children need to try to add as much information to their timeline as possible. Allocate names for periods of time, e.g. Viking, Anglo-Saxon. When the children have got as far as possible using their prior knowledge access to secondary sources should be given in order for them to try to allocate dates to the timeline.

Work made by the children in the last lesson is revisited and reused by the teacher – this helps to raise the status of the work produced by the children.

		Under the timeline the children need to try to make statements about the impact of changes in architecture (e.g. the Romans brought new building techniques and so some building started to look quite different from the Iron Age. New materials were used which brought advancements in the way buildings were designed and built).
10 mins	Question the children about their knowledge of the changes to houses through time. Ask the children to justify their answers using their work from the last three lessons.	More able children to sequence their pictures. Each child to take one picture and create a data card on the house that should include information about the architecture and dating information.

History 3 The framework for history

Purpose of study

A high-quality history education will help pupils gain a coherent knowledge and understanding of Britain's past and that of the wider world. It should inspire pupils' curiosity to know more about the past. Teaching should equip pupils to ask perceptive questions, think critically, weigh evidence, sift arguments, and develop perspective and judgement. History helps pupils to understand the complexity of people's lives, the process of change, the diversity of societies and relationships between different groups, as well as their own identity and the challenges of their time.

Aims

The national curriculum for history aims to ensure that all pupils:

- know and understand the history of these islands as a coherent, chronological narrative, from the earliest times to the present day: how people's lives have shaped this nation and how Britain has influenced and been influenced by the wider world
- know and understand significant aspects of the history of the wider world: the nature of ancient civilisations; the expansion and dissolution of empires; characteristic features of past non-European societies; achievements and follies of mankind
- gain and deploy a historically grounded understanding of abstract terms such as 'empire', 'civilisation', 'parliament' and 'peasantry'
- understand historical concepts such as continuity and change, cause and consequence, similarity, difference and significance, and use them to make connections, draw contrasts, analyse trends, frame historically-valid questions and create their own structured accounts, including written narratives and analyses
- understand the methods of historical enquiry, including how evidence is used rigorously to make historical claims, and discern how and why contrasting arguments and interpretations of the past have been constructed
- gain historical perspective by placing their growing knowledge into different contexts, understanding the connections between local, regional, national and international history; between cultural, economic, military, political, religious and social history; and between short- and long-term timescales.

Attainment targets

By the end of each key stage, pupils are expected to know, apply and understand the matters, skills and processes specified in the relevant programme of study.

Schools are not required by law to teach the example content in [square brackets] or the content indicated as being 'non-statutory'.

Subject content

Key stage 1

Pupils should develop an awareness of the past, using common words and phrases relating to the passing of time. They should know where the people and events they study fit within

a chronological framework and identify similarities and differences between ways of life in different periods. They should use a wide vocabulary of everyday historical terms. They should ask and answer questions, choosing and using parts of stories and other sources to show that they know and understand key features of events. They should understand some of the ways in which we find out about the past and identify different ways in which it is represented.

In planning to ensure the progression described above through teaching about the people, events and changes outlined below, teachers are often introducing pupils to historical periods that they will study more fully at key stages 2 and 3.

Pupils should be taught about:

- changes within living memory. Where appropriate, these should be used to reveal aspects of change in national life
- events beyond living memory that are significant nationally or globally [for example, the Great Fire of London, the first aeroplane flight or events commemorated through festivals or anniversaries]
- the lives of significant individuals in the past who have contributed to national and international achievements. Some should be used to compare aspects of life in different periods [for example, Elizabeth I and Queen Victoria, Christopher Columbus and Neil Armstrong, William Caxton and Tim Berners-Lee, Pieter Bruegel the Elder and LS Lowry, Rosa Parks and Emily Davison, Mary Seacole and/or Florence Nightingale and Edith Cavell]
- significant historical events, people and places in their own locality.

Key stage 2

Pupils should continue to develop a chronologically secure knowledge and understanding of British, local and world history, establishing clear narratives within and across the periods they study. They should note connections, contrasts and trends over time and develop the appropriate use of historical terms. They should regularly address and sometimes devise historically valid questions about change, cause, similarity and difference, and significance. They should construct informed responses that involve thoughtful selection and organisation of relevant historical information. They should understand how our knowledge of the past is constructed from a range of sources.

In planning to ensure the progression described above through teaching the British, local and world history outlined below, teachers should combine overview and depth studies to help pupils understand both the long arc of development and the complexity of specific aspects of the content.

Pupils should be taught about:

- changes in Britain from the Stone Age to the Iron Age

> **Examples (non-statutory)**
>
> This could include:
>
> - late Neolithic hunter-gatherers and early farmers, for example, Skara Brae
> - Bronze Age religion, technology and travel, for example, Stonehenge
> - Iron Age hill forts: tribal kingdoms, farming, art and culture

- the Roman Empire and its impact on Britain

> **Examples (non-statutory)**
>
> This could include:
>
> - Julius Caesar's attempted invasion in 55–54 BC
> - the Roman Empire by AD 42 and the power of its army
> - successful invasion by Claudius and conquest, including Hadrian's Wall
> - British resistance, for example, Boudica
> - 'Romanisation' of Britain: sites such as Caerwent and the impact of technology, culture and beliefs, including early Christianity

- Britain's settlement by Anglo-Saxons and Scots

> **Examples (non-statutory)**
>
> This could include:
>
> - Roman withdrawal from Britain in c. AD 410 and the fall of the western Roman Empire
> - Scots invasions from Ireland to north Britain (now Scotland)
> - Anglo-Saxon invasions, settlements and kingdoms: place names and village life
> - Anglo-Saxon art and culture
> - Christian conversion – Canterbury, Iona and Lindisfarne

- the Viking and Anglo-Saxon struggle for the Kingdom of England to the time of Edward the Confessor

> **Examples (non-statutory)**
>
> This could include:
>
> - Viking raids and invasion
> - resistance by Alfred the Great and Athelstan, first king of England
> - further Viking invasions and Danegeld
> - Anglo-Saxon laws and justice
> - Edward the Confessor and his death in 1066

- a local history study

> **Examples (non-statutory)**
>
> - a depth study linked to one of the British areas of study listed above
> - a study over time tracing how several aspects of national history are reflected in the locality (this can go beyond 1066)
> - a study of an aspect of history or a site dating from a period beyond 1066 that is significant in the locality

- a study of an aspect or theme in British history that extends pupils' chronological knowledge beyond 1066

Examples (non-statutory)

- the changing power of monarchs using case studies such as John, Anne and Victoria
- changes in an aspect of social history, such as crime and punishment from the Anglo-Saxons to the present or leisure and entertainment in the 20th Century
- the legacy of Greek or Roman culture (art, architecture or literature) on later periods in British history, including the present day
- a significant turning point in British history, for example, the first railways or the Battle of Britain

---

- the achievements of the earliest civilisations – an overview of where and when the first civilisations appeared and a depth study of one of the following: Ancient Sumer; The Indus Valley; Ancient Egypt; The Shang Dynasty of Ancient China
- Ancient Greece – a study of Greek life and achievements and their influence on the western world
- a non-European society that provides contrasts with British history – one study chosen from: early Islamic civilisation, including a study of Baghdad c. AD 900; Mayan civilisation c. AD 900; Benin (West Africa) c. AD 900–1300.

💬 12 Languages

Planning languages in the national curriculum

Kelly Stock

Languages 1 Principles of planning

This section looks at the key factors which are specific to planning effective language lessons. It builds on the generic factors for planning found in Chapter 1 and should be read in conjunction with these ideas.

This chapter is designed to give you *confidence* – confidence in the knowledge that you can plan to teach primary languages lessons that are enjoyable to teach and fun to learn.

If you ask children what makes an outstanding teacher they say, without exception, someone that is 'enthusiastic' and 'makes learning fun'. Secondary students feel that the modern languages teacher is 'more important than in other subjects' and identify the teacher as the main reason why they like (or dislike) learning a language (Chambers, 1999 and Fisher, 2001). Not surprisingly, OFSTED links the quality of teaching primary languages to the teacher's confidence (2013). When you teach a subject in which you lack confidence there can be, understandably, a sense of dread and need to 'get it over with' as soon as possible. As a result, children sense *your* unease making *them* feel uncomfortable. So the stakes are high – not just in terms of children's learning and progression, especially now that primary languages are statutory, but also in terms of relationships with children and their attitudes to the lesson and their respect of you, their teacher (Jones and Jones, 2001). With OFSTED school inspection now looking at pupil attitudes in lessons it is likely head teachers will take this into account in performance management reviews and lesson observations. Mujis et al. (2005) and McLachlan (2009) identified the principal issues arising from the 2010 entitlement of primary languages as being subject-specific pedagogy and linguistic competence. This chapter is written to address the first.

Planning is key and arguably one of the factors that can change 'good' teaching to 'outstanding'. For the non-specialist it is equally critical to ensure your confidence in teaching the content (Bernhardt and Hammadou, 1987) as it is to ensure content is accurate and builds children's skills and understanding over time. *Confident* knowledge can facilitate effective scaffolding leading to high levels of language proficiency (Lantolf, 2009) and can increase flexibility in lessons such as developing unpredicted questions or points raised by children.

Vocabulary

It is helpful to list the vocabulary and structures you aim to teach for a number of reasons. First, it is a practical support if your mind goes blank under pressure; even a specialist will sometimes think of the word in French when they actually need the Spanish. It is useful to have quick reference to gender, spellings, etc., and you can also tick off what has been learnt well and mark those that need reinforcing next lesson. Second, it makes it easier to track what you have covered over the weeks and months; ensuring prior knowledge is considered and skills and understanding can be reinforced in new contexts. It is important to note both previous and new vocabulary so that tracking is a focus.

If you are going to try to use the target language in class, resist the temptation to immediately translate into English. If you do, children will learn to ignore the French and just wait for the English translation. Instead use other children to check understanding or have a puppet that only speaks one language that the children can ask questions. It is important to create a safe learning environment in which children feel comfortable speaking the target language.

Remember, you are not a human dictionary. Even a specialist will not know every word – so be upfront. Have dictionaries in classrooms and encourage children to find out for themselves.

Structure and sequence

There are several approaches to teaching languages – however, many favour the 3 Ps approach: presentation, practice, production. It gives a clear structure to lessons (particularly helpful to non-specialists) but also gives children the opportunity to reinforce and apply skills necessary to make good progress over time. Combined with careful sequencing of the four skills (listening, speaking, reading and writing), children will be able to manipulate new language to make it their own to use in a meaningful and relevant way. By keeping to this structure you will ensure children make progress in all four skills.

Second language acquisition is arguably no different to how a baby learns to communicate. It listens, repeats, speaks, read and writes. The 3 Ps approach looks like this:

- **Presentation**: you present – they listen. This is *passive* listening as children listen for pronunciation. They then speak, repeating what you say. This is *passive* speaking as they are simply repeating.
- **Practice**: children can practise what they have learnt through *active* listening (listening for information or communication), *active* speaking (to communicate through conversation) and reading.
- **Production**: this is when children make the language their own through speaking and writing.

One of the main recommendations of the MFL OFSTED report (2011) was to introduce reading and writing earlier in modern language learning. Think ahead; you want to prepare children for transition to secondary school. By giving equal focus to all four skills, children will be confident and competent in all skills. In theory this should put an end to secondary school teachers having to 'start from scratch' and in doing so wasting all your and the children's hard work and efforts.

Developing literacy

Writing can, no doubt, be a worry for non-specialists. How can I mark work accurately? How can I give quality next steps? To combat this, be specific in what you ask the

children to write. Initially only ask them to write what *you* know. For support, buy and use secondary school key stage 3 textbooks for clarification. Ideally set up a link with your local secondary school to regularly meet to moderate writing. Take advantage of primary hubs in your area to share ideas, check marking together and share *accurate* resources. If possible, anticipate misconceptions and predict curious questions with secondary specialists. This will help not only to deal with the unexpected but also to differentiate planning more effectively in order to challenge the highest attaining children.

Developing oracy

- In presenting new language try to resist showing the written word too early before the children's pronunciation is secure, otherwise *je m'appelle* will sound like 'je m'apple' and *hola* will be pronounced as 'ho-la'. Encourage children to sound out and guess spellings before showing them the word.
- Develop pronunciation through scaffolding using pictures and gesture. For example, say the word and show the gesture three times in a row. Then say the word three times and ask the children to show the gesture. Finally, you show the gesture three times and children say the word.
- Support weaker children by giving them the correct answer last – if the answer is dog you would ask, *C'est un chat ou un chien?* For higher attaining learners ask for the vocabulary without any support, *Qu'est-ce que c'est?*
- Use free online resources such as VOKI or Story Bird to motivate children to write independently and with creativity. Before they can produce the final piece they need to read it aloud.

Subject knowledge

While secure subject knowledge is a prerequisite for good teaching (Brant, 2006), *expert* subject knowledge is not synonymous with effective teaching. This is not to say subject knowledge does not have to be secure so that pronunciation and content is accurate – it means you do not necessarily have to be fluent or have a degree in a subject to teach it well. MFL subject specialists often comment that they are better teachers in their second or third language as they are able to 'go back to basics' more easily and are able to predict misconceptions, including 'false friends' or dissonance with other languages, based on their own (more recent) experience of learning the language. Nevertheless, as the teacher you are the linguistic model and it is vital you are able to quickly pick up mispronunciations to ensure accurate language acquisition (Chaudron, 1998) and are able to reshape explanations so that all children understand (Brant, 2006). Consequently, resources (detailed at the end of this chapter) that include sound bites from native speakers are invaluable. Good subject knowledge also enables you to understand the cognitive and language level of your planning which is particularly important when planning for years 5 and 6.

Relevance

In some parts of society, children (and their parents) will question the purpose of learning a foreign language 'when everyone speaks English'. Additionally, many children and parents view learning a language as notoriously 'difficult' (Morgan and Neil, 2001; Graham, 2004). Parents often have bad memories of their own French lessons when they were at school and these perceptions can sometimes lead to children not valuing the subject and becoming disinterested from an early age. As a result you will need to factor motivation into your planning. Children need to see

the point, the relevance in what they are learning, and why. If the purpose is meaningful, they are much more likely to be engaged and motivated. As a result, where possible use authentic resources that match children's interests. Be creative in what you ask them to do – for example, writing a Twitter entry (maximum 140 characters) can help children to redraft and perfect written work for a real audience that makes the communication meaningful. The British Council offers a myriad of opportunities to connect with schools in France, Spain and many more countries, enabling children to make real connections with children from other countries as well as showing children that languages are not monolingual entities. These connections can lead to your school being awarded the international school award which in turn can raise the profile of languages with senior management and parents.

Assessment

The most effective assessment is where it makes a difference. Verbally feeding back to a child when they are completing an activity enables them to make immediate improvements. Assessing learning in primary languages can be problematic given that schools have not previously had to assess the subject. Arguably one of the most comprehensive forms of assessment is Asset Languages which tracks progress across the four skills through certification, providing children with accreditation that can be taken with them to secondary school.

Just as teaching needs to meet the different learning styles of children, so does assessment, especially in languages when you are assessing four skills. When planning assessment ensure you provide opportunities for all children to succeed. When many teachers first start teaching there can be a tendency to teach the way you prefer to learn. This can result in missing out a third to a half of your children every lesson. A simple trick is to keep a seating plan of the class for every lesson. Tick each child when you are confident they have met the learning outcomes or you have given verbal feedback to them. It will not always be possible to feed back to every child so this is a practical way of tracking interactions in addition to marking in books. It can also help to identify children who are at risk of underachieving so these can be the focus at the end of the lesson or in the following lesson. You can also use this technique to track groups of children (e.g. children who receive the pupil premium, looked after children, or those with special educational needs).

Resources

Be wary of the accuracy of online resources and worksheets other teachers have created. If you do decide to use them check vocabulary is correct and spelt accurately. The websites provided at the end of this chapter are all trustworthy.

When choosing resources to support teaching about culture be wary of committing 'essentialism', where you encourage children to think that all French people eat croissants for breakfast, etc. If stereotypes and caricatures are murder, essentialism is manslaughter. Use organisations like the British Council (and the global gateway) and culturally valid resources such as Early Start. These resources will encourage children to think about their own identity as well as learning about other cultures.

Further reading

Bernhardt, E. and Hammadou, J. A. (1987) Decade of research in foreign language teacher education. *The Modern Language Journal*, 71 (Autumn): 289–99.

Bernhardt, E. and Hammadou, J. A. (1987) On being and becoming a foreign language teacher. *Theory into Practice*, 26(4): 301–6.

Brant, J. (2006) Subject knowledge and pedagogic knowledge: Ingredients for good teaching? An English perspective. *Edukacja*, 94(2): 60–77.

Chambers, G. (1999) *Motivating Language Learners*. Clevedon: Multilingual Matters.

Chaudron, C. (1998) *Second Language Classrooms: Research on Teaching and Learning*. Cambridge: Cambridge University Press.

Clinton, B. and Vincent, M. (2009) *Leading the Way: Co-ordinating Primary Languages*. CILT.

Fisher, L. (2001) Modern foreign language recruitment post-16: The pupils' perspective. *Language Learning Journal*, 23: 33–40.

Graham, S. J. (2004) Giving up on modern foreign languages? Students' perceptions of learning French. *The Modern Language Journal*, 88 (Summer): 171–91.

Hood, P. and Tobutt, K. (2009) *Modern Languages in the Primary School*. London: Sage.

Jones, B. and Jones, G. (2001) Boys' performance in modern foreign languages: Listening to learners. *Journal of Language and Linguistics*, 1(4).

Jones, J. and Coffey, S. (2013) *Modern Foreign Languages 5–11: A Guide for Teachers* (2nd edition). Abingdon: Routledge.

Lantolf, J. P. (2009) Knowledge of language in foreign language teacher education. *The Modern Language Journal*, 93(2): 270–4.

McLachlan, A. (2009) Modern languages in the primary curriculum: Are we creating conditions for success? *Language Learning Journal*, 37(2): 183–203.

Morgan, C. and Neil, P. (2001) *Teaching Modern Foreign Languages*. London: Kogan Page Limited.

Mujis, D., Barnes, A., Hunt, M., Powell, B., Martin, C., Arweck, E. and Lindsey, G. (2005) Evaluation of the Key Stage 2 language learning pathfinders. DfES.

OFSTED (2011) *MFL Achievement and Challenge Report 2007–2010*. London: HMSO.

OFSTED (2013) *Promoting Improvement in Initial Teacher Education (ITE): Secondary Modern Languages*. [online] Available at: **www.gov.uk/government/publications/promoting-improvement-in-initial-teacher-education-secondary-modern-languages**

Planning resources

Association for Language Learning: **www.all-languages.org.uk**

Teachers TV: **www.teachersmedia.co.uk**. A wealth of authentic videos here, particularly good for showing French- and Spanish-speaking countries such as Guadeloupe and Mexico.

European Playground Games: **www.bing.com/search?q=european+playground+games &src=ie9tr**

Languages 2 Examples of planning

The following three lesson plans are provided as examples of planning in language. They do not contain the detail you will probably wish to have on your plans but do illustrate some of the points discussed previously. The lessons show how the 3 Ps structure works for a year 5 class, based on previous learning in years 3 and 4.

Lesson One

Subject/topic: Weather	Date: 25/10/2016	Teaching group/set: Y5
	Time: 1.15 p.m.	No. of pupils: 28

Intended learning:

Children will learn to:

- listen for sounds, rhyme and rhythm (O4.3)
- use gesture and mime to show they understand (Learning Language Strategies, LLS)
- use action and rhymes to aid memorisation (LLS)
- imitate pronunciation (Knowledge about Language, KAL).

Success criteria:	Assessment strategy:
All children will be able to: - say and recognise five to eight types of weather with support and copy words. Most children will be able to: - say and recognise five to eight types of weather from memory and copy words accurately. Some children will be able to: - use a range of weather descriptions accurately, with good pronunciation from memory.	- Informal oral QA - Peer assessment - Level 1 asset writing

Key vocabulary:	Resources:
New: *Il neige, Il gèle* **Previous:** *Il fait chaud, Il fait mauvais, Il fait beau, Il y a du vent, Il fait froid, Il fait du soleil, Il pleut*	Flashcards (pictures and CD from Français! Français!) Flags from French-speaking countries Cut up months of the year

Time	Teacher focus		Pupil focus
10 mins	**Starter:** Recap weather from Unit 7 using flashcards or the IWB. G&T: introduce *Il neige* and *Il gèle* and ask higher attainers if they can guess meaning and spelling using prior knowledge of pronunciation.		Respond to prompts. Use prior knowledge to identify meaning and spelling.
30 mins	**Practice:** Put cut up months of the year and weather symbols on the board. Listen to the weather song from Français! Français!	This is an example of active listening.	Less able children to match the cards. Pupils gesture the weather when they hear it. Respond to flags shown and try to identify country on map.

	Show flags of different French-speaking countries and ask the children what they think the weather is like. Use a map of France to reinforce the new language and reinforce pronunciation rules (Paris, Nantes, Lorient, etc.). Once pronunciation is good, introduce the written word of weather, matching symbols with words, unscrambling the letters, lieiegn = *il neige*, etc. **Production:** Copying words (level 1 asset): they need to copy four to five words correctly.	Children can then say what the weather is like in different parts of France and French-speaking countries (e.g. *A Guadeloupe il fait chaud.*). To extend the more able, encourage them to include the temperature, and refer to the morning and the afternoon, or in the north, etc. (e.g. *Dans le sud, à Bordeaux il pleut le matin mais l'après-midi il fait beau.*)	Ask pupils to work out the pronunciation rule before telling them. This is the only example of when copying is a productive activity.
10 mins	**Plenary:** 'Simon says' using weather gestures, 'Bingo' using weather symbols or 'Good morning your majesty!' Follow up in week by asking the weather.	Children to play game to reinforce and embed learning.	This is a recall game to practise questions and answers.

Lesson Two

Subject/topic:	Date: 2/11/2016	Teaching group/set: Y5
Weather	Time: 11.30 a.m.	No. of pupils: 28

Intended learning:
Children will learn to: • listen with care for specific words and phrases • read and understand a range of familiar written phrases • read some familiar words and phrases aloud and pronounce them accurately • apply phonic knowledge of the language to support reading and writing.

Success criteria:	Assessment strategy:
All children will be able to: • say and recognise five to eight types of weather and understand basic temperatures using numbers 1–30. Most children will be able to: • say and recognise five to eight types of weather and understand temperatures including minus. Some children will be able to: • say (from memory) and recognise a range of weather descriptions accurately including temperature, with good pronunciation.	• Informal oral QA • Mark books • Listening/reading activity • Peer assessment

Key vocabulary:	Resources:
Previous: *les saisons, temperature, degrés, moins, aujourd'hui*	Flashcards and temperatures Listening grid Reading true or false

Time	Teacher focus	Pupil focus
10 mins	**Starter:** Recap prior knowledge of seasons. Then quickly recap numbers 1–30.	Ask pupils to stand if you call out a weather suitable for spring, sit if summer, hands on hips if autumn and hands on head if winter. If you have enough room pupils can run to the correct corner of the room (Starboard game).
30 mins	**Presentation:** Place pictures of hot and cold places with a temperature (some negative numbers) around the room. Model how to say *degrés*. Point to a picture of a hot place. Use a thermometer or number line to count, for example, from zero to 30 degrees with children. Say *Il fait 30 degrés* and mime 'very hot'. Repeat for some other hot places. Point to a picture of a cold place. Count down with the thermometer or number line. Stress *moins* before each number and stop at – 10 degrees. Then say, for example, *Il fait moins cinq degrés* and mime 'very cold'. **Practice:** Listening: play transcript	Pupils repeat throughout. In pairs, children practise asking *Il fait quelle température?* Partner A can respond in French and partner B writes down the answer. Pupils have to listen to the transcript and tick the grid if they hear the weather description. More able pupils complete the 'extra' column adding additional information they hear, e.g. town/country/season.
	Plenary: Games: 'Eleven' or 'Bingo' weather with temperatures.	Pupils engage in game to reinforce and embed learning.

This is an example of passive speaking.

And this shows how speaking can progress to active communication.

This can progress to a reading activity where pupils read the transcript and answer true or false statements.

This is an effective recall game to encourage confidence practising series of numbers.

Lesson Three

Subject/topic:	Date: 7/11/2016	Teaching group/set: Y5
Weather	**Time:** 1.15 p.m.	**No. of pupils:** 28

Intended learning:

Children will learn to:

- listen with care for specific words and phrases
- read and understand a range of familiar written phrases
- read some familiar words and phrases aloud and pronounce them accurately
- apply phonic knowledge of the language to support reading and writing
- memorise and present a short spoken text (O4.1)
- use a dictionary to look up spellings (LLS).

Success criteria:	Assessment strategy:
All children will be able to: - say, copy and understand weather phrases and say which clothes they might wear in different conditions (with support). Most children will be able to - say what they wear depending on the weather with support - say weather phrases from memory, match weather conditions to clothing and be able to predict the meaning of unknown vocabulary using context, cognates and knowledge about language.	- Informal oral QA - Peer assessment - Asset Speaking Grade 3

Some children will be able to: • say what they wear depending on the weather with good pronunciation and intonation • understand extended descriptions and accurately write weather conditions from memory and present their own weather forecast using the present tense.	
Vocabulary: *Un manteau, Un chapeau, Un parapluie, Une écharpe, Des gants, Des bottes, Des lunettes de soleil, Qu'est-ce que tu portes? Quand . . . je porte*	**Resources:** Clothes flashcards Clothes PowerPoint Clothes props Cut up cards for weather report

Time	Teacher focus	Pupil focus
10 mins	**Presentation:** Present new clothes vocabulary using flashcards or gestures. First introduce the items of clothing and then extend to *quand . . . je porte* and give options.	**GT:** Ask pupils what they think 'quand . . . je porte' means. Then model the questions, Quel temps fait-il? Qu'est-ce que tu portes?
30 mins	**Practice:** Sing the clothes to the song of 'London's Burning'. Use white boards or cut out items of clothing in felt. Ask a volunteer (preferably another teacher) to choose from the props and run into the room unannounced. Pair work: Speaking level 3. They need to perform it without notes so teacher can either go around and monitor or ask pupils to perform in front of the class for the Speaking Grade 3 Asset assessment.	Class divided into two. This allows further opportunity for less confident pupils to practise the pronunciation. Ask children to listen to the teacher, putting on the correct items of clothing. Instead of a whole-class activity you could have four children with four sets of clothes/props. When the teacher calls out the items of clothes, the quickest one to put it on keeps the item on. The child with the most clothes on within the time limit wins. Pupils have to try to remember the items of clothing they were wearing. In pairs the children ask each other two questions (e.g. *Quel temps fait-il? Qu'est-ce que tu portes?*)
20 mins	**Production:** Organise the class into groups. Give each group a selection of cards as above, weather symbols and items or pictures of clothing. Read out a weather report, e.g. *Bonjour, Je m'appelle Monsieur Brown. C'est mardi le 22 avril. Voici la méteo. Aujourd'hui, il pleut. Quand il pleut je porte un parapluie.* Children assemble the correct date, weather symbol and clothing. They feed back their answers in French. It is important to choose your groups carefully so that all children can contribute and feel proud of their achievement.	Children work in groups or pairs to create a weather report for a French-speaking country. These are performed to the rest of the class who comment constructively using two wishes and a star format. Children who are not confident in speaking can participate by saying single words or saying words in chorus. Some children may need lists of key vocabulary (some supported with pictures) to use. Children who are able to do this without using their notes can be assessed for Asset Languages Speaking Grade 3.

With most able pupils, insist on the full answer: Quand il fait de soleil je porte des lunettes de soleil.

An example of passive speaking.

A more creative approach is to give children the time to prepare a visual A6 map with their own drawings of weather symbols, and town names. They can dress up when presenting etc.

Extension: Children extend the weather report by including the temperature, adding morning, afternoon and evening and referring to the coordinates. Model this first and show how the level can be scaffolded.

e.g. *Bonjour, Je m'appelle Monsieur Brown. C'est mardi le 22 avril. Voici la méteo. Aujourd'hui, à Dieppe il pleut. Quand il pleut je porte un parapluie. Dans le sud à Bordeaux il fait froid, il fait 2 degrés. Dans l'ouest le matin il fait beau, mais le soir il pleut etc.*

FROM THE FRAMEWORK

Languages 3 The framework for languages

Purpose of study

Learning a foreign language is a liberation from insularity and provides an opening to other cultures. A high-quality languages education should foster pupils' curiosity and deepen their understanding of the world. The teaching should enable pupils to express their ideas and thoughts in another language and to understand and respond to its speakers, both in speech and in writing. It should also provide opportunities for them to communicate for practical purposes, learn new ways of thinking and read great literature in the original language. Language teaching should provide the foundation for learning further languages, equipping pupils to study and work in other countries.

Aims

The national curriculum for languages aims to ensure that all pupils:

- understand and respond to spoken and written language from a variety of authentic sources
- speak with increasing confidence, fluency and spontaneity, finding ways of communicating what they want to say, including through discussion and asking questions, and continually improving the accuracy of their pronunciation and intonation
- can write at varying length, for different purposes and audiences, using the variety of grammatical structures that they have learnt
- discover and develop an appreciation of a range of writing in the language studied.

Attainment targets

By the end of each key stage, pupils are expected to know, apply and understand the matters, skills and processes specified in the relevant programme of study.

Schools are not required by law to teach the example content in [square brackets].

Subject content

Key stage 2

Teaching may be of any modern or ancient foreign language and should focus on enabling pupils to make substantial progress in one language. The teaching should provide an appropriate balance of spoken and written language and should lay the foundations for further foreign language teaching at key stage 3. It should enable pupils to understand and communicate ideas, facts and feelings in speech and writing, focused on familiar and routine matters, using their knowledge of phonology, grammatical structures and vocabulary.

The focus of study in modern languages will be on practical communication. If an ancient language is chosen the focus will be to provide a linguistic foundation for reading comprehension and an appreciation of classical civilisation. Pupils studying ancient languages may take part in simple oral exchanges, while discussion of what they read will be conducted in English. A linguistic foundation in ancient languages may support the study of modern languages at key stage 3.

Pupils should be taught to:

- listen attentively to spoken language and show understanding by joining in and responding
- explore the patterns and sounds of language through songs and rhymes and link the spelling, sound and meaning of words
- engage in conversations; ask and answer questions; express opinions and respond to those of others; seek clarification and help*
- speak in sentences, using familiar vocabulary, phrases and basic language structures
- develop accurate pronunciation and intonation so that others understand when they are reading aloud or using familiar words and phrases*
- present ideas and information orally to a range of audiences*
- read carefully and show understanding of words, phrases and simple writing
- appreciate stories, songs, poems and rhymes in the language
- broaden their vocabulary and develop their ability to understand new words that are introduced into familiar written material, including through using a dictionary
- write phrases from memory, and adapt these to create new sentences, to express ideas clearly
- describe people, places, things and actions orally* and in writing
- understand basic grammar appropriate to the language being studied, including (where relevant): feminine, masculine and neuter forms and the conjugation of high-frequency verbs; key features and patterns of the language; how to apply these, for instance, to build sentences; and how these differ from or are similar to English.

The starred (*) content above will not be applicable to ancient languages.

🏃 13 Music

Planning music in the national curriculum

Alison Daubney and Duncan Mackrill

Music 1 Principles of planning

This section looks at the key factors which are specific to planning effective music lessons. It builds on the generic factors for planning found in Chapter 1 and should be read in conjunction with these ideas.

This chapter explores the implications in the context of planning for musical learning in primary schools. The fine detail within the national curriculum for music is not extensive, yet there is considerable depth in order to get children ready to start key stage 3 with a broad-based musical education behind them, provided throughout key stage 1 and key stage 2.

Don't be fooled into thinking that if you don't give a child a musical education in your class then it is okay because someone else will take responsibility for this. One of Paynter's (1982: xiii) guiding principles is that *Classroom music is the core activity and extra-curricular music should develop from here.* It is only through 'classroom music' that we can ensure that music education is accessible to all, and not an elitist pastime available only to those that can afford to pay for it.

Musical planning

What is it that you value in a musical education? Why is it that you think a musical education is important within the curriculum? In thinking through these questions, most teachers and pupils come up with a series of answers which relate to enjoyment, inclusion, collaboration, developing a sense of community, valuing diversity, opening up pathways, development of social skills and transferable skills, exploring and nurturing individual and collective identities and preferences, celebration, and many other extremely worthy aspects of education. Answering these questions for yourself is an important step in working out your philosophical underpinning of music education within and beyond the curriculum and will guide you in your curriculum planning, delivery and assessment.

As the national curriculum states, *a high quality music education should engage and inspire pupils to develop a love of music and their talents as musicians.* A core principle of music in the curriculum is that *making music is more important than musical information* (Paynter, 1982: xiii). This means that the core activity in music lessons

comes about through making music – playing together, singing, making up music (composing), experimenting with sound – coupled with integral opportunities to respond to music physically, musically, artistically and through language, encouraging children to think *in, through* and *about* music.

This active learning comes through in the content of the national curriculum. In key stage 1 there is a specific mention of playing tuned and non-tuned percussion (although music education does not need to be limited to these), singing, experimenting with sounds, and listening and responding to music, as well as the aim that every child will have the opportunity to play a musical instrument. Through key stage 2 this becomes more formalised; pupils should have opportunities to perform in solo and ensemble contexts, and the quality and complexity of their music-making increases. As the teacher planning the curriculum, decisions about what is included in terms of repertoire, musical focus and so on are entirely up to you. Therefore it is important that you think about the order in which you introduce concepts and ideas, the suitability and difficulty of repertoire chosen and how to develop the quality of the music. Since learning is not linear, there are no easy answers to these points, but, as the teacher, you need to be clear how you are planning for a wide range of musical progression suitable for the pupils in your class. For example, when are they ready to start singing in harmony? How do you encourage them to refine their musical material to give it a clear structure?

When thinking about music in education, it is easy to think that we teach music because it might create better learners with transferable skills which are desirable in education, such as working well in groups or improving school results. Indeed, there is a lot of compelling evidence about this (see Hallam, 2010). Yet the reasons we teach music are related to music itself. Excellent music lessons support children's development *as musicians* – the development of musical skills, knowledge and understanding through the immersion in sound (learning through doing) – and also support the improvement of the quality of the work and depth of responses. Instead of just playing through together from beginning to end, rehearse short sections such as beginnings and endings, encourage clearer diction and greater fluency, and communicate emotions. In their own music, help children to structure their musical ideas coherently, and assist them in developing their creative ideas by trying things out and accepting and rejecting ideas.

Each learning opportunity needs to have a musical purpose – the learning for each lesson, unit and year needs to be thought through in advance. Each lesson or series of lessons should be based upon specific learning objectives and perhaps some questions for pupils to consider. Defining the learning first helps to overcome the issues of a teacher planning a nice set of activities without a specific purpose. Skill development should be central to the planning – what are the musical skills which pupils are working on and how will the quality of these be improved? The other important parts of music education (e.g. communicating your ideas, learning to use different notations, gaining understanding about the historical, cultural and social aspects of music) all arise from learning about music from the inside out and with a real purpose. For example, notation only begins to make sense when there is a sonic connection, developing the skills to work out the relative rise and fall in pitch of particular phrases of the music, or the rhythm, through internalising the sound first.

Children should be encouraged to think and act in musical ways and teachers need to model these behaviours. This can be facilitated through, for example, using your voice or instruments for call and response patterns, asking groups of pupils to demonstrate, and using something as simple as an mp3 file to support singing or instrumental work. The assessment of music should also be inherently musical.

Relevance

It is inconceivable to think that there is anyone in your classroom that does not engage with music in some way outside of school. Music is integral to our individual and collective identities. Young children sing songs as they go about their everyday lives. They make up music in the playground, play skipping games, and sing on the swings, often changing the words of well-known songs. They dance and move to music, play musical video games such as *SingStar*, sing along with the radio, bang rhythms on surfaces and instruments, play music with their mates, sing along in football crowds, for worship, and at birthday parties. It is clear, therefore, that music has great relevance in children's lives and that music education in schools needs to recognise and develop the learning that children bring to the classroom.

It is certainly the case that children arrive in a music class with a wide range of musical experiences from outside the classroom. As well as an extensive internal 'play-list' and a memory bank of music, many children will have had access to lessons on a particular instrument, either through the whole-class instrumental and vocal tuition programme funded through the Department for Education (DfE) grant to music hubs, or through individual or small group tuition. Children may have also taught themselves to play instruments, to sing or to dance outside of school, all of which contributes to their musical identity. It is important that the music education offered in the classroom recognises and builds upon this in order to help to join up the musical parts of a child's life and make these experiences valuable and progressive. This means, for example, encouraging children to bring in instruments they play and use these in the work undertaken in the classroom. To do this, you will need to find out how your pupils engage in music outside of school. It also means bringing familiar music into the curriculum at some points in order to try to minimise the distinction children make between 'school' music and what for them is 'real' music in their lives.

The purpose of music education in school, therefore, is to perpetuate what children already know and can do or to extend their experiences of music to other genres, styles and traditions which they have not necessarily had contact with before. The phrase *the best in the musical canon* in the aims of the national curriculum includes music from a wide range of *historical periods, genres, styles and traditions*. The interpretation of this is very wide, which is excellent. There should also be access to *high quality live and recorded music*. This could (and should) include live performances from other pupils in your school or perhaps those from a local secondary school.

The best teachers of music are the ones who successfully manage to build bridges backwards and forwards to help children to see the relevance of new experiences in relation to their own sound world. This includes helping children explore the social and historical context of music across times, places and cultures, through engaging with this as musicians.

Taking creative risks

An overarching aim of a musical education is to encourage children to take creative risks, try out ideas, experiment, doodle, develop their work by working out for

themselves what works and what doesn't. One issue with this is that, in much of education, children think they are seeking the one 'right' answer that the teacher has in their mind. We need to do a lot of work as teachers to persuade them that their own creative and musical ideas are valued. The other main issue is that many children (and adults) are worried about fear of failure, particularly looking silly or incompetent in front of their classmates. A far too frequent example of this in adulthood is where, as a child, we were told we were 'not good enough' to be in the choir, or to stop singing as we were 'out of tune' – the child then grows up believing they are incapable of singing and are 'no good at music'. Therefore teachers need to be vigilant about the unintended consequences of their words and actions; an aspiration of music education in schools is to create a supportive and encouraging environment where children feel secure, grow to believe in their musical skills, and are happy to take creative risks. Such opportunities should be planned within every lesson. For example, when asking children to 'improvise', in the first instance make sure that everyone in the class is trying something out at the same time. Plan to use a song or piece of music everyone can learn together and then have 16 beats of 'free-styling' where children are encouraged to try out their own ideas, often using a restricted range of notes, at the same time as everyone else before coming back together with the learnt material. This critical mass of noise, along with some elements of structure, help promote an inclusive and supportive environment. The teacher is crucial to this – you should model and demonstrate the creative behaviours and be willing to join in and experiment in front of the class. Planning opportunities for supported peer learning is also important.

Assessment

OFSTED have frequently criticised the poor and inappropriate use of assessment in music education. In order to be useful, assessment needs to be 'musical' and avoid the use of arbitrary sub-levels. Robin Hammerton, HMI for music at OFSTED, wrote *A powerful creative act cannot be contained by a neat spreadsheet of numbers and letters. As national curriculum levels disappear, I'd ask you respectfully not to replace them with another set of numbers* (Hammerton, 2014).

Instead, OFSTED and others urge the capture of 'sound' as part of the process. This means making audio and (with permission) video recordings of children's work over time. These should be used as part of the musical process, for example to play back to children as 'work in progress' recordings and to ask for comments or suggestions to improve the work. Indeed, formative 'developmental' assessment in music is far more important than making summative judgements as it helps pupils and teachers understand the learning process better and to work out the range of possible next steps.

Assessment in the arts is often subjective and it also leads people to make assumptions about themselves that may not be valid. A teacher is a very powerful person and what they say and the messages they give through the design of their curriculum and the assessment send messages about the accessibility of music to all. In order to prevent music having an elitist position in your school, your assessment of music, like your curriculum and teaching, needs to send messages about inclusion and celebration.

Once you have worked out what it is you want to assess, you need to work out how you are going to do this. In most cases, the purpose of the assessment is to provide the scaffolding for developmental feedback to improve pupil learning. There is

seldom any need for 'tests' in music lessons; a thoughtful teacher will pick up the evidence they are looking for through talking and listening to children responding to, creating and making music, asking and answering questions, observing their engagement with the learning process and with each other and through the awareness of what they write down informally. Planning questions and developing formative strategies to help to elicit the learning is crucial as there are many ways in which formative, developmental assessment can be implemented. Find out from the children themselves what they think, and involve them in the assessment of their own and others' work. You may be surprised just how insightful they are.

Most primary schools only expect a short formal comment to be sent home to parents at the end of each academic year. Nevertheless, you should have an idea of the range of musical development in each year, in relation to a child's playing, singing, composing, responding to music, ability to work with others, applied knowledge and understanding of music, and what this might look like across different years. Recent advice for helping teachers to plan and assess is given on the Incorporated Society of Musicians (ISM) website (**www.ism.org/nationalcurriculum**). This subject association is keen to support music education and has issued a substantial amount of guidance on planning for the new curriculum, all of which is available through this link.

Cross-curricular learning

Music is also excellent for helping to unlock and support other areas of the curriculum, as discussed further in Section 3 of this book. It can be the catalyst for cross-curricular work based on an area of local study, for example through developing local social and cultural history, literacy and geography from broadsides, songs and tunes collected by folk collectors across the UK in the early twentieth century. Music should commonly be used to support the curriculum in other ways, for example in learning songs about the water cycle or the wives of Henry VIII in order to memorise facts. This supportive role for music is not, however, a musical education unless there is a developmental *musical* purpose to the learning. As with all learning, the musical learning needs to be planned for in advance, rather than just being a nice set of activities to support learning.

Developing musical language

As with any subject, music has its own subject-specific vocabulary which you should encourage children to use as appropriate. This can be promoted by the teacher using specific language related to the music; it is not a case of learning language for the sake of it, but instead for musical language to emerge from musical learning experiences. In music, children do not always need to verbally demonstrate their understanding of the language; showing you through musical demonstration or movement, for example, may be more appropriate at times. You should plan to develop the use of appropriate musical language and terminology wherever possible. In the new national curriculum, the *inter-related dimensions of music* are what were previously referred to as the 'elements of music' – pitch, dynamics, tempo, timbre, texture, rhythm, duration, etc. which describe various features of the music. Help in deciphering some of this musical language, along with many practical teaching activities, is available on the DfE Expert Subject Advisory Group webpages listed in the further reading section.

Using information and communications technology (ICT) in music

Technology is cited as an important aspect of music in key stages 1 and 2. Digital technologies are certainly part of most children's everyday lives and their use of these in music is no exception to this. Increasingly, mobile technologies are part of how children access, store and make music, yet the use of digital technologies in primary schools for music appears limited. There are many ways in which digital technologies can be included – for example, in the use of apps, software or hardware for making, recording and mixing music. Encouraging children to make their own recordings, use microphones, and explore and change digital sounds are all ways of giving children autonomy. Some schools are also working towards the regulated use of mobile phones. Tablets too can be a valuable teacher tool to collect and organise audio and/ or video evidence of pupil work. Pupils also usually enjoy watching themselves back via a data projector and this helps them understand how they can improve. You should consider what you want from the technology and make sure that there is a pedagogical reason for using it, which may be related to the music making itself or to capturing of sound for developmental feedback or for an e-portfolio. In other words, the reasons for using technology should:

- have clearly identifiable benefits for either the teacher or pupils or both;
- allow pupils to do something that would otherwise not be possible, would be less effective or take longer to complete if technology was not used;
- improve the quality or capacity of the work;
- have a clear musical purpose.

Resources

Resourcing music does not have to be expensive. However, good resourcing needs careful thought and a well-planned lesson needs to consider the following.

- What instruments are available in the school? Tuned and non-tuned percussion instruments are specifically mentioned with the national curriculum.
- Which resources would best support the intended learning?
- Does your school follow a particular scheme or system for music learning? How will you get access to this?
- What technology is available for you and the children to use?
- How will you store recordings? Spreadsheets on Excel are useful with hyperlinks, and there are a number of intuitive low-cost apps which are designed for this purpose.
- Will you have access to online sources of music such as from YouTube or are these filtered out? Talk to your IT manager about how you might be able to gain access to these.
- What instruments do children play at home or have lessons on that you could bring into the music lessons?
- Who is the music coordinator in your school and what planning and teaching resources do they have which you would find useful?
- How will you structure the learning to make sure that, over time, every child gets to develop their skills and experiment on different instruments if there are not enough for one each?
- Who is your music education hub? What help, support and resources are offered?

Further reading

Beach, N., Evans, J. and Spruce, G. (2011) *Making Music in the Primary School: Whole Class Instrumental and Vocal Teaching.* Abingdon: Routledge.

Burnard, P. and Murphy, R. (2013) *Teaching Music Creatively.* Abingdon: Routledge.

Daubney, A. and Fautley, M. (2014) *The National Curriculum for Music: An Assessment and Progression Framework.* Incorporated Society of Musicians, London. [online] Available at: **www.ism.org/nationalcurriculum**

Duffy, B. (2006) *Supporting Creativity and Imagination in the Early Years* (2nd edition). Open University Press.

Hallam, S. (2010) The power of music: Its impact of the intellectual, personal and social development of children and young people. *International Journal of Music Education* 38(3), 269–89.

Hammerton, R. (2014) Where words finish, music begins. TES community. [online] Available at: **http://community.tes.co.uk/ofsted_resources/b/weblog/archive/2014/06/16/music-in-schools-where-words-finish-music-begins.aspx**

Lehmann, A., Sloboda, J. and Woody, R. (2007) *Psychology for Musicians: Understanding and Acquiring the Skills.* Oxford: Oxford University Press.

Mills, J. (2009) *Music in the Primary School.* Oxford: Oxford University Press.

OFSTED (2012) *Wider, Still and Wider.* [online] Available at: **http://webarchive.national archives.gov.uk/20130731000001/youtube.com/watch?v=CdHlO-UPVZM**

OFSTED (2013) *Music in Schools: What Hubs Must Do.* [online] Available at: **www. northamptonshire.gov.uk/music/Info/resources/Documents/PDF%20Documents/ Music%20in%20schools%20what%20hubs%20must%20do.pdf**

Paynter, J. (1982) *Music in the Secondary School Curriculum.* Cambridge: Cambridge University Press.

Useful websites

BBC Ten Pieces: **www.bbc.co.uk/tenpieces**

Cross-curricular planning and ideas based on folk music: **www.efdss.org/efdss-education/ resource-bank/resources-and-teaching-tools**

Map of music education hubs: **www.ism.org/education**

National curriculum support materials from the DfE Expert Subject Advisory Group: **www. sites.google.com/site/primarymusicitt**

Sing Up: **www.singup.org**

Music 2 Examples of planning

The following three lesson plans are provided as examples of planning in music. They do not contain the detail you will probably wish to have on your plans but do illustrate some of the points discussed previously.

Lesson One

Subject/topic: Do you believe in magic?	Date: 23/9/2016 Time: 1.15 p.m.	Teaching group/set: Y5 – mixed ability class No. of pupils: 28
Intended learning: Children will learn to: • create musical soundscapes from a given starting point • critique their work through the cyclic use of audio-based recording.		**NC reference/context:** Improvising, performing, creativity, playing instruments Links to literacy, drama and visual arts

Success criteria:	Assessment strategy:
All children will be able to: • select appropriate sounds for the musical purpose and explain why they were chosen • perform with appropriate control and awareness of the audience. Some children will be able to: • successfully combine and adapt sounds, justifying their choices of sounds and relating these effectively to the purpose/ image.	• Observation, probing questions and listening during rehearsal, performances and discussion • Making aural recordings and playing back; listening to pupils discussing their own work

Key vocabulary:	Resources:	Risk assessment:
mood, texture, timbre, feeling, dynamics, start, stop, rest, silence, improvise	*Leon and the Place Between* by Angela McAllister Copies of pictures from the book Range of tuned and non-tuned percussion instruments, plus children's own instruments Video recording capability (e.g. mobile phone, flip camera, iPad)	Clear the space so that children can work on an uncluttered floor

It is often useful to 'hook' musical learning around a source, e.g. a picture, book or song.

It is important to encourage children's musical lives from beyond the classroom into your classroom work.

Classroom layout is important. Have the class standing together in a bunch of people or a horseshoe.

Time	Teacher focus	Pupil focus
10 mins	Stunning starter – dim the lights, draw curtains. Teacher (in costume) to read the opening of the story. Hot-seating – pupils ask questions of 'Leon'. Finish with a discussion on words to describe the mood.	Pupils seated together on the floor, room laid out as a performing space. Pair and share – think up interesting questions to ask Leon/the magician. One sticky note each – write words that describe the mood set. Share. Think about the kind of music that would be needed to accompany each scene. Share ideas with the class.

10 mins	Join in with whole-class improvisation based on an image from the book:	Thinking of the words written down, which part of the image do these go with?	
	Put up the image on the whiteboard screen.	Taking a musical instrument, 60 seconds to explore the different and unusual sounds it can make.	
	Record the resulting soundscape. Take suggestions for cues to start/stop.	Focusing on the different parts of the picture (as the frame moves around) try to add in the sounds together to create a soundscape.	
20 mins	Split pupils into groups – support groups to create, perform and critique the effectiveness of their own work.	Working in groups of four pupils, each group will have a different image from the book to create music to 'tell the story' (no more than 1 minute per group). 3 mins – discuss ideas, 5 mins – try them out and refine, one group to perform 'work in progress', share ideas for improvement then continue to develop.	
20 mins	Direct a performance of the whole book. Make recording to share. Lead discussion/ critiquing of work.	Each group to perform their soundscape while they tell the story. Video this. Watch the video back and critique the work, each group commenting on their own intentions and others commenting on whether these were met.	

Really important that the teacher joins in/models/ demonstrates.

Exploring the instrument with a critical mass of noise going on is a useful strategy to overcome fear of failure. Make sure the class know the cue to stop exploring and praise them for adhering to this.

The mini plenary is a great way to move work on for the whole class when groups are working independently – it encourages children to reflect upon, discuss their work and find solutions.

Ofsted urge the use of video/ audio as part of the musical process and to show progress over time as part of a sound-based portfolio.

Developing the quality by rehearsing parts/ techniques etc., not just singing through from beginning to end, is extremely important.

Lesson Two

Subject/topic: What kind of magic?	Date: 30/9/2016 Time: 10.30 a.m.	Teaching group/set: Y5 – mixed ability class No. of pupils: 28
Intended learning: Children will learn to: • respond to music through art, using this as a prompt to discuss thoughts and feelings about music heard • rehearse and develop the quality of singing through learning new material aurally.		**NC reference/context:** Rehearsing, singing, performing, creativity, listening and responding to music, discussing music Links to visual arts
Success criteria: All children will be able to: • memorise most lyrics and sections of melody of a new song; perform broadly in tune and time • respond to music through art and give reasons for choices with basic use of technical language. Some children will be able to: • sing with appropriate posture, good diction, tuning and sense of timing; be aware of others in the group and fit their voice in appropriately • ask astute and interesting questions about the music, justify their thoughts and feelings using sophisticated language to communicate their ideas effectively.		**Assessment strategy:** • Listening to pupils discussing their thoughts about the music • Listening, watching while children are singing without the pupils realising you are listening
Key vocabulary: singing, warm up, diction, tuning, soundscape, dynamics	**Resources:** Recorded music based upon a circus/magic/wonder theme Song materials (may include recording, lyrics on IWB) Evocative visual image	**Risk assessment:** Clear area for working; no electric cables running across the floor

Time	Teacher focus	Pupil focus
15 mins	Lead/co-lead an interactive vocal warm-up which also incorporates movement. Help pupils to create a whole-class vocal soundscape of a new image of awe/wonder/magic. Use a 'picture frame' of folded paper to isolate parts of the picture. Teacher should join in.	Warm up bodies and voices. Focus on the sound production and following the 'leader'. Pupils to respond to the changing images through vocal improvisation, body percussion and sounds from the environment. Think about which parts of the images will be loudest/softest and adjust their sounds accordingly.
20 mins	Teacher directs pupils to respond through drawing to the music extracts played. Be sure to explain in advance that there are no right/wrongs – also that they will be 'asking interesting questions' about the music. Use probing questions, particularly around 'why'.	Pupils respond to the two short extracts through drawing. In groups of four, discuss their own images and reasons with each other and then think up two really interesting questions about the music they would like to ask another group about the music. Bring two groups together to share questions and responses.
25 mins	Teach the whole class a song based upon the theme of circus/awe/wonder/fantasy worlds, e.g. 'Magical Mystery Tour' (Beatles), 'Sound of Silence' (Simon & Garfunkel), 'It's a Kind of Magic' (Queen). Lead the rehearsal of different parts to improve the quality, based upon children's suggestions.	Pupils learn song, probably the chorus first. Rehearse parts to improve the quality – particularly phrasing, diction, beginning and endings (as opposed to singing through without working on any parts). Pupils make performing suggestions/lead sections. Make a video recording of an 'in progress' performance of the song at the end of the lesson to use in the next lesson; write a suggestion for improvement on a sticky note bank as they leave.

Pupils might help to lead this. This strategy also takes away the focus from the teacher.

Make sure children know what they will need to do before they listen to the music. This engages them as critical listeners with a purpose, rather than springing questions on them afterwards.

Listen in on the questions asked – these are at least as enlightening as the responses to the questions!

Find a strategy for teaching a song that you feel comfortable with.

You might also take a suggestion from the children about this – it is best to do this in the previous week so that you have time to prepare it.

Lesson Three

Subject/topic: Rapping magic!	Date: 7/10/2016 Time: 1.15 p.m.	Teaching group/set: Y5 No. of pupils: 28
Intended learning: Children will learn to: • construct and refine lyrics for an 8-bar rap 'break' • perform in a rap style and practise keeping in time.		**NC reference/context:** Rehearsing, refining, inventing, performing, critiquing, creativity Links to literacy and visual arts
Success criteria: All children will be able to: • suggest lyrics and key phrases for a short rap 'break' • perform broadly in time. Some children will be able to: • sequence the lyrics to make an interesting, coherent and musically satisfying rap 'break' • perform the rap section with a good sense of timing, metre and vocal clarity.		**Assessment strategy:** • Observation of children working on development of rap and in rehearsal/performance and negotiating with each other about content • Listening to the discussions and questioning • Taking suggestions for improvement based upon comments from the video in the previous lesson

Links to the NC requirement to use voices in different ways.

Key vocabulary:		Resources:	Risk assessment:
rap, metre, timing, break, chorus, verse, structure, rhyming, rhythm		Paper and pens Song materials Looped track at 60 beats per minute Images drawn by the children in the previous lesson	No trailing cables, clear area for working

Time	Teacher focus	Pupil focus
15 mins	Scaffold the conversations. Teacher to write these on whiteboard. Lead a very short vocal warm up then facilitate the singing of the song with a focus on improvement.	Working in teams of four, each group to come up with their 'top tip' for improvement (what to improve and suggestions for how to do this) based upon the video from the end of previous lesson. Sing through the song, trying to make the suggestions suggested by other pupils.
10 mins	Teacher extracts information on 'what makes a good rap' by modelling/demonstrating/ for a range of good/not so good ideas. Teacher writes list based upon pupils' suggestions. Model the process of constructing a 4-line rap (8-bar), showing ideas of different rhyming structures.	Pupils make suggestions about what makes a good rap and make suggestions to improve things they feel could be better/write the next line from the demonstrations.
30 mins	Teacher facilitates groups to write their own short raps. TA to support pupils with the literacy as required. Teacher should oversee the scribing, rehearsal and performances, make video recording for use at the start of the following lesson (where all of these parts will start to come into one arrangement).	Based on the pictures of the previous week and the post-it note words from lesson 1, pupils work in groups of four to create an 8-bar rap (this is likely to be 4 lines) about one of the fantasy worlds and linked broadly with the theme of the song learnt. 'Phone a friend' if needing a line finishing. 'Rehearse, perform and record.

You can easily make one of these on a program such as AcidXpress or Soundation, or using the pre-recorded loops on an electronic keyboard.

What to improve AND how to do this are key points relating to good practice in promoting developmental feedback.

'Good' modelling and 'bad' modelling both offer opportunities for children to see what is possible and make suggestions.

Get everyone to share their first line, then the first 2 lines – this offers plenty of opportunity for peer feedback and suggestions and keeps the momentum going.

The modelling should have made it clear to the children that there is a great deal of creative freedom and that they can put their own individual 'stamp' on this.

This might not necessarily be performed to the whole class – groups might make their own informal recordings to use in the following lesson.

Provide the children with home-made paper 'caps' to wear when they perform – watch how this changes the mood of a performance due to providing a little more authenticity.

Music 3 The framework for music

Purpose of study

Music is a universal language that embodies one of the highest forms of creativity. A high-quality music education should engage and inspire pupils to develop a love of music and their talent as musicians, and so increase their self-confidence, creativity and sense of achievement. As pupils progress, they should develop a critical engagement with music, allowing them to compose, and to listen with discrimination to the best in the musical canon.

Aims

The national curriculum for music aims to ensure that all pupils:

- perform, listen to, review and evaluate music across a range of historical periods, genres, styles and traditions, including the works of the great composers and musicians
- learn to sing and to use their voices, to create and compose music on their own and with others, have the opportunity to learn a musical instrument, use technology appropriately and have the opportunity to progress to the next level of musical excellence
- understand and explore how music is created, produced and communicated, including through the inter-related dimensions: pitch, duration, dynamics, tempo, timbre, texture, structure and appropriate musical notations.

Attainment targets

By the end of each key stage, pupils are expected to know, apply and understand the matters, skills and processes specified in the relevant programme of study.

Subject content

Key stage 1

Pupils should be taught to:

- use their voices expressively and creatively by singing songs and speaking chants and rhymes
- play tuned and untuned instruments musically
- listen with concentration and understanding to a range of high-quality live and recorded music
- experiment with, create, select and combine sounds using the inter-related dimensions of music.

Key stage 2

Pupils should be taught to sing and play musically with increasing confidence and control. They should develop an understanding of musical composition, organising and manipulating ideas within musical structures and reproducing sounds from aural memory.

FROM THE FRAMEWORK

Pupils should be taught to:

- play and perform in solo and ensemble contexts, using their voices and playing musical instruments with increasing accuracy, fluency, control and expression
- improvise and compose music for a range of purposes using the inter-related dimensions of music
- listen with attention to detail and recall sounds with increasing aural memory
- use and understand staff and other musical notations
- appreciate and understand a wide range of high-quality live and recorded music drawn from different traditions and from great composers and musicians
- develop an understanding of the history of music.

14 Physical education

Planning physical education in the national curriculum

Kristy Howells

Physical education 1 Principles of planning

This section looks at the key factors which are specific to planning effective physical education lessons. It builds on the generic factors for planning found in Chapter 1 and should be read in conjunction with these ideas.

Working physically

Laker (2001) extended Kirk's (1993) ideas and proposed that a physically-educated child would develop within three domains and learning would occur within and between these domains. These domains, which will help within the planning stages, are: practical, cognitive and social (see Table 14.1). It is important to consider all three domains, and not just focus on the practical domain without considering

Table 14.1 The three domains in physical education

Practical	Cognitive	Social
• Mastering basic movements • Running • Jumping • Throwing and catching • Balance • Agility • Co-ordination and control • Dance • Strength • Flexibility	• Tactics and principles for attacking and defending • Applying and developing skills to link to make actions and sequences • Understand how to improve • Recognising success • Playing competitive games • Compare performances and demonstrate improvement	• Communicating • Collaborating • Challenges both individually and within a team • Compete with self and with team against others • Cope with not winning • Confidence

(Adapted from Laker (2001) to reflect the elements of the national curriculum)

the cognitive and social elements. The National Association for Sport and Physical Education (NASPE) highlighted that educating the whole child within physical education lessons enables them to have the *knowledge, skills and confidence to enjoy a lifetime of physical activity* (NASPE, 2004) which links to the aims of physical education to ensure all pupils lead healthy, active lives (DfE, 2013).

High-quality physical education lessons have four core elements to consider when planning: pace, structure, transferable skills and competition.

Pace

Pace of the lesson is key to keeping the children engaged, positive and inspired and experiencing a broad range of physical activities. The national curriculum (DfE, 2013) states that children need to be physically active for sustained periods of time; therefore, pace needs consideration when planning. Ensure your planning does not result in you stopping and starting the lesson too much. For example, when do you discuss the purpose of the lesson or the learning objective? Can you tell the children the learning objective while they're getting changed in the classroom rather than stopping straight after the warm up? Videos and pictures can help support the children's understanding of the learning that will occur within the physical education lesson. The World Health Organization (2008) has proposed that in order to increase children's physical activity schools should increase the number of physical education lessons provided. McKenzie and Kahan (2004) suggested that the teaching profession was obliged to provide children with adequate moderate to vigorous physical activity within physical education lessons, particularly as these lessons may be the main source of physical activity for a child within the school day.

Structure

It is important to ensure that your activities link within the lesson to develop progression and skills. One key question to consider is 'Does your main activity link to your warm up and cool down, and if not why not?' You want to have progression of learning throughout the whole of the lesson, not just the main learning activities. This is particularly vital if you have limited time for physical education lessons. The children need to see the links between all activities within the lesson as this will help them be inspired as they form habits, likes and dislikes (Howells, 2007). The flow of the lesson will be important in ensuring that the children are motivated and engaged. For example, if you give the children balls, rather than stopping them and asking them to hold the ball, set them off with a task to explore different ways to use and move with the ball. The children will be intrigued and excited rather than being told off for not being able to hold the ball still. Kyriacou (2009) refers to successful teaching as planning for keeping the children actively engaged in the lesson, thereby reducing the amount of time when children are bored, frustrated or restless. (Rink (2005) and Bunker and Thorpe (1982) offer ways to link and develop progression.)

Transferable skills

Within the national curriculum children should develop fundamental movement skills in key stage 1 and then develop and apply these skills to enable them to link movements. The key within planning is to ensure that the children are able to understand that they are developing transferable skills which will enable them to develop in all areas and all activities; this is particularly important in athletics and

swimming. As a teacher it is important to understand how these skills are transfer-rable across activities and to plan to highlight these to the children. These transferable skills include:

- sending;
- receiving;
- travelling (with/without a ball);
- balance/stability;
- timing;
- confidence;
- co-ordination;
- combination;
- challenge.

Responding to challenges both individually and within a team within outdoor and adventure activity (DfE, 2013) is in key stage 2. You can plan for responding to challenges through developing team building, communication and collaboration skills as well as problem-solving skills, linking to both the cognitive and social physical education domains. The key is to allow the children time to plan, do and then to review and evaluate – this could then be repeated to replan, do and then review so that it becomes a cycle (Martin, 2000). There is a tendency to rush through this process but children need time to solve the challenge set. It is also important for children to feel comfortable enough within physical education to get the wrong answer and then to be able to reflect on how to be successful as this supports them in becoming increasingly confident and able to work co-operatively within a team.

Competition

There has been a shift towards focusing on children playing competitive sports and activities. Careful planning is needed to ensure that children can explore how to cope with winning and losing (Laker, 2001). It can be quite difficult for children, particularly in key stage 1, not to run around shouting 'losers' at those who have lost. This is a key area of the social domain of physical education that needs to be developed to enhance emotional development. Care and consideration is also needed for the amount of times that competition is a planned focus within your physical education lessons as the House of Commons Education Committee (2013) proposed that competition in school sport 'deters some young children from par-ticipating in sport and physical activity' (page 2). Competition could also cause children to become overwhelmed and not able to perform competently or to their full potential (Passer and Wilson, 2002), which may also deter some children from lifelong physical activity. Therefore, within your physical education lessons the way in which competition is perceived is important. If you develop and focus on indi-vidual improvement and encourage and inspire the children to succeed, this will develop their capacity for resilience and perseverance (Woods, 1998). There are two main ways in which planning for competition can be completed. The first is indi-vidual target setting, where the children have their own goal that they are trying to beat. The second is to compete against another child or to be part of a team, the focus being to set team or individual targets so the emphasis is, again, on the children's improvement rather than winning the competition. This would involve planning and focusing on the children's tactics and problem-solving skills linking to the cognitive domain of physical education.

Assessment

Assessing learning in physical education can seem daunting but it can be broken down and planned for in much simpler terms than many teachers think possible. Almond (1989) suggested the need to plan for progression through measuring, recording and comparing in order to move from 'who is best' to 'what is my best and how much better can I get?' It is important to have clear objective measurements such as time, distance and weight. The key is to ask yourself questions that can be completed through observations of the movement or through written records of individual and team performance. Questions can link to your planned description of the activity and your teaching points which would allow you to compare the actual movement to the expected movement and provide next steps. Also, you can plan for assessment through using ICT and technology such as videos, photographs and drawings of, for example, choreography or balances. ICT can help self- and peer analysis. Guo et al. (2010) warned about the need to allow the children to acclimatise to the equipment to overcome the initial inquisitive manner they may experience with new technology to ensure that it supports the learning. Using ICT within a series of lessons would allow for this acclimatisation and enable the children to focus on the cognitive and practical domains of physical education.

Vocabulary

Teaching physical education vocabulary is an important aspect of effective physical education although not identified in the national curriculum to the same extent as other subjects. It is important to identify key words that are used within the lesson (e.g. counter balance, counter tension) and for the children to understand the differences. This will ensure that the children develop the cognitive domain of their physical education and become physically educated.

Health and safety

Akin to science, the practical and active nature of physical education means it is important to identify any hazards associated with planned activities. This could be the equipment being used, the groups allocated, or the space or area used. However, in attempting to minimise risk it is also important to ensure children are still presented with challenges. For example, in rounders there are at least four different bats that can be used, all differing in size, shape and surface area, and this needs to be planned for prior to the lessons. The key text from the Association of Physical Education for support in physical education health and safety is Whitlam (2012).

Further reading

Almond, L. (1989) (ed.) *The Place of Physical Education in School*. London: Kogan Page.

Bunker, D. and Thorpe, R. (1982) A model for the teaching of games in secondary schools. *Bulletin of Physical Education*, 18(1) (Spring).

Guo, S., Zhang, H. and Zhai, R. (2010) A potential way of enquiry into human curiosity. *British Journal of Educational Technology*, 41(3): E48–E52.

House of Commons Education Committee (2013) School sport following London 2012: No more political football: Government Response to the Committee's Third Report of Session 2013–14. House of Commons, London: The Stationery Office.

Howells, K. (2007) A critical reflection of the opportunities and challenges of integrating the Every Child Matters (ECM) agenda into teaching physical education (PE). *Primary Physical Education Matters*, 2(1): ii–iii.

Kirk, D. (1993) Curriculum work in physical education: Beyond the objectives approach? *Journal of Teaching in Physical Education,* 12(3): 244–65.

Kyriacou, C. (2009) *Effective Teaching in Schools: Theory and Practice* (3rd edition). Cheltenham: Nelson Thornes Ltd.

Laker, A. (2001) *Developing Personal, Social and Moral Education through Physical Education: A Practical Guide for Teachers.* London: Routledge.

Martin, B. (2000) Teaching outdoor and adventurous activities, in Bailey, R. and MacFadyen, T. (eds) *Teaching Physical Education, 5–11.* London: Continuum.

McKenzie, T. L. and Kahan, D. (2004) Impact of the Surgeon General's report: Through the eyes of physical education teacher educators. *Journal of Teaching in Physical Education,* 23(4): 300–17.

National Association for Sport and Physical Education (2005) *Moving into the Future: National Standards for Physical Education* (2nd edition). New York: McGraw-Hill.

Passer, M. W. and Wilson, B. J. (2002) Motivational, emotional, and cognitive determinants of children's age readiness for competition, in Smoll, F. L. and Smith, R. E. (eds) *Children and Youth in Sport* (83–103). Dubuque, IO: Kendall/Hunt Publishing Company.

Rink, J. (2005) *Teaching Physical Education for Learning.* New York: McGraw-Hill.

Whitlam, P. (2012) *Safe Practice in Physical Education & Sport.* Worcester: Association of Physical Education.

Woods, B. (1998) *Applying Psychology to Sport.* Oxford: Bookpoint.

World Health Organization (WHO) (2008) School Policy Framework: Implementation of the WHO global strategy on diet, physical activity and health. [online] Available at: **www. who.int/dietphysicalactivity/SPF-en-2008.pdf**

Physical education 2 Examples of planning

The following three lesson plans are provided as examples of planning in physical education. They do not contain the detail you will probably wish to have on your plans but do illustrate some of the points discussed previously.

Lesson One

Subject/topic:	Date: 27/10/2016	Teaching group/set: Y2
Shape and flight	Time: 1.15 p.m.	No. of pupils: 28

Intended learning:	NC reference/context:
Children will learn: • different shapes that can be used at different heights and within flight.	**KS1** Developing balance, agility and coordination, (transferable skills) applying to range of activities (within gymnastics), in a range of increasingly challenging situations Master basic movements such as running and jumping

Success criteria:	Assessment strategy:
All children will be able to: • complete a sequence that includes shape, flight and travel • use large body parts to hold shapes. Some children will be able to: • have height within their flight and shapes in flight.	• Observation of individuals and groupings throughout the session, through the use of questions to help focus the observations

Key vocabulary:	Resources:	Risk assessment:	
star, straight, tuck, pike, large body parts	Mats for landing on and for comfort. Benches/table tops for jumping off from	Moving into space – get the children to look into the empty space and move towards it. Stopping – get the children to focus on stopping either with two feet together, or one foot then the other. Practise this with your children. Have a signal for stopping for those who need more support. Landing from height – introduce landing before take off – landing on balls of feet, squishy landing with knees bent and arms forward for balance.	

Section of lesson	Description and organisation	Teaching points	Assessment for learning
Introduction and warm up	Introduce three of the basic shapes – star, tuck and straight shapes – to the children.	Straight – body straight from fingers to feet, when lying remember to say reaching out to the walls (not reaching up). When sitting this will be a pike position (introduce language here).	Can the children complete the different shapes?

Key vocabulary.

Transferable skills – combination, coordination, balance, stability, challenge.		Play 'Shape Statues'. At walking speed ask children to walk round the room, calling out the different shapes, children to stop and move into the shape, hold for 3 seconds (plus height to complete the shape at – lying, sitting, standing). Progress the speed of the activity onto jogging and calling out the different shapes (plus height), children to stop and move into the shape, hold for 3 seconds. Progress the speed further to skipping, then running, repeat the shape call. Stretch out using the three shapes, at lying, sitting and standing level.	Star – when sitting, this will move into a straddle position (introduce language here). Tuck – when tucking while standing, this will be a jump into the tuck position, knees bent, and landing on balls of feet. In sitting, knees close to chest.	Can the children complete the different shapes in sitting, lying and standing? Can the children remember the different names of the shapes? Are the legs coordinated at the same time in jumping and landing tuck while standing? Can the children move at different speeds? Can the children stop?
Transferable skills – combination, coordination, balance, stability, challenge. Key vocabulary.	Lesson Activity 1 Floor work (Exploring)	Using different large body parts (back, tummies, sides), explore different ways to perform star, tuck and straight shape while on large body part. (Mats may be used for comfort here.) Set individual challenges, e.g. moving between shapes while on tummy.	Straight – stretch out fingers and toes. Point the toes to extend the straight position. Tuck – bringing knees up close to chest, bringing ankles close to bottom. Star – stretch out as far as possible, control and hold position. Highlight how children have used both sides – increasing their confidence.	Can the children complete tuck, star and straight on tummies, back and sides? Do the children use both sides? Do the children extend their bodies within the shapes?
Transferable skills – timing, travelling, stability.	Lesson Activity 2 Small apparatus work (Selecting)	Using benches and table tops, form the shapes in the air. Select favourite shape (tuck, star, straight) and take off from the bench or table top onto the mat for comfort in landing.	Focus on shape. Extend out the shape, point toes. Bring legs and arms back out of the shape. Take off by pushing up and off the small apparatus and land on a mat. Landing on the mat on balls of feet, squishy landing, bending knees and putting arms out forwards for balance.	Can the children take off and up into the air? Do the children form the shape in the air? Can the children land without toppling forwards?

Lesson Activity 3 Floor and small apparatus work (Combining and refining)	Using benches and/or table tops. Children to start on the floor, choose their favourite shape and large body part, use this as a starting point, then travel along, up onto the small apparatus and then jump off in one of the three shapes. Landing on a mat. So the children complete a sequence.	Hold the first shape for 3 seconds, before moving to the small apparatus. Focus on shape. Extend out the shape, point toes. Bring legs and arms back out of the shape. Take off by pushing up and off the small apparatus and land on a mat. Landing on the mat on balls of feet, squishy landing, bending knees and putting arms out forwards for balance.	Can the children land on balls of feet? Do the children have a start, middle and end to sequence? Can the children hold the first shape for 3 seconds? Do the children extend the shape in the air? Can they transfer the skills learnt in the shape to flight?
Plenary and cool down	Celebrate successes within the lesson – focus on the type of travel used, the shapes used and the height of flight. Recap the knowledge that the children have developed. Use the three shapes to move round the room at ever-decreasing speed – this could be as 'Mr Men': Mr Small in tuck shape, Mr Tall in the straight shape and Mr Wide in the star shape. Come together as a group and stretch out using the three shapes.		

Transferable skills – confidence.

Lesson Two

Subject/topic:	Date: 3/11//2016	Teaching group/set: Y2
Shape and flight	Time: 1.15 p.m.	No. of pupils: 28

Intended learning:	NC reference/context:
Children will learn: • different foot patterns that can be used to take off and land.	KS1 Developing balance, agility and coordination (transferable skills) applying to range of activities (within gymnastics), in a range of increasingly challenging situations Master basic movements such as running and jumping

Success criteria:			Assessment strategy:
All children will be able to: • complete a sequence that includes different foot patterns, flight and travel • describe and use different foot patterns. Some children will be able to: • have height within their flight from their foot pattern take off and shapes in flight.			• Observation of individuals and groupings throughout the session, through the use of questions to help focus the observations

Key vocabulary:	Resources:	Risk assessment:	
Two feet to two feet (jump). One foot to two feet. Two feet to one foot. One foot to one foot (hop). One foot to other (leap/skip)	Mats for landing on and for comfort Benches/table tops for jumping off from	Moving into space – get the children to look into the empty space and move towards it. Stopping – get the children to focus on stopping with either two feet together, or one foot then the other. Practise this with your children. Have a signal for stopping for those who need more support. Landing from height – introduce landing before take off – landing on balls of feet, squishy landing with knees bent and arms forward for balance.	

Clear signals minimise potential for risk.

Section of lesson	Description and organisation	Teaching points	Assessment for learning
Introduction and warm up	Introduce five basic foot pattern jumps (take off and landings): two feet to two feet; one foot to one foot; one foot to two feet, two feet to one foot and one foot to other to the children. Play 'Jump and Squash': At walking speed ask children to walk round the room, calling out the different foot pattern jump shapes, children to jump, land and hold for 3 seconds. Progress the speed of the activity onto jogging and calling out the different foot pattern jumps, children to stop and move into the shape, hold for 3 seconds. Progress the speed further to skipping, then running, repeat the jump foot pattern. Stretch out while standing in the various foot patterns.	Land on balls of feet, land with squashy legs and bent knees. Could shout squash when land, to encourage children to land correctly. Introduce language and key vocabulary (hop, skip/leap, jump). On take off push off from balls of feet and reach as high as possible.	Can the children complete the different foot patterns? Can the children complete the different foot patterns to take off? Can the children complete the different foot patterns to land? Can the children remember the different names of the foot patterns? Can the children stop?

Transferable skills – balance, stability and co-ordination.

Lesson Activity 1 Floor work (Exploring)	Using a mat, explore the different ways to take off and land while moving across the mat. Explore how to make a tuck shape and a straight shape. What foot patterns make these? How can we use one-footed take off?	Straight – stretch out fingers and toes. Point the toes to extend the straight position. Tuck – bringing knees up close to chest, bringing ankles close to bottom. Highlight how children have used both sides – increasing their confidence.	Can the children complete tuck, and straight jumps? Can the children identify what foot patterns are being used? Can the children extend this further to make a jump that is one footed? Do the children extend their bodies within the shapes?
Lesson Activity 2 Small apparatus work (Selecting)	Using benches and table tops, complete the take off and landing of different foot patterns in the air. Select favourite foot pattern, and shape, take off from the bench or table top and complete shape in the air, land onto the mat for comfort in landing. Describe the take off and landing.	Focus on shape. Extend out the shape, point toes. Bring legs and arms back out of the shape. Take off by pushing up and off the small apparatus and land on a mat. Landing on the mat on balls of feet, squishy landing, bending knees and putting arms out forwards for balance.	Can the children take off and up into the air, using the foot patterns? Do the children form the shape in the air? Can the children land without toppling forwards?
Lesson Activity 3 Floor and small apparatus work (Combining and refining)	Using benches and or table tops. Children to start on the floor, choose their favourite foot pattern, use this as a starting point, take off and travel along, up onto the small apparatus and then jump off in three shapes, concentrating on the foot pattern. Landing on a mat. So the children complete a sequence. Repeat the sequence.		

Transferable skills – balance, stability and co-ordination.

Transferable skills – confidence, combination and challenge.

| Plenary and cool down | Celebrate successes within the lesson – focus on the type of foot patterns, travel, shapes used and the height of flight. Recap the knowledge that the children have developed.

Use the foot patterns to move round the room at ever-decreasing speed – this could be as walking, hopping, skipping.

Come together as a group and stretch out using the shapes straight and tucked, this could be lying and sitting. | | |

Transferable skills – timing.

Lesson Three

Subject/topic:	Date: 12/11/2016	Teaching group/set: Y2
Shape, flight and foot pattern	Time: 1.15 p.m.	No. of pupils: 28

Intended learning:	NC reference/context:
Children will learn: • different shapes that can be used at different heights and within flight and how these can be produced using different foot patterns.	**KS1** Developing balance, agility and coordination (transferable skills) applying to range of activities (within gymnastics), in a range of increasingly challenging situations Master basic movements such as running and jumping

Observations are linked to success criteria.

Success criteria:	Assessment strategy:
All children will be able to: • complete a sequence that includes foot patterns, shape, flight and travel • describe movement that is occurring in sequence. Some children will be able to: • have height within their flight and shapes in flight.	• Observation of individuals and groupings throughout the session, through the use of questions to help focus the observations

Key vocabulary:	Resources:	Risk assessment:
star, straight, tuck, pike, one to one, two to two, one to two, two to one, one to other	Mats for landing on and for comfort Benches/table tops for jumping off from	Moving into space – get the children to look into the empty space and move towards it. Stopping – get the children to focus on stopping with either two feet together, or one foot then the other. Practise this with your children. Have a signal for stopping for those who need more support. Landing from height – introduce landing before take off – landing on balls of feet, squishy landing with knees bent and arms forward for balance.

Section of lesson	Description and organisation	Teaching points	Assessment for learning
Introduction and warm up	Revisit basic shapes and foot patterns. Spend time reminding the children of the foot patterns used last time and the basic shapes used in lesson 1. Play 'Jump and Shape': At walking speed ask children to walk round the room, calling out the different foot pattern and shape to be made in the air, children to stop on landing and hold for 3 seconds. Progress the speed of the activity onto jogging and calling out the different foot patterns and shapes (emphasis on height within the shape), children to stop and hold for 3 seconds at end of landing. Progress the speed further to skipping, then running, repeat the shape call. Stretch out using the three shapes, at lying, sitting and standing level.	Land on balls of feet, land with squashy legs and bent knees. Could shout squash when land, to encourage children to land correctly. Introduce language and key vocabulary (hop, skip/leap, jump). On take off push off from balls of feet and reach as high as possible. Straight – body straight from fingers to feet, when lying remember to say reaching out to the walls (not reaching up). When sitting this will be a pike position (introduce language here). Star – when sitting, this will move into a straddle position (introduce language here). Tuck – when tucking while standing, this will be a jump into the tuck position, knees bent, and landing on balls of feet. In sitting, knees close to chest.	Can the children remember the different shapes? Can the children complete the different shapes in the air? Can the children hold after landing? Can the children land on balls of feet? Can the children remember the different names of the shapes? Are the legs coordinated at the same time in jumping and landing tuck while standing? Can the children move at different speeds? Can the children stop?
Lesson Activity 1 Floor work (Exploring)	Explore the number of tuck jumps that can be performed in a row with correct take off and landing. Repeat for straight. Repeat for star. Challenge and increase the number completed by the children, to move from one isolated jump to several jumps in a row.	Straight – stretch out fingers and toes. Point the toes to extend the straight position. Tuck – bringing knees up close to chest, bringing ankles close to bottom. Star – stretch out as far as possible, control and hold position. Highlight how children have used both sides – increasing their confidence.	Can the children complete tuck, star and straight several times in a row? Do the children use more than just two foot to two foot, foot pattern? Do the children extend their bodies within the shapes?
Lesson Activity 2 Small apparatus work (Selecting)	Using benches and table tops, complete the take off and landing of different foot patterns in the air. Select favourite foot pattern, and shape, take off from the bench or table	Focus on shape. Extend out the shape, point toes. Bring legs and arms back out of the shape.	Can the children take off and up into the air? Do the children form the shape in the air?

Transferable skills – combination, confidence and challenge.

| | | top and complete shape in the air, land onto the mat for comfort in landing. Describe the take off and landing. (This is a repeat of lesson 2 to ensure that balance and stability is developed on apparatus.) | Take off by pushing up and off the small apparatus and land on a mat.

Landing on the mat on balls of feet, squishy landing, bending knees and putting arms out forwards for balance. | Can the children land without toppling forwards?

Can the children transfer into second jump on the floor after the apparatus? |
|---|---|---|---|---|
| Transferable skills – balance and stability. | Lesson Activity 3

Floor and small apparatus work (Combining and Refining) | Using benches and table tops, take off from the apparatus and land then add another jump once landed, so select favourite foot pattern, add shape for in the air (tuck, star, straight) and take off from the bench or table top onto the mat for comfort in landing, then add second on the floor. So the children complete a sequence. | Focus on shape. Extend out the shape, point toes.

Bring legs and arms back out of the shape.

Take off by pushing up and off the small apparatus and land on a mat.

Landing on the mat on balls of feet, squishy landing, bending knees and putting arms out forwards for balance.

Second take off pushing up and off the mat. | Can the children land on balls of feet?

Do the children have a start, middle and end to sequence?

Can the children hold the first shape for 3 seconds?

Do the children extend the shape in the air?

Can they transfer the skills learnt in the shape to flight? |
| Transferable skills – combination, confidence and challenge. | Plenary and cool down | Celebrate successes within the lesson – focus on the repetition of the jumps on the mat. Focus on the shapes used and the height of flight. Recap the knowledge that the children have developed.

Use the three shapes to move round the room at ever-decreasing speed – this could be as 'Mr Men': Mr Small in tuck shape, Mr Tall in the straight shape and Mr Wide in the star shape.

Come together as a group and stretch out using the three shapes. | Star – reach out towards the wall, making the body as wide as possible.

Straight – reach out and up towards the ceiling, up onto tip toes, think about tummies being pulled in.

Tuck – curl into a tight ball, curve back. | Can the children move round the room at a decreasing speed?

Can the children hold the shapes while moving? |

Physical education 3 The framework for physical education

Purpose of study

A high-quality physical education curriculum inspires all pupils to succeed and excel in competitive sport and other physically demanding activities. It should provide opportunities for pupils to become physically confident in a way which supports their health and fitness. Opportunities to compete in sport and other activities build character and help to embed values such as fairness and respect.

Aims

The national curriculum for physical education aims to ensure that all pupils:

- develop competence to excel in a broad range of physical activities
- are physically active for sustained periods of time
- engage in competitive sports and activities
- lead healthy, active lives.

Attainment targets

By the end of each key stage, pupils are expected to know, apply and understand the matters, skills and processes specified in the relevant programme of study.

Schools are not required by law to teach the example content in [square brackets].

Subject content

Key stage 1

Pupils should develop fundamental movement skills, become increasingly competent and confident and access a broad range of opportunities to extend their agility, balance and coordination, individually and with others. They should be able to engage in competitive (both against self and against others) and co-operative physical activities, in a range of increasingly challenging situations.

Pupils should be taught to:

- master basic movements including running, jumping, throwing and catching, as well as developing balance, agility and co-ordination, and begin to apply these in a range of activities
- participate in team games, developing simple tactics for attacking and defending
- perform dances using simple movement patterns.

Key stage 2

Pupils should continue to apply and develop a broader range of skills, learning how to use them in different ways and to link them to make actions and sequences of movement. They should enjoy communicating, collaborating and competing with each other. They should develop an understanding of how to improve in different physical activities and sports and learn how to evaluate and recognise their own success.

Pupils should be taught to:

- use running, jumping, throwing and catching in isolation and in combination
- play competitive games, modified where appropriate [for example, badminton, basket ball, cricket, football, hockey, netball, rounders and tennis], and apply basic principles suitable for attacking and defending
- develop flexibility, strength, technique, control and balance [for example, through athletics and gymnastics]
- perform dances using a range of movement patterns
- take part in outdoor and adventurous activity challenges both individually and within a team
- compare their performances with previous ones and demonstrate improvement to achieve their personal best.

Swimming and water safety

All schools must provide swimming instruction either in key stage 1 or key stage 2.
In particular, pupils should be taught to:

- swim competently, confidently and proficiently over a distance of at least 25 metres
- use a range of strokes effectively [for example, front crawl, backstroke and breaststroke]
- perform safe self-rescue in different water-based situations.

Section 3

Putting the curriculum together

This section will explore how planning is done in schools and how schools can create a curriculum which draws on knowledge and understanding across the curriculum. Examples of creative approaches to planning are provided.

Section 3

15 Planning across the curriculum

Keira Sewell

As you become more confident in both your planning and your teaching you will move from planning individual lessons to planning sequences of lessons. It is unlikely that you will be involved in longer-term planning during training as many schools will provide you with the long- and medium-term planning already in place. However, you will be expected to contribute longer-term planning in your induction year and it is important to understand how curricula are put together. It is also important that you develop your own personal philosophy about how the curriculum is developed so that you can begin to put in place some of the principles of this in your own planning.

The planning process

In Chapter 1 we looked at the structure and requirements of the national curriculum and how developing a philosophy of education underpins the development of a school curriculum. It is useful to return to this concept when considering how schools plan.

Most schools will have four stages in planning their curriculum.

- Policy development.
- Long term.
- Medium term.
- Short term.

Each of these stages leads to the next and each is important. They may be called different things in different schools but essentially the process is the same.

Policy development

This stage is the one which most defines and reflects philosophies of education. Schools have policies on all sorts of things from assessment to financial procurement and each of these defines the rationale behind an approach and, often, the approach itself. They will often be developed by key people in consultation with other stakeholders, including local authority representatives, advisers, governors, parents and children, and should be reviewed and updated regularly.

Policies will usually reflect the 'ethos' of a school and define what makes it distinctive. Consider the schools you have been into. What were your first impressions? Did the school portray who and what it is from the moment you walked in through the door? What kinds of schools would you like to work in (and not work in) and why? Often these very instinctive impressions are based on the ways in which the school portrays its philosophy of education and how easily your own philosophies can relate to this.

Although it may be named differently in different schools, each school will have a policy for the curriculum. It will outline how the curriculum is organised and why. Some schools choose to have a very subject-specific curriculum while others combine subjects into a more thematic approach. Others will have a combination of the two with some subjects, particularly English and mathematics, taught separately and other subjects being put together in themes or topics.

In recent years there has been a move to a more 'creative' curriculum. This is interpreted differently by different schools and varies from a very thematic or cross-curricular approach to children determining what it is they want to learn. Chris Quigley (see further reading) defines a creative curriculum as having three overall aims, which are that it:

- has clear educational purpose;
- is delivered with imagination;
- has measurable educational value.

The aims and requirements of the national curriculum reflect this, encouraging schools to go beyond the statutory requirements and develop a curriculum which is broad and balanced and driven by the needs of children, the local community and the values of the school. There is scope for schools to develop concepts, skills and attitudes and for these to help define the philosophies and ethos of a school and its educational purpose. This is important as it encourages children to see the relationships between subject areas and to use learning in a more holistic way. Some critics argue that children need to know what subject they are learning in order to make sense of it and there is some truth in this, but there are also some skills and areas of knowledge which permeate all learning and there are risks in trying to compartmentalise ideas. The creative curriculum does not advocate 'losing' subjects within a thematic approach but, rather, encourages schools to consider how relationships between areas of learning in specific subject areas can enhance the potential of the curriculum offered.

A creative curriculum should be flexible, able to adapt and respond to emerging needs and new agendas. It should use contexts which are real to the children in the school and reflect their interests and expertise. It should engage children in a love of learning and allow them time to explore new ideas and develop deep understandings.

Central to these ideas is that any curriculum should enable children to make progress; therefore the value of any curriculum should be measurable. This will require schools to develop outcomes which go beyond the parameters of the national curriculum programmes of study.

Long-term planning

Once the philosophical approach to the curriculum has been established then the school can move forward in putting this into practice. The first step is possibly more logistical than the following two in that it organises the content of the curriculum into subjects or themes and decides which year groups will do what in which school term.

Some themes are particularly easy to place in that they require a specific year or time of year, access to resources or off-site environments or booking of outside visitors or visits out. Others can be more flexible and take account of the need to spread demand for specific resources, teachers or rooms across the academic year. However content is organised, schools will want to map curriculum content to ensure that they are delivering the statutory programmes of study from the national curriculum at relevant points and that the organisation of content encourages progression.

Medium-term planning

Often called a scheme of work, medium-term planning usually covers a sequence of lessons lasting a period of time (e.g. a half term) or a theme or topic. Plans may focus on one subject area only or include a number of different subjects where they fit naturally together (e.g. a topic on houses may draw on science, design and technology, art and design and mathematics). It is important that intended learning is made clear at this stage as medium-term plans should show progression by demonstrating the way each area of learning is developed. They should also give an indication of the teaching approaches and assessment strategies used and are a good way of evaluating whether you are providing opportunities for the different needs within your class. It is also useful to identify key vocabulary and note resources, particularly those which need to be prepared or booked in advance. This may include booking specific places in the school environment, such as the hall, or even off-site visits.

Medium-term plans should reflect the same principles as those outlined in both Chapter 2 and the subject-specific chapters within this book. There are some examples provided at the end of this chapter to help you develop creative approaches which have the benefit of enabling learning in a range of subjects within one longer-term focus.

Short-term planning

These plans are more detailed and specific. They may cover a single lesson or, if a learning objective or activity is more long term, may cover a specific period of time. You should refer to Chapter 2 and the subject-specific chapters from this book to construct your short-term plans.

At first your short-term plans are likely to be very detailed. This is important as beginning teaching can be stressful and you are likely to forget key inputs. As you become more experienced your short-term plans will become less detailed and you may find more experienced teachers work mainly from plans which are more medium term. It is common for English and mathematics plans to be weekly rather than daily, reflecting the longer-term nature of the intended learning.

The creative curriculum: some examples

The following examples are designed to inspire your own ideas of how to put an exciting, broad and balanced curriculum together which will stimulate children's interests and support their learning across a range of subjects. However, there is a note of caution here. When planning in a cross-curricular way it is easy to get carried away by the 'fun' aspects and forget the key point of the curriculum: learning. Make sure you only put subject areas together which fit within the learning aims of the theme. Ensure you can justify how the learning from one subject area supports or enhances learning in another and be explicit about the links between the skills, knowledge and understanding drawn from each subject. Make these links clear to your children; remind them that they are using a range of ideas drawn from different disciplines so that they may make sense of this and continue to develop these in their future learning.

Natural sculptures

Year group: Key stage 1

Subject foci: Science, art and design, geography

Children could begin to explore a local outdoor environment and consider what plants grow there. They could map out their findings, building up a profile of the habitat and beginning to identify and name common plants found. They could look at how nature can be represented through art and consider the work of Andy Goldsworthy in creating their own natural art. Through this they could explore characteristics which enable us to group and classify plants and describe basic structures. This could lead to large-scale art by covering parts of the school field with shapes of black plastic (e.g. the centre and petals of a large flower) for around a week. This will make the grass turn yellow and leads into thinking about photosynthesis as well as making striking art.

Seed germination

Year group: Key stage 1

Subject foci: Science, art and design, design and technology, English

In this activity children research how best to germinate seeds (large seeds such as broad beans work well with this age group). Once the enquiry has been completed children should design a seed packet and write instructions as to how best to germinate the seeds. This activity can be extended by growing plants the previous year and collecting the seeds for sale in the spring. (Sunflowers, tomatoes and broad beans all work well for this.) This provides an opportunity for children to market their seeds and work out costings, bringing mathematics into focus.

Buildings around the world

Year group: Key stages 1 and 2

Subject foci: Mathematics, English, geography, design and technology

Using the picture book *My House Has Stars* by Megan Mcdonald and Peter Catalanotto, children explore different housing designs from around the world. They re-build and draw them and look for the similarities and differences in the geometry within them. This could also move into looking at architecture around the world, particularly the mathematics to be found in ancient buildings such as the Acropolis.

Weather

Year group: Key stages 1 and 2

Subject foci: Mathematics, science, geography, English

In this activity, children create a class weather station and, in groups, collect data about different aspects of the weather over a period of time that can include measurement of temperature and rainfall. They then collate that data and represent it in different ways, agreeing on how best to represent the data in order for it to be interpreted easily by the rest of the class. They can then write and perform weather reports for the school based on what they've found out and their subsequent predictions.

Maths from stories

Year group: All ages

Subject foci: Mathematics, English, and potentially every other curriculum subject, depending on the book

There is a rich vein of cross-curricular mathematics work to be tapped in the form of picture books for all ages. A comprehensive bank of these can be found at Books Kids Love: **www.the-best-childrens-books.org/math-for-kids.html**. A couple of good ones to start with are *One is a Snail, Ten is a Crab* by April and Jeff Sayre, and *365 Penguins* by Jean-Luc Fromental.

Roman market place

Year group: Key stage 2

Subject foci: Mathematics, history, English, design and technology

In this activity, children work in groups to create a market stall for a Roman market. They research the kinds of items that would be bought and sold on a typical market stall and make trays and products to sell. They use Roman numerals to label the price of their items and design their own money and devise calculation systems in order to charge and pay for them. Finally, they can create posters to advertise their market to potential customers.

Islamic art

Year group: Key stage 2

Subject foci: Mathematics, art, RE

In this activity, children explore the 2D and 3D shapes, symmetry, tessellation and tiling inherent in Islamic design. The symbolism of the shapes and patterns can be researched and leads to understanding of some of the fundamental concepts of Islam. A good starting point is the V&A website, accessed at **http://www.vam.ac.uk/content/articles/t/teachers-resource-maths-and-islamic-art-and-design**.

The X-factor

Year group: Lower key stage 2

Subject foci: Music, science, design and technology, computing

Children could start by considering the ways in which music is made through a variety of different instruments. Through studying these they could develop an understanding of vibration in sound production and consider how they could use this to change pitch and volume. They could use their emerging knowledge to make musical instruments to play. Using a computer sound recording program they could compose a piece of music and record each element separately. Children could then explore how recorded music can be manipulated to improve sounds and change pitch or volume. This work can be extended into thinking about recording studios and how they are constructed to both insulate sound and improve sound. For example, there are some artists who choose to record in certain studios because of the materials they are made from and the effects on the sound produced.

Marketing a 'des res' for a woodlouse

Year group: Lower key stage 2

Subject foci: English, science, computing, geography

This activity requires children to investigate where woodlice choose to live and then design an estate agent's details which might market a desirable residence for a woodlouse. The activity could begin by searching for woodlice in the school grounds and mapping where they are found. From this, children could develop a hypothesis about the conditions woodlice choose for their preferred habitat and devise an investigation to test this out. They could research the life processes of woodlice and relate these to the habitats in which they are found. Children could research estate agents' details to explore structure and language used and then use their findings to construct their own online or hard copy agent's details for woodlice choosing a new home.

Decorative tea light holder

Year group: Lower key stage 2

Subject foci: Design and technology, science, English, mathematics, RE

Children evaluate a range of tea light holders and then draw their own design which they will give as a gift. They will need to consider the likes and preferences of their chosen recipient – colour, shape, stability, amount of light emitted – before modelling their own design using salt dough. The dough can be left to dry naturally or baked in an oven to speed things up. Tea light holders can then be decorated according to the original design and subsequently evaluated. The activity can be used to support a festival such as Diwali, and as a teaching opportunity in science, looking at properties of light, and also properties of salt dough.

Candle-style night lights can be used; however, for safety considerations inexpensive electronic night lights are also readily available.

The force of the Egyptians

Year group: Upper key stage 2

Subject foci: History, science, design and technology, mathematics, physical education

In this activity children will explore the methods used by the ancient Egyptians to build the pyramids. They will look at the architecture used, considering why structures were built in the styles and using the materials selected. They will explore how the Egyptians used their knowledge of forces, levers and pulleys to move the stones across considerable distances and place them in the building process and calculate the effects of using these approaches in reducing the forces involved. The children could also explore the effects of balance and opposing forces in physical education and experiment with alternative movements.

Making and marketing cookies

Year group: Upper key stage 2

Subject foci: Design and technology, mathematics, computing, geography, history, science, English

This activity works well with all ages of children but with upper key stage 2 children as 'managers' it lends itself to being a whole-school marketing project. Children can design, make and package cookies made to a variety of recipes, costing them and working out profit margins so that they can plan a coffee morning for parents, end of term assembly or perhaps a tea party at the local care home. They can collect and evaluate a range of packaging styles before deciding on their own – having considered their target users. They can use a YouTube clip to design and make their packaging, using their science knowledge to select appropriate materials – greaseproof, aesthetic appeal, theme of their work. They can use science to consider calorie values, healthy eating and dietary requirements (e.g. Coeliac disease) to vary recipes. They can also consider making their cookies from a history perspective (e.g. what ingredients/spices would have been available in Tudor times?), or from a geography perspective they could consider names and availability of ingredients in their chosen region of study. Throughout the project children will be using their speaking and listening skills to negotiate, evaluate and market their cookies.

Further reading

Quigley, C. *Planning a Creative Curriculum*. [online] Available at: **www.teachprimary.com/ learning_resources/view/planning-a-creative-curriculum**